PUPIL POWER

Issues in Education and Training Series: 2

PUPIL POWER

Deviance and Gender in School

Lynn Davies

 The Falmer Press

(A member of the Taylor & Francis Group)
London and Philadelphia

UK	The Falmer Press, Falmer House, Barcombe, Lewes, East Sussex, BN8 5DL
USA	The Falmer Press, Taylor & Francis Inc., 242 Cherry Street, Philadelphia, PA 19106-1906

First published in 1984

Library of Congress Cataloging in Publication Data

Davies, Lynn.
  Pupil power.

  (Issues in education and training series)
  Bibliography: p.
  Includes index.
  1. Classroom management.   2. Deviant behavior.
3. Sex differences in education.   4. Problem children—
Education.   I. Title.   II. Series.
LB3013.D37   1984   371.1′024   84-14713
ISBN 1-85000-007-7
ISBN 1-85000-006-9 (pbk.)

Typeset in 11/13 Bembo by
Imago Publishing Ltd, Thame, Oxon

Jacket design by Leonard Williams

Printed in Great Britain by Taylor & Francis (Printers) Ltd, Basingstoke

Contents

Figures and Tables

Part I
Gladstone High

1   *Deviance and Gender Compared*

When I came to leave my first teaching job, I received a note from one of the pupils. 'Dear Mrs Davies', it read, 'I am sorry you are living. Love Janette.' My interest in pupil deviance must stem from those early days of experiencing fear of failure: at worst I had alienated Janette completely; at best I had failed to teach her to spell. Assuming the best, I was in fact absurdly gratified, since she had been one of my most troublesome pupils, far worse than any of the boys; subsequent experiences over the years have served to confirm three related notions. First, that anxiety and problems of 'success' as a teacher were not confined to myself; second, that a large measure of such success is seen as related to questions of order and control; and third, that boys and girls often present different challenges in the classroom.

There is no shortage of books dealing wholly or in part with pupil discipline; there are now a number of texts or papers on the more specifically sociological question of pupil deviance. What is curious about these volumes is that either they do not tackle the sex difference, or they are — quite unashamedly — simply about boys. The invisibility of women in much sociological research has been commented on, and rightly somewhat modified of late. With regard to the school, however, while differences in achievement between the sexes have been investigated and even acted upon, differences in deviance have received much less attention. Yet these disparities are not insubstantial: either girls are seen to present less of a problem on the whole than boys, or the girls that *are* difficult prove in the end to be more intractable than their male counterparts. 'When she was good she was very very good, and when she was bad she was horrid' would perhaps sum up the phenomenon, and the documented evidence for such perceived divergences in pupil reaction will be presented later. The question is why this difference has not been seized upon in deviancy studies. If medical research had noted that of two groups one was markedly more prone to a disease than another, or reacted to a given treatment differently, then this difference would be the first thing to be investigated. Would it be dietary fibre, exercise, cholesterol, smoking, obesity; what could we learn from this difference; and what could be inferred about the prevention and cure of the disease?

Hence this book, in highlighting the gender difference in pupil deviance, does not aim merely to fill a gap in the literature; it maintains that such a difference could be a prime clue in investigation of pupil response to schooling. The interest is then twofold: to provide or attempt more comprehensive explanations of pupil deviance, but also to draw inferences for action. I am not suggesting that deviance is a 'disease', for which we must find cures; but that it is a phenomenon, a social construct, which requires illumination. And the power of such illumination should be tested by probing the dark corners into which it shines. Fortunately, the field of sociology is no longer, in the interests of the 'scientific' approach, required to remain dispassionately objective, and 'radical' sociology certainly leans towards the interventionist. However, the adjective 'prescriptive' is still the most effective insult in the vocabulary of learned criticism (even if there is only a thin dividing line between suggesting radical change and being prescriptive); and I certainly want to avoid yet another manual on The Craft of Teaching. Yet I would like to address myself firstly to a potential readership of pre- and in-service teachers, who (at least in my experience of teacher training) rightly want to test the relevance of any theory in terms of classroom practice. Researchers and theorists may also be interested in the approach; but I want to resist as far as possible the temptation to make covert appeals to academic approval by the use of obfuscating jargon, oblique references and statistical complexities. Such rigour can be detected, if required, in Davies (1980). Here the pursuit is of readability.

I will at this point further alienate another section of the readership by intimating the general tenor of the conclusions here: that it is not the teachers, but the pupils who need more power, in other words that much pupil deviance can be seen as the result of a power struggle which the pupil is in danger of losing. Hence springs the not particularly original but seemingly paradoxical recommendation that teacher control is enhanced by relinquishing certain dominative aspects of it. For those seeking to consolidate a clearly recognizable authority role, this may prove a disappointment.

A definition of what will be understood by the term 'power' is necessary at this stage. Parsons' interpretation is traditionally quoted with reference to schools: 'the capacity of persons or collectivities to mobilize resources for the attainment of goals, especially when these goals are obstructed by some kind of human resistance or opposition' (Musgrove, 1971). Yet power has to be more than the ability to make others do what you want, or allow you to do what you want, for I am not convinced that pupils are necessarily aware precisely what they want teachers to do, although the reverse *may* be true. Thus, although the concept of power to be used here does include the ability to evoke a response from another — which is, of course, the bedrock of human relationships — this does not mean that the other's response is unwilling. Pupils will react to teacher power quite happily in answering questions, in submitting to discipline; but it means that without such impetus from the more powerful, that response would not have been made. A pupil who 'cheeks' a teacher into reaction, however punitive, is temporarily successful in feeling power over events. Power is not the same as status, for neither feelings of self-worth nor respect from the other necessarily accompany the exercise of power; but status may be an alternative to power, as we shall see with pupil identity. In its broadest sense, power is the ability to alter the course of events, to create a happening, *whether or not a particular end is in view*. A teenage mother was quoted in a Sunday paper recently: 'Some of the girls won't use any sort of contraception, just for the thrill. It's like when we were kids running across the road in front of the cars, it's like breaking a school rule, like jumping down the corridors and screaming something rude' (*The Observer*, 16 August 1981). The concept of power being goal-directed does not somehow capture the flavour of this type of Russian roulette. Here power is the creation of possibilities where none existed before. It is this definition of power as the creation of possibilities that I shall be using throughout.

The major thesis of this book is, then, that boys and girls *may* seek to exercise power in different ways in the classroom; and that recognition of the basis and source of these power struggles is the key to teacher-pupil relationships. The final framework was pieced together from the usual mixture of theoretical possibilities matched against field research. However, this volume will itself take on a deviant format. The case-study and my conclusions from it are presented almost immediately; the review of the literature, analysis of relevant theories of deviance and discussion of the methodology of researching deviance come afterwards. This may appear illogical, in that the more normal pattern is for theory and previous research to be discussed, hypotheses formed, and case material then presented which tests those hypotheses. Yet no research is ever actually conducted in that smooth and linear way; and such a written format involves the reader wading through shoals of past studies and veritable seas of conflicting theories before getting to the 'live' subjects marooned and waiting to be rescued somewhere around chapter 4. The decision here was to reverse the process. The pupils, the teachers and their variegated deviance appear 'cold', without much preamble; the catalogues of thinkers and thoughts form a sort of reference or review section at the back. The aim is that of readability; and also to allow for some flexibility in the way the second section might be used, or dipped into, or treated as a glossary. Page references will be made to it during the first part, indicating where a fuller treatment might be found; but it is to be hoped that the anthropological account will stand on its own at the initial reading. This research now needs a brief outline.

Gladstone High

Over a period of two years I pursued a study in depth of a large Midlands comprehensive school, a study which had the joint aims of seeing whether boys' and girls' deviance was qualitatively or quantitatively different, and of considering which sociological perspective(s) on deviance would best inform any differences, if found. The school had a predominantly working class intake from a heavily industrialized area with strong community loyalties; it was not chosen because it had particularly notorious behaviour problems (on the contrary), yet it had various features which signalled it as rewarding for study. One was a support unit for pupils with problems; another was a ladies working party which had been set up specifically to examine and deal with girls' behaviour; most important was an openness to research and willingness to permit access and intrusion. The school was relatively traditional, however, in its ordering of pupils, and in its emphasis on examination achievement: the lower school, for the 11–13 year olds (housed two miles from the main site) used a five band system, while the upper school used six. The head admitted that transfer between the streams was rare, and it was clear that the use of different option choices for upper and lower bands meant a degree of identification with being a member of either the 'top classes' or the 'lower classes' (as the pupils denoted the streams). The buildings were a mixture of designs dating from 1928 onwards, and while the entrance hall had plants and usually a

4

current display, the rest of the school did not appear to demonstrate any overt concern with visual appeal, the usual painted brick and stone floors of the corridors being generally unrelieved by pictures or pupil work. On the other hand it was in good order and mostly free of graffiti. Some classrooms had carpeting on the floor; most were traditional transmission style units with pupil desks facing the teacher and blackboard. There were very few extra-curricular activities, this being attributed to the fact that most pupils and teachers preferred to get away at four o'clock. There was a school uniform, flexible in terms of a range of choices, but with relatively stringent attempts to enforce it. Overall, therefore, the hidden curriculum gave certain messages about expected roles and relationships of teachers and pupils, although the possibility of a wide variation within the interpretation of these will be a source of discussion later.

Research in the school took a variety of forms over the two years. At the beginning there were relatively structured interviews with a large proportion of the fourth year, probing their views of school, of pupil behaviour, of discipline. I spent a week following the first year intake around, acting in the role of 'cultural stranger', and learning with them the official and the hidden curriculum of the school, and noting how it was transmitted. All the staff in the upper school were invited for interview individually, to elicit their comments on pupil behaviour, on sex differences, and on school policy. Pupils and staff filled in banks of questionnaires, and participated in informal discussions and 'chats'. Approximately 400 hours were spent in classroom observation across age and ability ranges. In the second year I concentrated particularly on a group of girls identified by the school as 'difficult', and spent time 'hanging around' with them in and out of lessons, accompanying them on school trips, and recording conversations. Overt investigation of the school was supplemented by a more behind-the-scenes delving into school records and policy statements, interviewing the Educational Welfare Officer and monitoring the attendance, detention and punishment books. A fuller discussion of this and other methodologies of researching school deviance will be found in chapter 8.

The usual disclaimer will have to be made about generalizing from a unique case-study. Of course one attempts *some* degree of generalization: there would be little point in the research otherwise, except perhaps from the individual school's point of view. What one aims at is either keeping the inferences tentative, or using the school study as a base-line to test broader theories. Of great value is the comparison with existing surveys and research. Chapter 6 provides the detailed account of what is already known about sex differences in pupils' behaviour, but a brief summary of the evidence might help at this point.

At the primary school level, the norms and the rules that define the 'good pupil' seem more in line with girls' behaviour and attitudes. They are seen to work harder, and concentrate more; they are cleaner, quieter, more submissive, more mature and less maladjusted. Hence girls are perceived as less problematic, as less deviant according to criteria for 'success' at school. At the secondary level, the scene is more complex. Questionnaires asking pupils themselves to log their behaviour, to admit their 'crimes', show fewer sex differences than do surveys requiring teachers or heads to comment on discipline, where girls are overall still seen — being less disruptive, violent or delinquent — to present less of a 'problem'. However, there is little agreement on whether boys truant more, and teachers at the secondary level appear to show greater appreciation of boys' outward-going and casual characteristics, and to find their deviance easier to cope with than they do the 'deep-seated' emotional resistance of girls. They unconsciously give boys more time and attention in mixed-sex classrooms. Girls may be preferred at primary level; but the majority of secondary school teachers, if forced to choose, would prefer to teach boys. There appear to be 'extremes' of behaviour demonstrated by female pupils; girls by this stage seem to be developing their own dubious or irritating strategies for disruption; and the question emerges of whether the incidence of girls' misbehaviour is increasing. So while the evidence points to girls in general taking on the appearance of greater conformity, the picture is complicated by age, by individuality and by social change.

It also starts to become clear, by the range of terms used, that pupil 'deviance' encompasses a wide field. The crucial question to ask is the labelling theorist's query regarding who defines what as behaviour that deviates from 'normal'. In the field of crime and delinquency, official statistics show a distinct, if declining, sex ratio for 'persons found guilty of or cautioned for indictable offences'. Although with criminality the questions about the cultural base of definitions of 'law infringement' still apply, at least rule-breaking can be recognized or identified as an infraction of a written code. In schools, 'deviance' is clearly more than the breaking of codified or even overtly agreed rules: investigation has to include not only the spectrum of disruption, defiance and disaffection, but also passive resistance, 'working the system' and alienation. The prediction is therefore that not just amounts of trouble but definitions of a 'normal deviant' will vary according to sex.

Deviance in Gladstone High

My first task, then, was to sort out the actual nature and comparative extent of boys' and girls' deviance in a particular school setting. For this I probed school records, logged teacher and pupil verbal ideas and compared written admissions from pupils on an anonymous self-report schedule listing a range of offences from 'chatting in class' to 'setting fire to something' (see Figure 7 at the end of the Review Section).

Initially the impression was of contradiction between these various sources of information. School records showed boys receiving more detentions than girls and being thirteen times more likely to be caned. On the self-report schedule (hereafter referred to as SRS) there were either similar rates of offences for the sexes or again boys exceeding girls in more categories than girls exceeded boys. The education welfare officer, who did not keep records, thought truancy greater among boys, which agreed with the SRS. Scrutiny of one year of pupil records revealed similar numbers of letters sent home to parents regarding pupil behaviour, and similar numbers of court appearances for outside school offences. Yet in contrast to all this, the majority of both pupils and teachers, male and female, saw girls as being 'more trouble'. Girls received more suspensions. Pupils were twice as likely to see girls rather than boys breaking rules; only one teacher, a female PE teacher, saw boys as 'probably worse' in behaviour.

To accommodate this apparent disagreement three tasks seemed to need tackling: to break down categories of 'trouble', or definitions of 'deviance'; secondly to identify what *stage* of a rule-breaking episode was being referred to; and thirdly to clarify the actual proportions of each sex involved.

Five broad categories of offence emerged. Three were initially 'victimless crimes' involving breaking school rules about work, about timetables, about the institutional ethos; two involved direct relationships, between pupils, and between pupil and teacher. There is obvious fuzziness and overlap between these categories: is 'not bringing a pen to a lesson' or 'not doing a detention' taken as a personal affront by a teacher, or seen as indicative of a pupil's general attitude towards school? Under what category does one place the offence (noted occasionally in the detention book) of 'arrant stupidity'? But by using categories we can begin at least to sort out where the dissent lies; the areas where there is some agreement will be disposed of first.

Work

These offences relate to the 'instrumental' or 'technical' goals of academic success and so refer to violations of the expected means to these goals: failure to do homework or classwork; copying; cheating; lack of effort or conscientiousness. There was no disagreement from any of the four sources that boys transgressed work norms more than girls. Boys were twice as likely to be put into detention for work-related offences — 'not doing homework' being the largest category. Interestingly, this particular detention was much more prevalent in streams 2, 3 and 4, for both sexes: presumably the top stream did theirs, and with the bottom streams teachers either did not set it, or did not enforce it. When interviewed, teachers agreed distinctly that girls were more conscientious about academic tasks, being harder workers and more consistent. They took a pride in their work, and were neater, whereas the boys could be 'careless', 'slapdash', leaving things to the last minute, doing the minimum. The fact that the boys obtained more O and A level passes is initially a puzzle; but teachers put boys' success down to their 'native wit' or enthusiasm, to their being less passive and regurgitive, to their ideas, their eventual greater ambition. No teacher mentioned the possibility, now backed by evidence, that boys received more pressure and attention from *them*; the picture is always of the conscientious plodding girl, the happy-go-lucky intuitive boy.

Timetables

This refers to violations of organizational 'rules' which structure the pupil's daily life, in terms both of time and space. Offences include truancy; being late; missing lessons, assembly or registration; skipping detentions; and the vague illegality of 'loitering'. As mentioned, truancy figures seem to show a preponderance of boys, but the creation of timetables round the school seems to be more the girls' domain; they were almost twice as likely to be put in detention for missing lessons or assemblies, for being late for lessons or skipping 'short detention' (a separately recorded 10 minute sentence for lateness). The SRS revealed similar rates for boys and girls 'skipping lessons', but some teachers did in fact refer to girls as 'trying to get out of lessons'. One male teacher related this to girls bearing grudges longer: 'She'll have you for the rest of the year, and she'll skip your lessons, although you know she's in school, so you have to go and find her.' Ways of displaying power begin to emerge.

Institution

Whereas the previous section referred to the pupils' creation of time and space, now we will look at the creation of meaning or excitement; and here there are some similarities as well as divergences between the sexes. Similar rates for smoking appeared, whether admitted by pupils or perceived by teachers; the detention book showed no differences and a similar proportion of canings related to smoking offences (with the proviso that girls were far less likely to be caned anyway). Girls were 'obviously' more likely to break the no jewellery, no make-up rule (although the school was at that stage pondering what to do about boys who sported one earring); but in general pupils infringed dress rules with equal impunity.

However, boys were three times more likely to be put into detention for noticeable misbehaviour around the school — damaging property, kicking furniture, 'disturbance by the toilets', misbehaviour during assembly, and some fascinating categories like 'dangerous driving of trolley'. There was a significant difference between the sexes on the SRS for 'damaging or breaking something deliberately', both in school and out of school, and also for 'setting fire to something'. One teacher did see girls as 'more trouble round the school', but expansion of this remark — 'smoking, getting on your nerves, answering back, getting stroppy generally' — indicated relegation to personal interaction rather than infringement of institutional rules. Teachers were generally inclined to relate differences in school misbehaviour to sex roles, in the sense that boys were more likely to break rules about riding bicycles in the playground because more of them came on bicycles; they were prone to cause damage by kicking footballs around, 'whereas the girls with their tennis balls will just throw them from one to another — they're just living out their separate roles'. From the pupils' point of view, whereas boys were the ones to 'kick windows in, throw bricks', girls were the phantom daubers: pupils saw them as the ones to write on the walls, and the girls themselves admitted to more graffiti, and to far more carving of desks (a not insignificant theme we must return to later).

Pupil/pupil

It is in this first area of relationships that we begin to see the real anomalies. The detention book and the SRS revealed boys as more prone to fighting, either individually or as part of a gang fight. Boys were caned for bullying, and more often admitted 'hurting someone who hadn't done anything to you'. No girls had been put into detention or caned for fighting or bullying; they were three times more likely to say they had never fought. Yet when interviewed, pupils were quite emphatic that girls were the same and more often worse than boys with regard to fighting or bullying. Girls' behaviour towards other girls was seen as extremely problematic. Older girls were 'bigheads' who 'looked down on you'; 'girls are worse than boys, they always seem to pick on each other more than the boys do'; they are 'always having arguments and falling out'. Moreover, girls' persecution of each other seems longer drawn out; whereas boys have a fight and forget about it, girls 'keep on at people, catty and that'. Nor is it just verbal aggression, as the boys point out: 'There's just been a fight with two girls . . . one girl busted the other girl's nose.' Some boys did see their sex as fighting more in general, but claimed that when girls did start they were worse. This might partially explain the contradictions, and point to the need (as with work) to distinguish between quantity and quality.

Both pupils and teachers saw girls' fighting as resulting from jealousies over boys, while boys fought over football teams, presumably showing group allegiances, or using this as a symbolic arena for displays of what the pupils called 'being big and hard'. Some boys mentioned physical exchanges between boys and girls, but mostly to draw attention indignantly to the fact that they would get punished for it more harshly than the girls even if the girl had started it:

> They (the teachers) always go on, the girls are marvellous, don't start the fighting — it's *them* who start the fighting, we get the blame for it. Anything that happens, we get the blame.

It seems that the understanding that girls are not expected to show aggression makes toughness, especially physical toughness, stand out and appear more important. A female teacher commented:

> Only when you get an aggressive girl, she's far worse than a boy, it's noticed far more . . . when a girl gets aggressive, she will use absolutely every part of her body — her teeth, her nails, the hair-pulling and so on. It isn't just a question of being given a thump, you know. I think it's noticed far more, too, we tend to think more children are aggressive than actually are.

But this insight is linked to the perception that girls are getting worse;

whereas they used to be 'on the periphery of violence', they are now joining in — because of emancipation or television were the usual theories. Phrased sorrowfully by a pupil, it was 'Girls don't act like ladies any more, go around acting bigheaded.'

Thus whether girls actually 'equal' boys in their aggressive behaviour remains open; the question of *interpretion* of behaviour according to previous expectations and experiences begins to be underlined.

Pupil/teacher

The arena for deviance of greatest impact for both teachers and pupils was the one in which they both spent the major proportion of their time in school: the classroom. Over half the teachers mentioned discipline issues first when asked about differing sex reactions to school; when questioned on 'causing trouble' the pupils too were most likely to draw attention to 'cheeking' teachers. And it is here that we begin to understand the contradictory evidence: girls appear to cause many teachers of both sexes more problems than do boys, but (and this is part of the problem) the encounters are those the teachers feel they should be coping with on the spot, rather than referring to a higher authority or to further discipline procedures like detention, where the deviance may become officially recorded.

What are these particular problems posed by girls? It is not so much general classroom behaviour; there were no significant differences on the SRS for the categories 'fooling about in class' or 'throwing things in class'. Teachers felt there were *some* 'rough' girls as much as there were some 'rough' boys — it was 'even stevens'. It is instead in *responses* to discipline attempts, once rules have been broken, that the troubles lie. 'I wouldn't say that girls are more badly behaved than the boys — they're far more sensitive to what their rights are than boys are.' This 'sensitivity' is not a delicate passive Victorian stance, but manifests itself in particular behaviour postures agreed upon by all participants. Girls were quicker to 'take offence', more reactive to personal remarks:

> MT:* To a boy, in a friendly way, you could actually say to him, actually refer to him as ugly, you could say, 'come on ugly, over here', where you could never say that to a girl,

---

* Throughout, MT refers to male teacher, FT to female teacher, and LD to author. B is boy; G is girl.

unless she looked like Racquel Welch, I suppose, then she
would know that that was just being.... (LD: Ironic?) Yeah.

They also 'take offence' at deviance imputations:

> *MT:*   If you tell a boy who's doing something he shouldn't do,
> if you tell a boy, stop, then he will — but a girl will far more
> easily turn round and tell you what you can do.... They're
> far more defiant than the boys.

The old favourite — 'bearing grudges' — crops up again; girls do not
take a reprimand 'for what it's meant', but appear to get mileage from
reading into it more than was intended. The expression of such
'resentment' takes peculiarly female forms, with the stock descriptions
from both teachers and pupils containing not only the stereotypical
verbs whine and complain, but the adjectives and phrases 'bitchy',
'catty', 'aggressive with the mouth' and 'spiteful'. One girl's recollection sums up the pattern of difference:

> Girls can be worse than boys. They can be gossipy, niggly,
> disrupt a lesson, just by acting stupid, laughing and giggling in
> a corner, and a teacher can't do anything with them; on the
> other hand, the boys can jump over desks and act silly, things
> like that. They used to act like monkeys last year, didn't they?
> Girls used to disrupt the lesson though, they used to shout over
> the other side of the room, and if we had a teacher who wasn't
> very strict, they knew they could practically do what they
> wanted. They wouldn't do any work at all. Terrible.

Both the SRS and the interview showed pupils regarding girls as more
prone to 'telling the teacher what you thought of them'; and boys drew
particular attention to girls' use of language:

> *B:*   They swear at the teachers and everything. A wench walks
> in, and a teacher says, you gotta see Mr V, something like
> that, her goes, oh fucking hell, I don't want to see him. I've
> always gotta see him, something like that. (LD: Boys don't
> do that?) No, they just go.

The boys were far more likely to mention girls swearing than the girls
themselves were, but again this may be related to particular cultural
sensitivity to language from females, rather than necessarily a greater
incidence. Girls would in fact react very strongly to being *accused* of

swearing, and many incidents of such false accusations were highlighted. One girl was incensed at finding herself in the support unit one day because she was reported to have told a teacher to 'shit off' when she claimed she had 'only' responded 'shut up'.

Teachers did not report swearing quite so much (perhaps because it reflects badly on them, or pupils exaggerate, or the swearing is *sotto voce* anyway) but one important area where pupils and teachers agreed was on the linkage between girls' impertinence and teacher's difficulties in disciplining girls. Girls cheek teachers, said the pupils, 'because they can get away with it', and so said the teachers too, if not in so many words. Pupils pointed out that the degree of 'playing up' was directly related to the strictness, or lack of it, of the teacher, but described the 'lack of discipline' with some amazement at times:

> B: They [the girls] only do it to show off. When they start playing up, they really do. Swear at him, call the teacher names, and everything. Write on the board when he ain't looking. Write names on the board. He takes no notice, I don't know how he stands for it.

That girls are treated less harshly in general, and that male teachers have particular problems in disciplining girls, will be crucial issues; at the moment we can merely note a circular, self-reinforcing situation whereby the perception is that girls do not take their punishments as well as boys, and fewer punishments are used or are available. Do teachers not use as many sanctions for fear of not being able to implement them, or of causing long term resentment? Or are girls merely capitalising on the effect of *claiming* greater grievance?

But finally we can at least confirm that we may not be talking about girls as a category, but merely a prominent section. Pupils are quite precise in emphasizing *some* girls; the raw scores on the SRS revealed that girls tended to be more polarized for some items, ticking either 'never' or 'quite often', whereas the boys were more spread among the four frequencies. And teachers' remarks again always seemed to support the notion of 'extremes' of behaviour — typically 'On the whole I think that girls are more amenable to discipline, but if you get bad ones they can be stinkers.' Nor are these 'stinkers' confined to the lower streams:

> MT: Boys tend to be a bit more boisterous than what the girls are, the O level set I've got at the moment, where I find if you get a bad girl she's a damn sight worse than a bad boy.

Summary

Examination of one particular school adds a gloss then to the previous generalities about patterns of pupil deviance. A *résumé* of this localized picture shows girls as more conformist only in certain areas — the institutional rules of the school in terms of attendance, misbehaviour and damage, and the technical goals of achievement in terms of conscientiousness and presentation of work. Rule infringements such as smoking and lack of uniform are here equally likely for both sexes, and girls seem to assert *more* independence in the creation of personal time and space around the school. It is in the arena of interpersonal relationships that *some* girls can present different or greater 'problems' in their heightened, longer-lasting reactions to both affront (whether from peers or from teachers) and to attempted or actual disciplinary treatment from teachers. In short, if problems arise, they will not so much actively kick out at or avoid the institution, but they will be concerned to assert and protect their individual status.

Now the detective work begins. Whether or not the scene in Gladstone is at all typical, any theory of pupil deviance would appear to need to explain a) the fact that there were indeed overall differences *between* the sexes in response to school control; b) that *within* each sex there is selectivity as to which types of rules are broken; and c) that there may be starker contrasts between 'conformists' and 'deviants' for girls than there are for boys. The detail, and critiques, of current possible explanations are to be found in chapter 7; as I move into presentation of the pupils and their teachers at Gladstone, I will for the moment merely call up the spectres of five main suspects. There is the obvious issue of biological or genetic differences. There is the possibility of different socialization and control practices, with children brought up to have differing orientations towards authority, towards institutions, towards the display of aggression or emotion. A sub-cultural approach on the other hand would locate behaviour in the membership of groups, and would produce in evidence the fact that boys are more conditioned by, or reliant on, the larger peer group to provide status and identity than are girls. Then there is labelling theory which is concerned with how we categorize people and behaviour, and invites us to suspect that girls' and boys' conduct may be subject to different interpretations and different treatment in schools. Finally emerges social structure, where the analyses insist that socialization, labelling and subculture derive ultimately from the economic under-pinning of society, from patriarchy, or capitalism or indeed patriarchal capitalism. Clearly we are not searching for a single 'cause' of sex difference, but a way to synthesize these possibilities and test them against the day-to-day reality of an urban comprehensive school.

Another deviant feature of this book will now become apparent: it uses girls as the base-line for comparison. The aim is not just to chart the relatively unexplored field of girls' resistance in school, but to demonstrate that the female *can* provide a central focus for analysis in a mixed-sex situation. The female 'bias' will hopefully act as a counter to the male-oriented deviancy studies of the past, but, unlike them, it is not to be an exclusive focus. It invites comparisons with such studies, and with boys in the school itself; and it is to act as a constant reminder that women are not necessarily a 'specialized' field for investigation but half the world. While one hopes that the book would be useful to those working in the women's studies area, the intended implication is that analyzing from the female perspective gives new insights into pupil deviance in general.

2 Individual and Group: The Response From The Pupils

Outlining theories is of course much easier than testing them. One cannot do vivisection on pupils to examine genes; one cannot accost a schoolchild and enquire 'do you see yourself as a longterm victim of the reproductive capitalist infrastructure?' What is possible is some attempt to monitor immediate pupil and teacher reactions to each other and to institutional constraints. In this chapter I want to present some of the tentative findings, and a few of the many dead ends, in my exploration of pupils as individuals and as members of a group.

SOCIALIZATION AND CULTURE CONTACT
The aim here was to get at the very basic question of whether the sexes display different 'attitudes' towards self, school, teachers and peers — attitudes which would then occasion a conformist or deviant front. For this I used, in addition to semi-structured interviews, a bank of questionnaires to probe: self-concept and esteem; important concerns to the pupil personally; perceptions of the purpose of school; and present orientations to the actual life of the school. These issues could be balanced against admissions made on the self-report schedule. All results were subjected to statistical analysis (see Figures 5–7 below), but it is enough here to comment on overall trends — or lack of them.

Institutional Attachments

Control theory can be tried out by examining pupil orientations towards school. Are girls more likely than boys to form attachments to institutions like education, or more to the institution of marriage? With regard to school, the overwhelming impression in fact was of almost identical expectations for the sexes. Both boys and girls took an

17

instrumental view, believing that the main task of school was to help you to pass examinations, teach you things to help you get a good job, teach you what jobs are like, and teach you things which will be useful to you when you have got a job. A range of subjects and interests, as well as clubs and outings were far less important. Essays on 'The Ideal School' revealed similar percentages of boys and girls wanting better and more equitable teacher-pupil relationships, less compulsion in lessons, more free time and better facilities. In the interview, both sexes appreciated and disliked the same qualities in teachers; equal numbers were averse to uniform, the length of the school day, or simply 'getting up for it'.

Yet in spite of similar opinions that school was not an interesting place, and girls sharing the boys' doubts as to whether teachers 'took an interest in you', twice as many girls as boys replied 'yes' to the statement 'Most days you look forward to going to school'. This would agree with other research findings of girls' more positive orientation towards school (see evidence cited at the beginning of chapter 6). The question remains of why this should be. Girls were not notably more academically successful; they were certainly not preferred by the teachers; and friends at school were equally important for both sexes. In fact in response to the question 'what do you like about coming to school', the most frequently mentioned advantage was the social side. Typical comments were: 'If you couldn't have friends, school wouldn't be anything, would it?' and 'You can have a laugh, when you're not doing lessons, like'. For self-concept, there were no differences in response to 'I find it easy to get along with people in the class'; both sexes would be just as inclined to 'talk' in boring lessons — admitted equally to 'chatting in class'. Yet girls were not unaware of peer group pressures in addition to the fun; some of their comments were reminiscent of those American studies of girls' hesitation about displaying academic aptitude or interest:

> G: I like maths the best. My mates think I've gone soft 'cos I like maths. They can't stand maths. I've been top of the class nearly all the time I've been through school.
>
> G: Some teachers let us do anything. I think they should be more strict with us. If they're not strict you don't learn anything. I don't like playing up. *I know it sounds a bit silly,* but I like to learn. (My italics)

Neither sex is immune to the fear that they will be considered 'creeps' or 'swots' if they appear to adhere too strongly to school values. Essays on the 'Ideal Pupil' revealed similar linguistic scorn. One girl wrote: 'The ideal pupil is usually a teacher's pet, a creep, a poof, a pest and I hate them. One such person is Michael Clark.'

The only difference (to explain girls liking school better) that I could find was the tendency, not commented on by boys, to realize that it was preferable to anything else, as the following comments suggest: 'I don't know what I'd do without school'; 'I wouldn't know anybody if it weren't for school'; 'If you're at home all day you get very bored, so it's a means of interest'. Even the notorious Lorraine (see next section) argued: 'Stopping at home's boring. Like to come to school, me mates are here. And I like cooking and some of me lessons.'

This is not so much commitment to school, as a lack of any viable alternatives. The involvement would not run to any prolongation of the school day. When asked on the questionnaire how they would feel if they had to stay later each day so that time for both hobbies and homework could be fitted in, only six girls (all top stream) said they would like this. Reasons given were that help with homework could be given and it could all be got out of the way before they went home. The rest reacted with anything from doubt to pure horror, mostly on the grounds that, first, school was long enough as it was, and secondly, they had other things to do with their evenings.

Girls' current attachments, or lack of them, to the institution do not, then seem markedly different from boys', and are vested in the same factors: learning as a source of marketable skills; relationships with friends; relationships with teachers; the place and time spent in learning. If more girls enjoyed coming to school, it was only because of its preferability to the 'boring' home culture. The next issue to examine is whether school may be perceived as preferable to the future, in other words, whether a gender role means different perceptions of work and marriage and the school's relationship to these.

As mentioned, there is no sex differential in perception of the school's function in job choice and job acquisition. The majority of both sexes thought school should teach for, and about, careers. While pupils thought its least important task was to take them on outings to places of cultural interest, most thought it *very* important for the school to 'take you on visits to factories or offices or other work places to see the different sorts of jobs there and what the work is like'. 'Getting a job which you like' and 'to be earning money' were equally and vitally important for both sexes. 'Starting work as soon as possible' also showed no sex distinction. The theory that paid employment has less salience for girls would appear to have little foundation.

In the fourth year interview, pupils had been asked what 'career' or job they envisaged. Either they understandably did not know (or simply wanted to leave as soon as possible), or they had clearly sex differentiated occupations in mind. Investigating where the pupils were to be found two years later, we did not see school disappointing its charges. More girls had thought they might 'stop on' than boys, and in fact more did. Similar proportions of girls went into hairdressing, secretarial and unskilled work as had expected to, although fewer boys went into the services than had hoped. Half the boys got apprenticeships or moved into skilled manual work, and one third obtained unskilled manual work, which contained no surprises as compared with their predictions. Although many pupils would have liked more or different sets of option choices, the relationship of school learning to career was rarely mentioned in the interview. At that stage, early in the upper school and just into option choices, pupils would not necessarily be able to assess relevance to work; it is difficult to link specific job choices with differences in pupil deviance.

Regarding other aspects of future life, some of the items on the purpose of school questionnaire do show up some differences, as Table 1 reveals.

Table 1   Purpose of school questionnaire items

School should	Proportions of pupils saying various school objectives are very important	
	Girls	Boys
10 Teach you how to manage your money when you are earning and about things like rates and income tax	82%	69%
14 Help you to learn how to get on with other people, for example those you work with, your future wife or husband	66%	46%
9 Teach you things that will be useful in running a home	58%	39%

We can see from this extract that significantly more girls thought it important that school should teach about money management, and about future personal relationships. This can be related to the female role of caring wife, and household and financial manager; they also believed it more important than did the boys that school should instruct in home management, although the girls in the bottom stream dispro-portionately contributed to this difference. Whereas sport was far more important to boys, 'your family' and 'getting married' attracted significantly more girls. This could indicate greater social control for girls, or a more caring concern for family relationships; either would relate to female sex role socialization. Marriage is, however, still less salient than getting a job. There were admittedly stream differences here, but even so, twice as many low stream girls thought getting a job very important as thought getting married very important.

It would appear at this stage that girls can be oriented both to work and to future relationships (as in essays analysed by Pahl, 1978 — see Chapter 7). Their options are in some ways wider, in some ways constrained by female sex role expectations and possibilities. The interaction with stream is clearly crucial here: pupils have learned not just a sex role but an 'ability' role which will weight the importance attached to future options. We have another chicken-and-egg riddle where we do not know whether girls look to the outside world of marriage because they are not successful at school, or whether they are less successful at school because their concerns lie elsewhere. The most one can say is that the process is interactive. And the overall impression is anyway that, in terms of perceptions of school life and of teachers, in expectations of education and work, there are few sex role differences which would account for the marked divergences in deviance.

Role Traits

Is it then something 'deeper' in the socialization of the individual? Are boys less likely to 'internalize' the values of school conformity? On the self-concept questionnaire there were no significant differences be-tween boys and girls with regard to the items 'I do things without being told several times', 'I like school jobs which give me responsi-bility', and 'I sometimes use unfair means to do my school work'. Nor, interestingly, were there many differences between the streams; however, the very bottom stream girls said 'Unlike Me' for the 'unfair means' question, presumably because they rarely did any school work, unfairly or otherwise, and conversely the top stream girls were twice as likely to say 'Like Me' for this item. This would indicate impression management for the achieving girl rather than moral obligation. I found no items to indicate that girls' greater 'conscientiousness' re-sulted from their finding school work more absorbing, or from believing that norms about the learning process were intrinsically just: presumably their application to work hangs on activities which are visible and gradable such as classwork and homework. The conclusion is that girls' greater 'conformity' is a carefully managed (rather than internalized) presentation; they have not so much learned the values, but have learned the approval from appearing to adhere to them. Typically one girl said in response to the interview question 'What do you do if the lesson is boring' 'I pretend to write — I don't interfere with the lesson.' A boy on the other hand would 'find something to distract you — like flicking bits of paper about'.

But is this then related to the supposed 'passivity' of females (p. 148)? With regard to physical aggression, there were indeed some nice instances of role socialization. One girl said 'Mind you, I don't think it's right for girls to fight. Especially if you're in a skirt — you've only got to be knocked over and your skirt's everywhere.' While pupils felt on the whole that boys and girls should be punished equally, some girls were aware of the female sex image: girls should be caned 'only if they're in trousers'. Apart from the implied indecency of striking a skirted bottom (and girls were in fact caned only on the hand in Gladstone), there is the 'weakness' clause: 'Boys are supposed to be harder than girls, girls would probably break down.' The boys were themselves torn between this masculine image — 'we can take it better' — and grievances about differential treatment. Usually the latter predominated.

Yet it is with verbal rather than physical encounters that some real indicators emerge. Both sexes claimed similar (doubtful) feelings with regard to talking in front of the class, to answering questions before anyone else; but the clue to passivity seems to lie in the *initiation* of pupil/teacher conflicts, and the emotional and personal significance attached to these. The slight majority of girls agreed 'I never ask teachers to explain something again', the majority of boys disagreeing, with top stream boys being the most confident group. More significant still was the marked difference in response revealed in Table 2.

Table 2   *Self-concept questionnaire item*

	Like Me		Unlike Me	
	Girls	Boys	Girls	Boys
14 I get tense when I'm called on in class	73%	58%	27%	42%

The interview revealed many top stream girls reluctant to question the teacher, for fear both of a lowered opinion from the teacher, and feeling foolish in front of peers. Very typical examples were:

> If you come across a problem, I feel that if you're put in an O level set, you feel silly if you go and ask them, 'cos the boys can probably do the science, but the girls seem to get stuck on things like that and get worried. I have asked them a couple of times, but you sit there trying to fathom it out. I haven't the confidence to go and ask, I'd rather work it out for myself.

> I don't like it when the teacher comes round with a ruler and just bangs it on the desk and points to something and just says 'answer the question'. You know it at the beginning of the lesson, but when he bangs the ruler it completely goes from your head and you feel such a fool.

The 'Ideal Teacher' essays showed similar concerns about exposure, with girls hating teachers walking round 'spying' on them when they were working: 'It gives you an uncomfortable feeling inside you.'

The *Young School Leavers* report (Schools Council, 1968) mentioned that girls more than boys 'complained that they did not understand the subjects, they were not explained enough and they were not good at them'. Although in Gladstone we encountered the view that girls cheeked the teachers more, in other ways (or for different girls) there seemed a fear of drawing attention to themselves, to their supposed inadequacies. The transcripts contain anxiety words: 'confidence', 'fool', 'silly', 'muddle', 'worried', 'uncomfortable', 'afraid'. Presumably the vicious circle of not understanding, not asking, understanding even less, would go some way towards explaining differential achievement, especially in 'boys' subjects like maths and science. It also ties up with teachers' perceptions of girls being more 'emotional', or 'taking things personally'. Girls were significantly more inclined to agree that 'I change my mind a lot' — which could be interpreted as stereotypical female lack of confidence in one's own judgments, or as the 'emotional insecurity' remarked on by teachers. While the item 'I often feel upset in school' elicited no overall sex difference, low stream girls were significantly more prone to say 'like me' than were top stream girls (or either stream of boy). The inference is that for top stream girls, 'emotion' would be channelled into anxieties about work and self-effacement, but for the bottom streams might also include 'attention-seeking' or upsetting exchanges with teachers.

While, as we have seen, friends at school are equally important to both sexes, we may have to question the actual impact of the large peer group (p. 173). Look at the two items from the self–concept inventory in Table 2a.

Table 2a *Self-concept questionnaire items*

	Like Me		Unlike Me	
	Girls	Boys	Girls	Boys
19 I take an active part in group projects and activities	30%	60%	70%	40%
3 Kids usually follow my ideas	19%	33%	81%	67%

But (19) suggests doing specific things – no question covers talking in groups etc.

There is a statistically significant sex difference, with boys more likely to concur. For boys, the group seems a more important source of activity and values; girls may be more independent, or oriented towards other people as individuals. Significantly more girls thought school should 'help you develop your personality and character'. If girls are more individualistic, then this might account for better orientation towards the individualism required in school achievement; or girls' conformity may arise because they have learned to seek and manipulate adult approval. For girls who have not learned this, or who have unlearned it, the group does not necessarily constitute a replacement pressure force, so that there may be an unpredictability interpreted as the 'extremes' of behaviour.

'Maturity' was another theme which contained some pointers. Boys and girls agreed wholeheartedly with the statement 'Teachers forget you are growing up and treat you like a kid', yet interestingly, the personal concerns section then showed up the sex differences apparent in Table 3.

Table 3 *Personal concerns questionnaire items*

	Proportions of pupils saying things were very important to them personally	
	Girls	Boys
4 Being treated as grown up	88%	68%
3 Clothes, hairstyles, appearance	74%	40%

It would seem that boys would be aware of the school's 'childish' treatment of them, but be less concerned about it. We can see the predictable divergences in concern about image, supported elsewhere in the questionnaire: regarding the purposes of school, significantly more girls thought it important for the school to 'help you make the most of yourself, for example with your appearance'; and we return to the self-concept section for an interesting extension to this greater comparative concern with appearance (Table 3a).

Table 3a Self concept questionnaire item

	Like Me		Unlike Me	
	Girls	Boys	Girls	Boys
5 I'm not as nice looking as most people	56%	33%	44%	67%

The significant sex difference arises chiefly because of the large number of top stream girls agreeing; low stream girls were markedly more confident (or less concerned). This refers us to analyses of 'teenage culture' (p. 174) and supports the findings there of an association between early maturity, extreme fashion consciousness and high ability for girls. In Gladstone, teachers saw top stream girls as, if anything, more fashion conscious than the lower streams, and the girls in the lower streams themselves also commented on the 'top classes' being snooty, bigheaded, because 'they have better haircuts'. While 'having a good time while you are young' predictably was a crucial personal concern for both sexes and all streams, pop music and dancing attracted many more girls than boys, which agrees with the teachers' views that girls went more to discos and clubs than the boys of their age.

Concerns about appearance, and the possible greater anxiety about themselves as individuals, seems tied up for girls with the question of personal identity and reputation. Not only did girls write more on the desks and walls, but from observation they tended to write their name, or their name plus the currently favoured boy; boys would scribble obscenities or the name of their football team. Girls seem concerned to carve out their identity, literally, on the institution. When wanting to look at school records one day, I was offered a desk outside the group tutor's room, facing a wall. This desk turned out to be the 'dunces' desk', where behaviour problems were put when thrown out of lessons and sent to the tutor. The wall was covered in graffiti, and was obviously the site of long-standing conversations between prisoners, with questions raised and answered in different handwriting about issues such as the sexual prowess of the teachers. There was the occasional snipe at a boy: 'Clive Parker is a wanker by myself', but the large proportion of this wall poster campaign was directed at girls: 'Debbie Parsons is a pro and a bag', or 'Trisha J is a cunt'. Many names had been furiously crossed out by their owners; one girl, whose name appeared many times, had been driven to inscribe 'Janie T is not a slag and if you think I am say it to my face OK boys or girls'. The question of moral rules and reputations is clearly to be a recurring theme in our investigation.

So far, then, from this number-crunching part of the the investigation, we can begin to link both the overall conformity and the conspicuous deviance of girls to personal concerns of identity, image, reputation and appearance. It is not to the attachments to institutional values and goals as such that we must look, but to the 'moral careers' offered by the school, by teachers and by peers. Immediate negotiations in the classroom have more impact in explaining sex differences in deviance than do long-term pupil perceptions of the function of schooling.

THE CHALLENGE FROM THE WENCHES

Above we were on the scent of individual interpretations of conformity; here we start from the opposite quadrant in exploring group expressions of deviance. Members of staff were unanimous in identifying one particular group of girls as 'difficult'; I accordingly focused for a year on them in the eager anthropological Quest For The Sub-culture. The admitted aim was to provide the female answer to Willis' 'lads', to Corrigan's 'Smash Street Kids', to Hargreaves 'delinquescent gang' (p. 165 ff.); these girls, now in the bottom streams of the fifth year, clearly posed certain longstanding 'problems' for the school, and were viewed as having some sort of group identity. My original intention was to 'discover' the norms, cultural styles, meanings and symbols attached to group membership, and provide a revelatory account of the deviant female group to counterpose to the literature on boys. That this aim was only partially fulfilled will become apparent as we continue.

I began spending whole days with the group, accompanying them to all their lessons, and participating in break-time activities and out-of-school trips. The girls were also released from classes at regular intervals to talk with me as a group in a spare room, when the conversations were recorded. The setting and option system meant that the same mix of girls was not always together, and decisions had to be made about which individuals to follow during the course of a day. Their own association choices were also variable (as with Furlong's interaction sets, p. 176) and it became obvious from the start that a tight controlling culture was not going to be identified. Nevertheless over this period I got to know a great deal about twelve girls who confronted teachers with problems and/or formed loose associations — the six comprising the remaining female component of 5F, five from the fourth and fifth streams, and one from the third stream. Two were of Asian extraction, one was half West Indian, with the rest white British. 'Wenches' was the local female appellation, and this is the term I shall use to distinguish the group under discussion.

Talking to the wenches was not only to elicit retrospective 'accounts' of what had gone on in school and outside; it also aimed to explore present and future worlds, to discover structural patterns. I wanted to know about the girls' perceptions of work — the desirability of it, the contrast with school. I wanted to check on their views on marriage and the home, and on their acceptance of patriarchy. How far would their social knowledge and skills in school be determined or influenced by the structural facts of being female in their home town (which we will here call Scrapton).

While the conversations 'overheard' ranged over a wide spectrum of issues — teachers, violence, boyfriends, children, drugs, work, parents, reputation — the central core could be seen to be relationships. The two arenas of school and out-of-school together provide a range of possibilities for interaction — on the one hand with teachers and with peers, on the other with boyfriends and the family. In the girls' accounts of action, all these relational aspects interweave into a complex network, for they do not necessarily talk about them separately. The themes which emerge show why: they all link to the crucial search for status which is underlined by the sub-cultural literature (p. 164). And status is a relational term: for these girls, status is not defined in tangible achievements or exploits, but in the day-to-day negotiation and interaction with adults and adolescents.

Observation of the wenches in many different educational contexts found that not only was the group different with different teachers, but that individual girls would be seemingly unpredictable in their encounters with teachers and in the extent to which they associated with the others at any one time. The amount of truancy of course determined how many of the group were present on any day, and thus the network would alter. Sometimes they would do some work, sometimes they would pay lip service to the idea without achieving much, sometimes they would blatantly do nothing. There were occasions when the teacher would be ignored, others when ritual games would be played to test parameters, yet others when direct confrontation would flare, apparently from nothing. The same request from different teachers might bring forth a whole range of responses: nor did the girls necessarily always agree on which teachers they liked or disliked. One has to examine the girls' accounts of observed and unobserved action to determine the themes and the shared meanings underlying their behaviour. Inter-group relationships much be seen against a backcloth of specific institutional and cultural contradictions which have to be managed by these girls.

Contradictions in Schooling

The wenches talked a lot about their teachers. Teachers were a source of interest, contempt, amusement, anger, affection, prestige. A perceptive remark one day by Terri provided the clue to the basis of their interpretations:

> But when you see some of the teachers, you wish you'd played them up worser. They're so bigheaded, they're like they're kids and all. The way they say, 'here you, come here'. You say 'wait, you don't say that to me. Who do you think you're talking to?' They say it as though they're kids to other kids.

What appears to arouse the greatest hostility and contempt from the girls is being presented with contradictions. Teachers are supposed to be authoritative adult models; instead they behave like their charges. The recurrent types of teacher behaviour selected for discussion by the wenches highlight the 'rules' which teachers are deemed to be breaking, and the criteria by which they are consequently deemed not to warrant the girls' reciprocal adherence to pupil rules.

The teacher as model

There are various behaviours which come under the heading of 'setting a good example'. The girls castigated teachers who, they said, shouted at them, used insulting nicknames like 'Maggot' for Margaret, bawled get that coat off, or never said please. They described the irony of how a teacher had reprimanded them: 'I've seen more manners in a packet of brussel sprouts than you layabouts', only to 'ask' them to leave by means of a pointing finger and 'You! Out!' Elaine commented: 'and if you say anything, they say 'shut your mouth or I'll get you out here'. I mean, that's the teacher, that is. I mean, you don't say things like that, do you, teachers to the kids.' Bad manners could be returned only by equally bad manners if status and principles of reciprocity were to be preserved:

> *Julie:* I had a go at the cooking teacher Monday... I said, I don't use manners to pigs.... I says, you teachers in this school think you're everybody, and when we're big enough, you're just scared of us. Tuesday morning, after me having a go at her, Monday, she give me ten out of ten for me sausage plait.

An important symbolic power victory for Julie.

In accordance with a sex-linked interest in appearance, girls were similarly incensed by 'dirty' teachers — any who wore scruffy suits, down-at-heel shoes, whose hair stuck up on end.

> *Donna:* He stinks, don't he? I wouldn't stand too close to him, he'd knock you out.
> *Julie:* He's supposed to set a good example to we, ain't he?
> *Debbie:* I had a shock once, he came in a different suit. After about ten years. He had that from a jumble sale, didn't he?

Female teachers likewise are supposed to be clean and respectable:

> *Debbie:* Mrs S was the one, her was about 82 years old ... her was filthy, her used to sit with her legs open, didn't her? All the chaps would be sitting in front of we on the floor lying down like this. Vultures. Every time I looked at her, I could kill her.

Mrs S's age presumably precluded the girls seeing her as a rival; it was her lack of propriety in fact which infuriated them. At the same time the girls were subject to teachers' comments on their own choice of dress and interpretations of uniform, and, worse still, implications that they were unaware of how to make an impression. They were warned to come 'looking respectable' if they wanted to go on a school trip, or if they were being interviewed for a job — a major insult for these shrewd and discerning girls.

There is a similar problem about examples for teachers who smoke and chew when pupils are not allowed to. Many of the girls have been smoking and drinking for some years, and in these practices, as in many others, see themselves as adults. The wenches work on the logical proposition that either teachers should not smoke themselves, or they should allow you to, in specified places. Smoking the girls' cigarettes which they have confiscated is perceived as the final insult. Dawn points to discriminatory rules in operation about lateness. too:

> When you come late, you have to stay till half past four — what about when the teachers come late? It's different then. And when the teachers are away, they don't have to bring a note, do they? They phone up.

Above all, the sexual morality of the teachers should be irreproachable. The wenches are, for some reason, faintly disgusted by male teachers who marry ex-pupils; and displaying an interest outside the teacher-pupil relationship is viewed with suspicion:

Debbie: Half the teachers today, they'm sex mad.
Julie: Ar, they're after the girls. They're in a car, right, like I never come on a Friday afternoon, put me posh clothes on, pencil skirt, and, you know, those funny half-inch stiletto shoes, and me and Lorraine had the same on, we was going somewhere, teachers went by in the car and blipped their horn at we! And they was from our school, they don't know it was me and Lorraine.
LD: You don't think teachers ought to do that?
Julie: No, specially the married ones.

The story may have been told partially to demonstrate Julie's fatal attractiveness, but it nonetheless throws interesting light on the mores still expected of teachers. The girls discuss sex education, and again expect the institution to give them a lead. As Linda said, 'They ought to give you lessons so as you can expect what's going to happen when you leave school and that. They should tell you what age not to have sex at, and that.' At first sight this does not square with their indignation on being gratuitously advised over appearance; but the importance attached by the girls to moral affairs (and to unwanted pregancies) will crop up again.

The same standards are expected of other adults in positions of semi-authority:

Dawn: You know the teachers, even if they're dinner women (sic) they shouldn't say bloody, should they. Well, the dinner woman was turning all that out, dinner time, saying I've bloody had enough of this, kids, they get on my bloody nerves, her kept saying that, but if that was we...

Expulsions from the dining room because of confrontations with dinner women were fairly commonplace amongst the wenches; the issue is never who started it, but the simple one, as in all these interactions, of whether those in control in the institution practise what is generally preached and enforced. The wenches' own 'language' was by no means unsullied by 'swear words', and they would even delight in one of the group 'giving someone a mouthful' yet they expect different conduct from those they might esteem. Julie had been most impressed by her new boyfriend making her wait outside the Crown because people inside were 'talking dirty'.

I was initially struck by the casual way the wenches treated school property: they would screw up work-sheets, drop test-tubes, push desks over, throw books up into the ceiling space, and, of course, deface surfaces. This was not done gleefully, or necessarily in defiance, but almost wearily, desultorily, automatically. An extract from my observation notes:

> Mr B gets papers etc given out. All do as requested — except Donna. Carole puts papers on her desk for her to give out, on an instruction from Mr B. She sits there watching them slide off onto the floor. 'I ain't picking them up.' Eventually she gives out the papers remaining on her desk.

Yet this apparent lack of respect becomes more explicable if we see the teachers through their eyes; teachers make them waste paper doing lines and then tear them up in front of them. 'I tell my mum sometimes, and she says what do they rip them up for, they keep on they ain't got no paper at school.' There are teachers also who do not show respect for pupil property:

> *Donna:* Her was looking at this book, magazine, takes the book off her, chucks it across the room, kicks it under the table! And the wench says, can I have me book back, at the end of the lesson, and he says, no, it's going in the bin. He's snotty. I don't like his lessons. That was too much.
>
> *Debbie:* Kick it under the desk and that, as though it's rubbish. If that was me, I'd have kicked it back at him.

Here my girls were not directly involved, but nonetheless the teacher had committed an offence: presumably the more rules the teachers break, the less the girls need to feel committed to institutional rules or institutional property.

Control

The first fundamental contradiction is that teachers are supposed to set a good example, yet some do not; a second is that they are supposed to be in control, and again some are patently not. The 'saft' teachers, those who cannot keep order, do not merit a great deal of respect from the girls. We should explore the interesting inversion of logic whereby it becomes the teacher's fault if pupils cannot resist playing them up. If a girl wins a confrontation, the teacher's right to sympathy is also withdrawn:

> *Linda:* He ain't said anything to me since.
> *LD:* Why?
> *Linda:* 'Cos he's too frightened. Thinks I'm frightened of him, but I ain't.
> *Debbie:* No, but it's a shame for him, though.
> *Linda:* Tis a shame, but he gets on your nerves.'

Similarly Janet observes:

> *Mr D:* He's saft, he is. He'll put the books on the desks and not one person does a bit of writing. So he fetches Mr Y, can't shout at you hisself, you know, has to fetch Mr Y.... We can answer him back, can't we. He ain't so strict as the other teachers.... I feel sorry for him in a way. 'Cos he's only little.

Are teachers in some sort of double-bind? If they shout, they are bad-mannered; if they do not, they are 'saft'. Yet the girls feel forced into contradictions themselves:

> *Kath:* It was all down to us, really, what made the one die, wasn't it? He was never here, he used to come and we used to play him up, and he used to be ever so nervous and he'd just go out, and he'd be ever so bad.
> *Terri:* He died not long after.
> *Kath:* We locked him in the classroom once, pulled the handle off, and he properly cried, really cried.
> *LD:* How did you feel?

> *Kath:* You feel great when you're doing it, 'cos it's funny to
> see them, but then afterwards you sit and think about it, and
> thought, oh, it was horrible.
> *Terri:* Like now, now you know he's dead, you think, oh
> dear.
> *Kath:* There was no need for it.

But the teacher was not blameless: he had pulled hair, chucked them
out, treated them 'like farm animals': 'When he keeps on, you can't
help it, you have to keep doing it, 'cos it makes you laugh.' The girls
may delight in their victories, but also may have to bear the responsibility of guilt. So 'techniques of neutralisation' are used which 'blame the
victim' for putting girls into positions where they have to create laughs,
or have to save face. Ten days before she left, Debbie was still saying
'There's nothing to miss in this school. It ain't the kids' fault, it's the
teachers' fault, 'cos they should have stricter teachers.'

Thus teachers who are supposed to contain deviance, but in fact
amplify it, cause problems for the girls. They are particularly sensitive
to teachers who attempt to 'show them up' in front of other kids, or
who 'stir trouble' by relaying publicly other teachers' comments on
them. There are, on the other hand, teachers the wenches will behave
for, who do not show them up, who don't 'make up things up what
you've done'.

> *Julie:* Like if we said to one teacher, oh Sir, Linda's been
> ripping the books, or something, he'd go, good for Linda; if
> it was another teacher — like you can't have a joke with Mr T
> — he'll have her in front of the class, shows her up, don't he?

In the end, it is not Linda's fault for ripping the books, or even the
group's for telling the teacher, but the teacher's for making an issue of
it. It is not that the girls are perverse, but that they have their own ideas
of proportion: a common phrase is 'there was no need', or 'I'd done
wrong, but that was a bit much.' Minor incidents to them seem to get
blown up. This can be a source of laughs, and the creation of power
possibilities. Donna conmented: 'Mr C, you can have a laugh with
him, 'cos you get him mad, just like that, you've only got to say "I ain't
doing my work", he'll say "Get outside, get to Mrs I, go here."' But
overreaction can also become a source of personal hostility and revenge
if girls feel themselves unduly scapegoated.

Teachers who are easily provoked, either for small offences, or by
rising to the deliberate 'getting them mad', thus cause more trouble;

they have only themselves to blame for future lack of cooperation. Teachers who are 'deviance insulative', on the other hand, are those who manage to keep the negotiations at a less intense level, or who enter into the spirit of things. The girls used to tease Miss T about her association with a male member of staff: the game was to make her go red, which she invariably did. Terri would take her on one side, say seriously: 'You've gotta get it sorted out, ain't you, Miss.' I asked, did that 'get her madder'. Linda said: 'No, like it gets her mad, she goes, "OK, fair enough, you've made me go red, let's finish with it for the day now." Like her ain't funny with you, like her has a game with you.' 'Games' in the classroom are, of course, not exclusive to girls; but the preferences amongst the wenches often centred round this individual role reversal, rather than the boys' 'team' performances to be discussed later. The science teacher wants them to try mouth-to-mouth resuscitation, but Sandra objects, on the grounds that 'I don't want to breathe into anybody else.' The teacher then offered to go on to something else, but Sandra then magnanimously agreed 'No, it's all right, we'll do it.' Such a stance by Sandra simultaneously demonstrates her own adult refinement and her influence over events. I was never sure who 'won' in these games, or if the point was not to win, but just to play the game; often these ploys in the classroom were ways to pass the time, share a laugh with each other or the teacher, test the teacher's control and role style.

Teacher's knowledge

Linked to teachers having to be 'in authority' is their having to be 'an authority': the third contradiction is that teachers are supposed to be possessors and purveyors of knowledge, yet appear neither to teach anything nor to know what is going on. Hence teachers who 'don't learn you nothing' are castigated by girls as much as boys:

> *Linda:* You know them records, Black Country, The Comics,
> he lets us listen to them, double lesson, that's boring, that is.
> *Carole:* He thinks we enjoy it, but we don't, it's boring.
> *Linda:* What does playing records learn you? What does going
> out to see them make buttons learn you?
> *Carole:* It don't learn you nothing.

Although girls may see school as irrelevant to marriage, they still deem it to have an improvement function. Teachers are supposed to be the arbiters of achievement; thus the over-anxious motivators who give undue praise to poor work are swiftly seen through, as in this example from my observation notes: '"Come on, Debbie, you've made a start", says Mr C, encouragingly. Debbie had written the title, fifteen minutes ago. She laughs, derisively.' And teachers should be in charge, yet appear dependent on pupils' good will and cooperation. Donna's view is that '*They* should supply you with the pens, *they* want you to do the writing.' Such alienated responses are a product of the girls' low stream status in a system organized for the certification of others. The Gladstone High official handbook states quite openly:

> Much work in the upper school is geared to external examinations. We make no apology for this. The examinations provide a goal for the pupils to aim at, and the results provide a valuable guide for employers when they interview applicants for jobs.

The wenches, though, reject if not the ends, certainly the institutionalized means of achieving them:

Sandra: Don't want to take exams, don't get you anywhere.
Donna: ... work even harder, they try and tell you, this'll get you a better job, but it don't, not in the end. You just end up in the factory like anybody else.

They are also cynical about the official careers guidance formula for approaching work, that of getting lists of firms and writing applications. Their immediate experience leads them to assert that 'you have to go there yourself', preferably when you know someone is leaving. As with McRobbie's girls (p. 175), it is how you look and dress which will impress an employer, not pieces of paper. Given that some of the wenches at least were capable of taking examinations, their comments could well be interpreted as cultural 'penetrations' (Willis, 1977) — that is, awarenesses — of the working class opportunity structures in the locality.

Thus teachers who do not give you marketable skills, or the unworldly ones who do not know what it is like 'out there' getting jobs, contradict their authoritative role; also in this category come the credulous teachers, easily fooled by the girls' strategies to create time and space for themselves. 'Her takes it all in, what you tell her', was a common refrain; Debbie even managed a cup of tea from the cooking teacher one morning by claiming she had had no breakfast. But lack of knowledge and awareness is more importantly demonstrated in the teacher who always 'picks on' the wrong pupil for offences: 'It's got to be the one they said it is, they can't be wrong.' The wenches are very sensitive to both the 'sibling phenomenon' and 'pupil biography' in deviance imputations. They see it as pointless 'being good' as the teachers always attribute responsibility, for example because their sister was 'bad', or because they themselves have gained a bad reputation. Again, this may be a technique of neutralisation, a way to shelve blame, but it was a frequently reiterated theme, as with Lorraine's comment: 'I've been suspended twice in one week, 'Cos of me background, me family what used to be here. 'Cos they were all the same. They don't give me a chance.'

Teachers are of course also subject to 'reputations'. Terri recounted: 'Like when I first came to this school, me brother says, like playing Mr J up, and Mr C, and then that's how it goes on, you spread rumours about and then they all do it, don't they?' But these rumours are only confirmed by the teacher's subsequent lack of teaching skill and perspicacity. Mr C 'puts one thing on the board and talks about something else'. He had come into another lesson one day and demanded from Debbie the lines he had given her on Thursday. She had not been in school that day, and told him so. 'He went bright red and went out of the room . . . one up for me.' In terms of one-upmanship, a twist which the wenches enjoyed was leaving school one afternoon when the teacher had not arrived for their lesson. They had taken their cooking things and gone to do community service in the old folks home, and 'naturally' they were thought to be, and later were accused of, playing truant (especially as they had marched out saying 'we're going home'). Being 'good' when people think you are deviant is a refreshing change from being deviant when people think you are innocent; but neither puts the deviance definers in a good light.

Status

All these perceived contradictions — not setting examples, provoking rather than containing deviance, lack of knowledge and awareness — would not necessarily be peculiar to girls' interpretations; but a final and most important school inconsistency has elements which are directly related to sex role identity. Both teachers and pupils are, of course, in the status game, but some teachers seek to promote their image when the pupils are not in a position to comment on this. Teacher insecurity is quickly noted, for example the teacher who talks 'normally' to the girls, but then puts on a 'snotty' voice to other teachers; or the teacher who 'treats the kids OK if they're on their own', but then 'shows off' if another class is in, 'showing folks up and that' by excessive disciplining. Teachers who are 'bigheaded' are a common source of complaint from all pupils; but the girls pointed to the sex image sometimes attached to this:

Rajinder: He thinks he's hard. Thinks all the wenches like him. Thinks all of them do.

Linda: Says, I've come in my new suit today, 'cos I've got to show some people round the school and I've got my new suit on, and he was going like this, warn't he? (flamboyant gesture), d'you like me new suit, that's why I've got it on.

Rajinder: He didn't have to tell us he'd got a new suit on, did he? Who wants to know?

Donna: If you go up to him in class, he thinks you fancy him, don't he?

The idea that they might fancy him is not only an insult to their taste, but also infringes the girls' rules about proper teacher conduct. Female teachers, too, have to be careful: 'Honest — her kept smiling at you, thinks her's beautiful. Can't stand her.' Arrogance, bigheadedness, and personal conceit are inexcusable in those who already have power and privilege, and especially in those who then attempt to downgrade the girls' own moral and sexual standing. A particular form of insult which has no equivalent for boys is slurs on the girls' moral character (see p. 184). Sandra said of a teacher: 'She gets on my nerves. Calling us scum and sluts. So I threw a pencil at her. Hit her glasses.' Linda tells me repeatedly one day how a male teacher had told her 'you'm nothing but common'. Donna joined in: 'He called her a prostitute', and Linda continued: 'He says, by the way you're going on, you'll have to get married before you're sixteen. I went mad, I did.'

The deputy headmistress herself was worried about this type of imputation, and thought staff who called girls such things 'asked for what they got'. One parent had threatened prosecution because his daughter had been called a slut; Linda's father had also reacted angrily when she told him about being called 'common'. There seems a need for the girls to check female identity against another male source after such stigmatisations; for the wenches it was also essential to react angrily themselves:

Janet: Her called Trudy an old bag, don't her?

Debbie: Ah. Teacher called her an old bag.

LD: (mishearing) You as well?

Debbie: No — I'd have killed her if her'd called it me — Trudy Cole. Her says, I'll tell Mrs I about her. I says, you must be mad, if her'd called me that, I'd have flung at her.

Solutions

The first prerequisite for the formation of a sub-culture is thus met: a group of people with common problems thrown together in a common situation. The problems for these girls seem to be the management of contradiction: against the basic 'status frustration' (p. 166) of being non-examination pupils in an examination-oriented institution are set glaring contradictions in the teacher–pupil relationship. They are being controlled for little purpose by those not seen as worthy of controlling. Against these anomalies they must manage their own presentation of self, whether as pupil or as independent young woman. The next step, then, is to examine whether common solutions are found to these problems, and whether the group is a counter-source of recognition and status, or provides guidelines for action and reaction.

    Certain group strategies, styles and activities are indeed in evidence. Some are geared to 'making their presence felt', others to the creative generation of freedom or meaning in their institutional life. Day-to-day classroom styles were wideranging, as mentioned, but often involved doing everything larger than life: moving chairs, calling for Sir, putting down books, all received exaggerated emphasis. A way to mock a role is of course to parody it, and thus distance yourself from it. They would feign anguish or indignation if they did not get a workcard or apparatus immediately (and then of course do nothing with it). Two typical minutes of an RE lesson:

Donna: I can't write, I've hurt me finger.
Teacher: Well, discuss it.
Donna: I *am* discussing it (she makes mouthing signs).

Teacher moves to Janet, who is doodling, suggests she write something.

Janet, stunned: I'm practising!
Elaine: I haven't got a sheet.
Teacher, mildly: You should have one from last week.

Elaine, thrusting file at him (forte): If you can find one in
    there.

Outrage is, of course, a good way to make a teacher back down.

Apart from controlling the management of a lesson, the girls
control time for themselves by being late for classes, skipping lessons,
leaving classes with or without permission, disappearing when supposedly out of school on community service, or simply not coming to
school at all. 'Playing trot' or 'blagging off' was sometimes an
individual withdrawal from school, but could also be a group activity,
with the wenches congregating at, for example, Lorraine's house.
Confrontations with the 'Trotter woman' were therefore frequent, as
she was viewed as the enemy, someone who threatened to prosecute;
she would 'twit on you', 'have you put away'.

Space is controlled by the use of certain territories in school, for
smoking or just hanging around. The smokers' corner, where I was
allowed access, did contain some boys, but it was mostly female.
Lookouts were posted, but these, plus the teacher patrols, had a ritual
quality about them: the teacher would come by, always just too late,
and joke, 'OK, fags out'. Although the girls were looking forward to
work in order to earn money, they recognized that at work they would
not be able to create so many freedoms, whereas 'here you can have a
walk about an' that'.

But it is not just the creation of time and space, but something to
fill it which is important. 'Having a laugh' and the generation of
excitement and mobility are not just confined to boys' gangs (p. 170);
the wenches, too, create their own excitement, their own life spaces to
allay the perceived boredom and futility of schooling. Breaking the
glass to set the firebell off is a predictable ploy. Debbie also recounts
how they 'rung up the school, saying there was a bomb planted, and
the school had ten minutes to get out, and the whole school went over
the park, getting the coppers in and everything.' Linda reenacts the
occasion when, tired of planting chewing-gum in the teacher's newly
permed hair, they started passing a lighted cigarette round, which
somebody finally put into the teacher's pocket: 'And she goes, ooh, can
anybody smell burning and we'd go, you can't, we can't smell nothing,
and she goes, ooh me pocket, it's me pocket!' There is partial
recognition that these events may by now be exaggerated or even
fantasized: Rajinder demurs 'The chewing gum never really stuck in
her hair', although Donna is adamant: 'It did, her had to have her hair
cut.' Yet the consensus that some version of these events did occur, and

NB [the concern to retell the myths, indicates the importance of shared reality transformers. 'Pinching', whether purses, sweets, cigarettes, vegetables from outside a shop, or even rhubarb from a garden, is done 'for a laugh', and is part of the accumulated repository of folk memories beginning 'That was a laugh, warn't it, when we . . .'. But these are more than just laughs, they are victories, small-scale triumphs over teachers, poofs, the Trotter woman, the institution.

Group rules

The need to create and maintain control entails certain rules of behaviour within the group. There are rules about interaction with teachers: 'creeping round' staff is frowned on, as is anything that smacks of allegiance, such as bringing a pencil case to school. It was not permitted to sit in front of the teacher's desk, and the girls would leave this space for the boys, positioning themselves round the sides or at the back. Following instructions immediately was also not allowed, as that gave undue authority to teachers; doing things in their own time also gave the impression of volition rather than constraint. Watching the end of a practical lesson, I noted that the wenches appeared not to hear the instruction to 'clear up', carrying on talking and looking at some Christmas cards. Yet a few minutes later they did in fact clear up: the message from them seemed to be that they were adult responsible persons who knew there was clearing up to be done, their movements having nothing to do with any command from outside.

Yet of course these rules and their interpretations varied according to the teacher the girls were with; favoured and liked teachers merited a softening of the stance, a remission of the need to make things difficult. Mrs K, who took them for basic subjects, was 'alright' — she was one of the few they might come back to see when they left. Here the relationship was played as if between equals. Mrs K took an interest in the girls, their friends, their out-of-school life, their appearance, and trusted them with confidences about herself and jokes against herself. They recounted to me how another liked teacher, Mrs B, had told them about going on her honeymoon, having a row with her husband, how funny it all was: 'That's the sort, ain't it, you don't want to play them up.' What impressed the girls most about Mrs K was the fact that she had told them she was pregnant before she told any of the staff. In return for Mrs K's trust, the girls confided in her: complaints about other teachers would be received and discussed; they took an interest in her (while playing role reversal at the same time):

Debbie: How many eye shadows you got on?
Mrs K: Two.
Debbie: Looks nice. I'll get you to come round and do my
make-up tonight.

And they would make an attempt at work, not react in outrage at reminders of manners.

It is curious to note the contrast with the girls' reactions to the self-seeking 'confidences' of Mr T, and also their appreciation of the teacher's interest in them in contrast to the more usual reaction of 'It's got nothing to do with them' and the insistence on privacy. Trying to find a common denominator for teachers who invited different rules of conduct, the key word seems to be 'humanity'. Acceptable teachers treated them as human adults who deserved explanations for requests or prohibitions, deserved consideration of feelings. They would apologise if they were late. They would share a joke without 'going barmy'. They were modest. They showed an interest in, for example, the girls' appearance, not for control purposes but as courtesy. In short, they followed the normal adult rules of social intercourse and exchange, while maintaining the teaching role of being in control and keeping discipline. That this is no easy task is evidenced by the number of teachers who 'failed' in the wenches' eyes.

What distinguishes 'difficult' girls is, then, their selectivity about teachers and their rules about reciprocation of perceived insult. A 'conformist' girl summed up the contrast:

I'm not sweet and innocent, I like a laugh and that, but I do respect my teachers, that's one thing I do do. I would say I don't think this is old enough for us to do, but I wouldn't go up to him and say I ain't doing this, and chucking my work about.

Again, consider this conformist accommodation to poor control: 'I can't stand the ones who can't keep order — like Mr G, it's awful in Biology — we're lucky, we sit on the front bench, he's right there in front of you, you can keep fairly good concentration.' There is a contrast with the wenches' 'you can't help playing up' reaction. It is not that conforming girls do not perceive contradictions: they disapproved of the maths teacher 'who didn't mark your books or anything', of the English teacher who said 'it doesn't matter to me whether you pass your exams or not', and they deplored the fact that the school

[margin handwritten note: But contrast with 'mature' girls at Hawthorpe — neither directly deviant or conformist]

41

didn't push enough people to do GCE. I think that's awful, we've got a year of 300, and only our class is doing GCE maths and English. They're always saying 'aim high' and then they put you down and don't let you aim for the high things, they tell you one thing and do the other.

But the difference is they are not moved to react personally to the teacher or the institution; by and large they shunt the contradictions aside in favour of the official school goals and the means to achieve them. Girls not having books to be marked, examinations to take, have of course nothing to lose, and possibly something to gain, by personal power struggles. Theirs is a more immediate logic.

Group relationships

A certain amount of loyalty was expected within the group: there were norms about 'twitting on your mates', and the wenches would automatically cover for each other's absences, or collude in excuse stories. Rajinder, the fighter, would heroically resort to fists if a friend were insulted by another girl; physical aggression was also her response to a girl who informed on her for smoking. She would not start a fight on her own, but was easily provoked if the norms governing relationships were infringed, even if most of this was ritual aggression, or 'threatening' behaviour.

There was naturally a lot of teasing and ribaldry within the group. Janet had given up going to church because of the girls' reaction to her sister, still attending at seventeen: 'Oh, her don't go to church, does her, at her age.' She admitted 'They'll take the mickey out of you.' The wenches would gently tease Balwinder about doing a paper round, about wearing a bra — long-standing jokes of unclear origin, but which Balwinder did not seem to mind. Badinage about boyfriends or reputations was common, but only if it was totally outrageous or non-hurtful, and could not be taken personally: 'Her goes in the shed every night, Miss, with her boyfriend.' Julie was attempting a serious discussion of a newspaper article about 'permissive Scrapton':

Julie: It was in the paper, warn't it? Wenches and chaps, having sexual (she has trouble with the next word, loud laughter) intercourse in the gardens, up entries, the lot.
Donna: What about you, Julie, you was one of them!

Julie: Get lost, I ain't like that (minor scuffle).
Julie promises to bring me the cutting.

But there is sensitivity to the timing and impact of teasing.

Julie: I don't mind being teased when I'm going out with him
... probably when I 'm going out with him they plague me.
But when he's finished with me they don't say anything.
Carole: 'Cos they know it'll probably hurt you.

For girls who were supposed to be 'rude' and antisocial, I found them
very tuned into each other's feelings, and reluctant to gossip about
absent members in consideration of confidence. Thus if they were
involved in some 'trouble', it was expected that responsibility was
shared:

Julie: I could have got out of it, say, I don't take anything, but
they noticed my mates, right, I didn't actually take the
things, but I was with them, like I was the watchout. I'm just
as bad as them, ain't I, I went in with it and all.

Conversely, if they were not involved, they expected absolution from
the others who were, demanding the teacher be told they 'weren't with
it'. While 'pinching', as mentioned, was not necessarily considered
immoral, there were agreed distinctions about who to pinch from.
Debbie would not like to work in a bank because of the 'temptation'
(she had been fired from a Saturday job for stealing money), but when I
pointed out that I had left my bag with them earlier, they were adamant
that they would not touch that.

LD: Why other sorts of pinching then?
Donna: But that's only kids, ain't it? If they say anything, you
just start a fight, that's it. But not out of your bag, I
wouldn't.
LD: What about teachers?
Rajinder: I don't think that's right, taking it, I mean, they *work*
for it.

We see the wenches having their own well-articulated, if flexible,
morality, based on earned rights, or on obligations within the group. A
shared language was used to describe pupils who had other rule
systems: those pupils who did not conform to the wenches' guidelines
for particular teachers were 'poofs', 'pets' or 'creeps': 'They're poofs
... they're stuck up ... they do it, don't they, if the teachers say do it.'

Nor should girls refuse to interact, they should not 'keep themselves to themselves' but 'mix with you'. They should not 'sneer at the other's feelings'. 'Looking down on you' is the worst pupil offence for these low stream girls. As Terri said, 'Some of them treat us like "oh look at those", nobody can be good enough ... they treat us like, they think they're at college.' However, even a low-status set, whose reference group cannot be college, must find others of even lower status by which to define themselves, and the wenches were equally scathing about 'scruffs' — girls who appeared not to care about their reputation and/or their appearance. Into this category came girls who did not wash or change their clothes frequently enough, or came to school in pumps, or 'slopped' when they chewed their gum. More importantly, scruffs were those who 'had a bad name'.

Reputation and Identity

It is in fact here that the clue to girls' group interactions lies: the control not just of daily life-spaces, but of one's reputation and status. Status was not going to arise for these girls in academic achievement; from teachers it came only from those sensitive enough to accord them adult worth or feelings. The major source of identity was peers, boyfriends in particular, but — because these girls are still home-based — against a backcloth of parental values and controls. Even though we were talking in school, girls' accounts were roughly equally divided between school-based issues and outside relationships and activities, the fusion of the two often occurring in talking of a pupil's 'moral career' (p. 188).

Again, the contradictions arise. Outside school these are the traditional female contradictions in many class cultures of having to be attractive and yet not too available; wanting a variety of relationships and yet maintaining a reputation; seeing marriage as the only long-term viable goal on the horizon and yet being aware of the enormous problems attached to that goal. Thus 'having a chap' was a source of status, but could also be a source of personal danger, or conflict with parents. 'If you go out with too many chaps, you get a bad name, don't you?' Kath was equally scathing about the motivation to achieve group status: 'They have one boyfriend one week, and another another ... they will, just for the sake of saying they've been with somebody.' Julie's parents in fact allow her out only two nights a week: 'They say it's not decent to be out, it's not right for a wench to be out at nights so much.' Reputation is guarded, if necessary, by verbal aggression:

> *Donna:* We was only walking up the road one day ... and Brooksy shouted 'you ain't no virgin, I bet you've had a good bit of ...' Julie says, 'get lost, I'm a virgin.' 'You ain't, look how you're walking, bow-legged!' Her gives him a mouthful!

Or by physical aggression, if the imputations, the 'nasty things' are said by a girl. A fight while I was there occurred when Norma had 'lamped' Jean, who had said not only that Norma's boyfriend was scruffy and looked a mess, but more crucially that he was 'having it off' with Donna. Norma was not defending his honour, but her own at being associated with a chap who could 'two-time' her.

A girl's reputation is also inextricably tied up with the peer group relationships and status indicators amongst the boys, as Julie explained to me one day:

> If the chap don't touch you, he'll go and tell his mates he has, just to make hisself look bigger. Or if some of the boys don't take to you, they tell him, you've got no chance with her ... I was with this D.J. and Gary called him over to him and said, I wouldn't bother with her, she don't do the game. Probably he knows. And when he comes back to me, I says, if that's all you want me for, you can piss off. And he said, if that's all I wanted you for, I wouldn't be dancing with you. See? That's how chaps find out what wenches are like.
>
> *LD:* Why do boys boast about it?
>
> 'Cos mates is mates, aren't they? If they go and tell a bloke who'll tell another chap, that chap is going to think more on them, it's great to them, but to the wenches it ain't, give you a bad name.

It is not that the wenches are against sex as such, on the contrary; but too young, too often and too many chaps, and in Scrapton, discredit results. 'Having to get married' is not a particular stigma, but it is best avoided, again because of the possible downgrading of one's personal value: 'That chap can say he had to marry you to his mates — some chaps say, oh, I had to marry her. Didn't want to, had to.' The aim is to remain a girl a chap *wants* to marry, and is proud to show to his mates.

Yet the female peer group is not without its dangers for the boy either:

> *Lorraine:* If he's just sitting there with his wench, and like a gang of her mates comes in, and you start talking to him, he's

hearing all the wenches looking at him (sic), seeing if he's nice
looking or if he ain't, embarasses the chap.

Depictions of adolescent gangs or groups tend to show the boys as in
control, the girls as passive hangers on; yet as Lorraine's point shows,
girls are aware of their power, especially in the group, and will talk of
boys in similar 'objectified' ways: 'He's been passed round, that chap
has, you know.'

Dependence and control

Thus if one contradiction in adolescent inter-sex relationships is status
versus intimacy, another is dependence versus control. Having a
boyfriend is important to adult recognition, but may define activities
too closely. That the boy traditionally pays also means that the boy
traditionally decides where the evening is spent. The girls argue
therefore about questions of equality. If you can get chaps to buy drinks
for you, that is a source of power, and also relates once more to
questions of reputation. 'I think it's more decent for the chap to buy the
drinks than the girl.' There are, however, problems with this type of
exchange, as financial dependence is integrally linked with other sorts
of dependence, especially in later (married) life: 'Put it this way, if he
wanted to go out with his mates, I'd want to go out with my mates.'
Terri talks of girls being 'ruined' by chaps — 'Everything they say,
they do' (the same terminology and tone used in describing poofs'
relationships with teachers). Linda reckons 'Your chaps don't rule you
anyway.' The alternative female control is not unproblematic either.
Julie reported: 'Our Dawn, her husband brought £80 a week, she give
him a fiver, and she kept the rest to herself! I don't think that's right, do
you? A chap's got to have his freedom same as a wench.'
  A revealing passage from Kath sums up the whole paradox:

  It's nice to have a chap sometimes what tells you what to do,
  'cos nowadays, some of them, you can go around telling them
  what to do, well that's good at first, ain't it, but it ain't so
  exciting as when they tell you what to do. If you say, do this,
  and they go and do it for you, it shows you up, don't it? You
  feel good sometimes, 'cos you can say, he'll do what I want him
  to do, but ... chaps, they think, oh he's saft, don't they.

I was reminded of Groucho Marx not wanting to join any club that
would admit him: a girl would not want to be associated with the sort

of chap she could control. The parallel is there, too, in girls' views of teachers: those that they can run rings round, who are 'frightened' of them, are in the end a source of contempt.

The other revealing word in Kath's account is 'exciting'. Yet another contradiction emerges: boys are a source of excitement, but also a source of trouble, violence, emotional hurt. For Linda, the excitement was riding motorbikes across fields, for Debbie smashing cigarette and chocolate machines, for Terri it was breaking and entering old houses (she was small, and therefore the one to be pushed through the window). As Donna put it, 'When you hang about the chaps, you have a laugh, don't you . . . 'cos they all do saft things.' But the 'laughs' meant, of course, that many of the lads had been in trouble with the police, and the girls involved too, if only for 'questioning'. The wenches neutralised all this, sometimes, by claiming there was 'nothing to do' in Scrapton, the implication being that excitement had to be created and then preserved in legend. Drugs and excessive drinking were not part of the wenches' own scene; they preferred to remain in control. Moreover, the police 'can't have you' for drinking shandy (the girls were of course under age, as I often forgot). But violence seemed an ever-present backcloth. When I first started 'hanging about' with the girls, Debbie had just had her front teeth knocked out by her (ex)chap — a constant source of amusement in class thereafter was Debbie removing her new false teeth at inappropriate moments. The chap was now in prison, but, as Debbie often recounted, he had asked her to write to him and to go out with him again on release. This was a source of outrage and firm denial from Debbie, but was also, I suspect, a source of some pride. A black eye and periodic bruises did not seem to prevent a steady relationship between Carole and her chap. Julie, on the other hand, gave up Mick because he used to punch her 'for no reason', and now has to abandon Kevin, not because he has been married, but because of him 'beating her up' for her objections to his two-timing her.

On these occasions, the girls would usually give as good as they got; but the initiation of physical aggression towards boys could produce the same double-bind as did over-control of the male. While a boy hitting a girl is justified if the girl is 'acting bigheaded', or insults his sister (very Sicilian, this) girls starting fights with boys would be 'terrible':

> *Terri:* Like when there's a wench in the corridor, and she says 'want to fight' to a chap, I think it's horrible, shows the chap up, don't it?

> *Kath:* If the wench wins him, it shows him up, right, but if he
> wins the wench, it shows him up just as much for hitting the
> wench in the first place.

Hence the major part of the wenches' own initiation of violence was
towards other girls. You did not punish the boy for two-timing you,
you punished the girl. This had the function of pure revenge and thus
catharsis, but it also had the function of demonstrating the extent of
involvement with the boy:

> *Julie:* Some chaps fall out with you, go out with another
> wench, just for you to lamp that wench. Then they come
> back to you.
> *Janet:* 'Cos they can see that you're jealous.

Sometimes this 'lamping' was confined to ritual sizing up or threats,
especially in public places such as pubs; but the fights were often real,
and, of course, could take place on school territory if both girls
involved were from Gladstone.

Groups of girls fighting was not unusual in discos, apparently
starting when 'they look at you and you look back'. Hence a girl would
be unlikely to go to a disco on her own. As Julie put it "'cos like if all of
we were sitting here, and there was a gang of wenches staring at we,
one of them wouldn't come over to all of we, would they, 'cos her
knows very well that her'd lose for we, wouldn't her, but her'd come
with a gang.' There is safety in numbers for reciprocating the insult of
'staring'. But girls admit that most of the 'trouble' is over chaps — if
the girls 'don't like someone you're going out with'. A ritual insult
about the boy will be delivered, and thus a fight invited. 'Throwing
down the gauntlet' is not confined to 19th or even 20th century males.

The family

Violence, of course, is nothing new to the wenches, for many of them
experience it in the home as well. This varies from routine smacks from
parents to Donna's recollection of being caught for stealing: 'I ain't got
no proper parents, me brother's looking after me, and he busted all me
mouth open.' There is controversy amongst the girls as to whether you
can or should hit your parents back, or swear at them, but generally
'being lamped' by the family seemed an accepted way of life.

Yet there was a wide range in types of family or parental control, and no patterns emerged which might be common to 'difficult' girls. Some parents (for example Carole's and Debbie's) appear to make few attempts to monitor their daughters' activities; others must negotiate in return for cooperation about babysitting. Indirect control is managed on occasions by the two generations in a family (typically Elaine's or Linda's) going out to the pub together. Both Terri and Kath concur that their fathers, like Julie's, are very strict with them. Terri sees this as possibly generating more trouble — 'Sometimes we used to do it just to get at them' — but they are basically glad their fathers are hard. Just as it was Kath's father who insisted she 'stick up for herself' and not cry in a fight, Terri's

> ain't brought me up rough, you know, but he's made me — like if we had a fight and we lost, he'd make me go and thump them ... he treats me like a chap really. Like when I was young, I never used to have a frock or anything. Never wear one now, do I? I wouldn't wear a dress now.

Is it then to 'weakness' in the mother's style that we must look (as suggested in the socialization literature p. 158)? The girls agree that the maternal role is housework and child care, and they are doubtful about working mothers, childminders and too many babysitters. Yet there are many examples of seeming 'aggression' from their own mothers:

> *Julie* (on the Trotter woman): She came to our mother's. Our mother slammed the door in her face ... 'not getting through my door!' 'I've a right to come and see her', and my mother said, 'You go and eff off somewhere else and go up to someone else's house, that chap over the road, he's never at school, and you come to somebody who's sick.' She ain't been since.

Terri remembers the support she received when she was suspended:

> Like our mother come in (to school) and said 'Oh we don't swear.' Oh, her do! Her was all posh and everything. Her ain't as posh as that, her's like all the rest of them round here. But to hear her talk! She had to though, you can't come back into school until they've seen your parents.

Mothers have even been known to get the police in after a fight between their daughters. Locally, mothers seem prepared then to defend their children's interests. They 'get on your nerves' for 'nagging you', and have to be told lies if the wenches want to stay out all night, but they attempt solace about troubles with boyfriends, and 'help you out' when you later have a family of your own. No girl ever expressed any real antipathy towards her parents, as she might towards teachers; Debbie even revealed remorse at the trouble she had caused them: '''cos the things I do, and they ain't done nothing to me, I mean, there ain't nothing wrong with the family, the house is clean ... I can't have much feelings for my parents, can I, to keep getting into all this trouble.'

Anticipations

The wenches' views of familial roles and relationships are then relatively 'traditional': men should go out to work, women should stay with very young children, and keep the house clean. However, more contradictions emerge when we move from the girls' current concerns to their anticipations of the future, of work and of marriage. Even towards the end of the year, the girls talked far less of work than they did of current relationships and interactions, although they would all be leaving relatively shortly. When we examine how the world of work presents itself to them, we realize why. It does not seem an exciting or meaningful prospect. It will be better than school, in that, crucially, they will be earning money; but there is no consensus that there will be greater freedoms or interests at the workplace. They were puzzled by my activities in the school — 'Is this your job, Miss?' — but when I explained my full-time occupation their only questions were about the 'hours' and whether I did it every day; they appeared not curious about its content or prospects, more important to me. Some rejected office work because it was 'boring' or 'just pressing buttons', but this may have been because they were not qualified for it anyway. They certainly had no 'higher' aspirations. They would mention *places* of work — the local factories, or shops — rather than job descriptions, if talking of the future at all. Conversely, they would discuss the processes of *getting* jobs — the right impression, the inside knowledge. If necessary, they were resigned to unemployment.

Is it then in marriage that concrete meaning lies? If it is, they will have to manage or reconstruct some of their own experiences and perceptions of married life. For Janet's mother, marriage is unexciting. 'She never goes out. Sits in the house.' Julie sees married couples out, but reckons romance has died: talking of pubs one day, she commented in parenthesis: 'In the pub, Sunday dinner-time ... I could tell how long they've been married, they just sit there, boring. S'right, you can tell married persons, 'cos they just sit there, quiet, they don't speak to one another. Once you're married, nothing to say.' On another occasion the wenches compared notes on jealousies, squabbles, sulks among married relatives. Debbie and Donna are the most scathing, reflecting their own experience of 'instability':

LD: So what do you think marriage is like?
Debbie: Rubbish. Nothing but arguments. And ending up in divorce.
Donna: You can't enjoy life anyway, you can't go out.
Debbie (who is aged 15):   That's what they don't see today, the young 'uns. They just think they can get married and it'll all be sunshine, ones getting married at 16, 17.
Donna: If you have a baby, you have to stop in.

With regard to children, then, only Terri and Kath specify that they do want them, although recognizing the constraints. Terri is unique in expressing the idea of work as an alternative: 'That's why we want to do a career, really, then you can go back to it when you have children ... I don't want to just work and have children, I want to enjoy myself as well.' Asked how children would fit in, she said, 'My mum'd have them!' Kath wants to have her children when she is young, apparently to preserve the female image: 'Otherwise you're old-fashioned towards them, ain't you like ... it's nice, ain't it, when you know your mother's younger looking, you're more proud, than going out with your Nan, think it's your Nan, say, "it's my mother!"'

This brings out clearly the dilemma of combining maternal with feminine attributes. There is no indication that any of the wenches wants to throw herself into full-time motherhood with all that that entails. Why then do they get married? To 'get away' from oppressive parents was often mentioned: 'Some of them get married 'cos they don't think they've got enough freedom while they're young.' Apart from escape, the major impetus might be the status attached. Just as the girls talked more of the skills of landing a job rather than the job itself, they were more expressly committed to the achievement of a husband, and to the wedding (churches, bridesmaids, wearing white) than to the state of marriage. Being 'on the mantelpiece' is a stigma still to be avoided in Scrapton. The moment of 'appropriation' of the marital ideology comes when turning an institutional commonplace into a personal triumph.

Interconnections between School and 'Outside'

The common 'problem' which links the girls, and which also links school and outside, is that of status: how to manage identity in the face of contradictory threats to prestige. These contradictions are found both in relationships with teachers (linked to the educational problematic of simultaneously 'warming up' and 'cooling out' pupils) and in relationships with boys (linked to the cultural contradictions of patriarchy). It would seem likely that girls would use similar strategies to test for power and control in both situations (although, as we have seen, it is a test they would prefer not to have to win). Another paradox noted is that, far from being 'immoral', these 'difficult' girls appear if anything to have a more explicit morality than their conformist peers: they judge teachers by more rigid standards, they react more strongly to rule-breaking amongst those in control. Given their perception of the way teachers manage their task, what needs to be answered is not why these girls are difficult, but why all pupils are not difficult? How is it that conforming pupils can manage to overlook the glaring anomalies in the school message system, or at least learn to live with them? Yet we have seen, too, the deviance amplification spiral (p. 182) that can ensue from reactions to competing interpretations of morality: both teachers and pupils recognizing infringements of their concept of 'good pupil' or 'good teacher', reacting adversely, and thus inviting further infringements of rules from the opposite party. 'Conforming' pupils and teachers keep a lower profile and avoid highlighting the contradictions.

If one paradox is that deviant girls seem in fact highly moral, another is that those least able to be controlled, in some ways would like most to be 'controlled'. They appreciate strength in parents, boys and teachers; not strength alone, but strength coupled with personal interest and concern. Their resistance stems, not necessarily from needing to be stronger (as possibly in the case of male supremacy), but from perceptions of weakness or insensitivity amongst those in a position to define the girls' identity and status. The wenches have to work at the management and presentation of self; others should also earn their right to respect. At school, the institutional authority of 'being a teacher' is not enough. The conforming girl respects 'teachers' as a body; the less conforming girl is far more selective. One reason why girls may 'bear grudges' is because they personalize the interaction: a conformist might see the 'insult' as representative of teacher-pupil relationships in general, or while a boy might seek solace in his group status, a girl may take every imputation as a personal affront, and thus something to be worked out personally.

The generic quest for status means interconnections between school and home worlds, interconnections which also throw light on girls' 'deviance'. Problems with boyfriends, as the teachers recognized, spill over into school in a variety of ways. Lorraine's behaviour was explained by Sandra and Kath as deriving from the fact that she constantly came to school 'upset' about her chap, not being able to help swearing — 'her couldn't talk, got to shout at you'. This should be contrasted with the girl whose work improved *because* she got involved with a boy: her fiancé encouraged and took an interest in her when her parents did not. As Janet commented in another context about the advantages of a boyfriend, 'You'm noticed'. The need for recognition and care is not peculiar to the wenches, but we begin to see how different types of received attention can have unpredictable results in school. For Terri, it accounted for truancy, for, unusually, she had been going out with a boy in her class: 'Like the chap I just fell out with, he's turned all the chaps against me. He says things what ain't true, it's my class and that, makes it worser, that's why I don't like coming to school.'

Apart from boyfriends, there is the direct importation of the home. Both Carole and Sandra had particularly high truancy rates because they were kept home for domestic duties including child-minding. Family attitudes obviously are reproduced in school. Julie, incensed at the late detention rules, argues 'Our mum tells me it's better to be late than not to come to school at all.' But more crucial home problems affect the wenches in different ways. With Donna, in the period before she transferred to the local authority home, it was withdrawal, and refusal to talk about it; with Debbie it was refusal to participate because, as she announced loudly and frequently, she was 'fed up' — all the trouble she was in, the coppers coming round all the time, her father was going to have her put in a Borstal. The message was that there was no way she could concentrate on school affairs given her personal loading.

Conversely, issues which the teachers may see as vital, the girls may not. Careers lessons and talks they dismissed as a waste of time, as was passing examinations to get a job. The wenches' view was that they could have taken examinations, but they had left it too late now anyway. Being 'clever' in their definition meant 'having put the work in', having little to do with any concept of innate intelligence. As we saw, getting jobs depended on other attributes in their opinion. Filling in careers forms in one lesson, the wenches were unsure of the meaning of 'positions of responsibility', let alone having held any in the school; they thought 'weak' at subjects must mean 'don't like them'; under 'careers you want to have information about' Carole wrote 'BSR, glassworks, packaging'. The linkages between school and work and the impact of school on 'career' perceptions were, at most, tenuous for these girls.

Overall, the 'real' world is outside school. 'Everything what happens different every week, that's got to do with outside. Not in school.' School, in contrast, is the same day after day, week after week, with this year's lessons and workcards seeming indistinguishable from last year's. Exaggerated reactions to power and contradictions may be a way of creating meaning, of passing time, or maintaining status, but the school (or teachers) do not really impinge on 'where the action is' in the long term. The impression that school is a pale shadow explains the wenches' blasé reactions to caning: their own experience of violence makes one stroke on each hand of little consequence. It amuses them to see the teachers taking it so seriously. Janet described how 'I had the ruler once — bump came up here — her was frightened to death, I showed the teacher, her was frightened to death, come on, let's bathe it for you.' The contemptuous reiteration of the teacher's fear shows what was memorable. Similarly for Elaine: 'Like when they caned me on me hand, the cane broke. I just had to laugh, I just couldn't help it. I don't feel it. I just thought of the cane breaking and flying through the air.' And anyway, as Sandra pointed out: 'There's really only our parents who ought to be hitting we and shouting at we.'

So responses to institutional violence (physical or symbolic) can be anything except remorse or increased conformity: it seems instead to invite principles of reciprocity or conversion into laughs or status enhancement. As the wenches do not equate teachers' rights with parental rights, they feel entitled to return 'physical' attacks — 'Miss C pulled my hair, so I hit her back', explains Rajinder. But physicality is not the only ploy. With boyfriends, violence may be converted to symbolic power by means of rejection which invites a pleading response; with teachers the conversion to power is achieved through nonchalance or humour. There is no question that the girls are prac-tised in responding to attempts at dominance, and may use similar strategies for personal recognition in any context.

But a Sub-culture?

Yet the final question — whether these strategies and styles can be said to constitute a 'sub-culture' — is hard to answer. The group does provide a useful means of support, both in and out of school. In school it supplies an audience and a base for character contests, and creates leisure opportunities for the management of boredom or alienation. Out of school it is again a supportive leisure base, for a wench would not go to a disco or a pub on her own unless she wanted to be either stared at or, worse, thought loose. Because of these mutual needs, the rules about group interaction arise: a girl should not pinch another girl's boyfriend, although pinching the boyfriend of a non-favoured or outgroup girl is a good way to demonstrate simultaneously your antipathy and your superiority. An interesting tie-up between school 'deviance' and outside status concerns came in a discussion of graffiti one day:

> *LD:*   Why *do* you write on the desks?
> *Julie:*   So's everybody knows who we are! Look, it's got Kevin and Janet. But I'll show you, that pair — see — there, she writes her name everywhere, Dawn and Bremmer. She called me an old bag, this and that, I don't like it. She just came up to me, she said, 'you've been going out with my chap'. I said, 'yeah, I have', 'cos I hated her, and I tried to get him to fall out with her, so I went out with him, and I thought I'd have me own back on her . . . she said, 'you've been going off with Bremmer, been writing his name, Julie and Bremmer'. 'Yeah, I have, what you going to do about it?' And she just carried on the fight with me.

Insults are reciprocated as above, or in a group fashion — 'I have to join in' is a typical phrase. But group allegiances are tenuous if they in any way threaten status; by the end of the year many of the girls were becoming cautious about particular associations. Donna commented on Sandra:

> I can't stand going about with people who's always going off with chaps. I used to hang about with her night-time, but her's an old bag now . . . [Sandra's mother had disputed her own daughter's virginity] That's why I stopped hanging about her, 'cos round here if you go about with somebody who ain't a virgin, they think you ain't, don't they, Debbie?

Kath, although by no means a 'poof', had similar doubts about ex-friends 'who've just gone low': 'That's the trouble with the lower ones, 'cos like they'm thick they think they're duffers, they think they're fighters and everything, think they're marvellous 'cos they're the hardest.' Being 'hard' was not part of Kath's image now, so she was dissociating herself from the fighting crew. Top stream girls were also rejected by the wenches because of their snottiness, but also because of different out-of-school activities: they either went to night clubs or stayed in and did their homework, neither of which was the lower stream's style. Yet Terri was beginning to be doubtful about some of the wenches' haunts like the Vic — 'used to be ever so nice, but now it's a right dump.' She was also starting to break away — in the third year she used to skip lessons with Carole, but now she was 'settling down': 'Mr A (the head) is pleased with me, I'd better have a good reference!' Carole in the fourth year used to truant with Rajinder and Lorraine; but with Carole and Lorraine now having steady boyfriends, and Rajinder retaining her tomboy image, there was far less association, in or out of school. The wenches do not reject Rajinder, but they are amused and worldly about her 'toughness'. As Terri said, 'You've only got to blow on her! Fall on the floor ... I thought, I should be telling her one of these days, I don't want to hurt her feelings, but her thinks her's the pick of the wenches.' Overall, mates are still important, and provide certain rules of behaviour and group definitions and boundaries; but the wenches are increasingly looking for individual rather than collective solutions to status concerns, whether in or out of school.

I suspect finally, that the term 'sub-culture' has been too uncritically accepted as an applicable explanation of pupil behaviour. It does not easily fit the girls. In this study they are not replacing commitment to school values with profound allegiance to the norms of the counter-culture. They have, like Willis' lads, shared partial insights into the way the school processes them, but they have no eager anticipation of work as an exciting release from school, and a place of new collective status. Hargreaves (1979) comments on how literature on pupil deviance has concentrated on oppositional cultures rather than the more interesting 'indifferent' pupils; the reason may be at least partially because of the emphasis on boys. Girls' response better accords with Durkheim's 'egoism and anomie'. The egocentricity of the achieving girl coincides well with the individualism of school effort; the 'private interests' of the less achieving girl are more likely to sit with an anomic response to school. The wenches may be the 'true' deviants — the loners, without even 'healthy' social solidarity for integrative support.

Or, we might take the view that the 'function' of the sub-culture has sometimes been misrepresented: it may be less a place to celebrate similarities as to demonstrate differences. The task for pupils in an anonymizing institution is to remember and prove that they *are* unique (although not too unique); the sub-culture provides a safe foil for this display, especially in the face of the inevitable depersonalization of the large classroom. Sub-cultures are not a kind of superglue where pupils must instantly 'adhere' to the rules of the group, but at most a cavity foam filling with plenty of air space to manoeuvre.

3 Labelling and Processing: The School Treatment of Deviance

I have a theory ... people who want to be naughty sit at the back, particularly if they are boys — girls don't seem to mind sitting at the front — I shall be keeping an eye on you two....
See if you can disprove my theory.

This was said by a teacher to 1C on their second day in school. This chapter attempts to trace the extent, the consensus and the effects of such expectations of different behaviour from the sexes. To see whether deviance is indeed typically defined and treated differently according to gender requires first some idea of definitions of 'normality' for pupils. We begin with how the institution and then the individual teacher interprets the 'good' boy or girl.

Institutional Rules about Gender

We can usefully start where I did — with a first-year intake into the lower school. Being with them continuously for the first week enabled me to monitor any communication of school 'rules' to these raw recruits. With regard to gender, many appeared to be about simple separation of the sexes — when lining up, giving books in, using boys' and girls' playgrounds — rather than expectations of qualitative difference. There were even double messages, as in the first assembly: 'I don't care if boys and girls are mixed, you're all pupils to me, but Mr G prefers to have girls one side, boys the other — it's good for sorting out teams.' Nevertheless, teachers expected and facilitated boys and girls wanting to sit and work in same-sex pairings in class; their 'understanding' conveys from the beginning the idea that such a gulf between the sexes might possibly inhibit learning.

Overlaying the basic divisions are, then, the more idiosyncratic gender expectations of the type quoted at the beginning. These were often transmitted in terms of how the sexes were seen to respond to the particular teacher's subject — for example art, or domestic science — and could not be termed common 'rules'. Others related to more general behaviour, and seemed shared amongst teachers — the likelihood of wearing uniform, or bringing the correct equipment to school, were common examples. Teachers claimed to be able to distinguish boys' voices from girls' voices when making deviance imputations. All these distinctions are of course minor compared to the major shared expectations of the good pupil; and boys and girls who deviated from these norms would not be sanctioned but merely considered eccentric. Nonetheless, fundamental parameters had been established, with the sexes expected to look, sound and behave in recognizably divergent ways.

Such differentiation is reinforced throughout the official curriculum — starting in the first week and continuing through a pupil's school career. Gladstone was not unusual in having traditional practices such as girls taking home economics and boys technical studies, whilst intending in the following year to let both sexes 'try' each others' subjects in the first year. The school was in the process of shifting its ideology of the domestic female and the technical male to a position more in line with current thinking and legislation. Some staff were opposed to this, and their acceptance of sex-typed subjects, together with the relatively few pupils choosing cross-sex subjects at option time, indicate school and locality assumptions about appropriateness. There were interesting stream differences here: a top stream girl complained:

> at this school they wouldn't let you do child care 'cos you was in the top class ... they think that if you're clever you're not going to go out and get married and have children, but if you're thick you are. (LD: Did they tell you this?) No, but they sort of drop hints about it.

The labels 'thick' and 'female' are of course not just additive but interactive; and they converge, too, with 'deviant', as when we contrast Janet's 'choice' of subjects: 'I had to wait for the new bed to come 'cos my mum was at work, and my dad, they couldn't afford to have the time off, and when I came back, I had to have the choices I don't want, do I. I couldn't have community studies, my favourite lesson, and I couldn't have that. Had to have child care.'

These could be classic examples of the school reproducing existing social or sexual divisions. Top stream boys suffered similar prohibitions on metalwork and woodwork. Certain subjects became more sex-typed as the perceived ability of their clientele decreased, so that home economics (a girls' subject, but with scientific leanings) became cookery on the option list for the non-examination groups, and craft was replaced by roadcraft (mostly about cars and motorbikes). Finally the official curriculum was also represented in careers lessons: the school was using the CRAC vocational choice book with its pictures of women associated with lists of jobs like office, social/people, computational, and men depicted against lists including practical/constructional, active outdoors, literary (sic) and scientific.

These instances of normative expectations for the sexes are part of the covert message system; the only gender differentiated official rules would be those applying to uniform, jewellery and make-up. Ties for girls had recently been made optional, and the amount of flexibility allowed would not point to an excessive 'masculinization' of the uniform, the possible consequences of which are discussed on p. 186. It is stated 'jewellery and make-up must not be worn', but the head intimated that 'discreet' or 'sensible' make-up might mean staff 'turning a blind eye'. However, 'it will come off if we find black eyes or bright red lips on a youngster' — in other words, the classic siren would not be tolerated. Various health and safety reasons were given for bans on eye make-up, over-wide trousers, 'dangling' jewellery; pupils generally did not seem aware of these reasons, and reported simply being told 'geritoff' if they tried to display individuality, or make the uniform 'more interesting'. The only rationale they were aware of was the escalation theory, that if rules were relaxed too far, inmates would go wild and 'come in anything'.

There did not seem in Gladstone at this time to be any symbolic revolts over uniform; pupils wore their own version, or relatively unostentatiously did not wear it. Nor was it replaced by a compulsory fashion dress amongst the wenches: they each had their own style. I could trace no one-up-manship amongst them about clothes, feared by some pupils and teachers; given the importance attached to out-of-school activities, they saved the real make-up and fashion-consciousness for the evening. They were even scornful of the top stream girls' predilection (in line with their reference group) for wearing college scarves to school. The wenches seemed to see these symbols as immature, a form of impression management which indicated school, not outside, as the central identity definer for the top streams. Overall, it would appear that each pupil would react to the uniform rules according to his or her perception of the need for individuality, variety or sex role presentation in school time. I could find no evidence that the actual rules themselves affected one sex more than the other.

However, the inseparability of rules from their enforcement means that the possibility of differential treatment must be briefly mentioned at this point. A teacher asserted: 'The girls are *really* in trouble if they don't have the correct uniform — usually they're sent home or put in isolation, whereas the girls know well the boys haven't been hauled up for this . . . I think the girls are in the limelight where that's concerned, the uniform.' And the girls themselves complained that their cardigans and coats received more attention than the boys' jeans. However, these are subjective impressions, and there is an equal likelihood that stream is as important in attempts at uniform enforcement. The top streams were often indignant that their own minor infringements were admonished while more frequent or glaring violations were ignored from the lower streams. As a teacher reiterated in another context: 'It seems the worse you are, the better life you have. The kids in the top classes complain bitterly — If they got caught smoking, they'd probably get caned; if you catch some of the lower streams smoking, they get them painting walls, walking round the school, generally enjoying themselves.'

The particular sex ideology which could be inferred from the uniform rule and enforcement is neither that the school is overtly promoting sex divisions, nor that it is devaluing female culture by means of a masculine girls' uniform; the inference is of a sexual neutrality as far as possible (in particular among high achievers). Extremes of dress which draw attention to sex role fashion and image will be frowned on throughout, however.

The joint combination of the curriculum options and uniform would point to a unisex ideology for the top streams, but an admission of sex differences for the lower ones. Each mixed comprehensive will manage the combined reproduction of social and sexual divisions in different ways, and it would be interesting to see at what point in any school's ordering of pupils, 'ability' becomes more important than gender. The 'normal' girl by whom deviance would be defined here would be one where sexuality was played down in favour of academic achievement, or channelled into domestic or mothering tasks (for instance, child care or cookery). Present ways of displaying sex were to be neutralised in favour of future orientations: the girls might learn about cosmetics in science, but they were not permitted to wear them now. The type of sex division seen as appropriate in school was perhaps best symbolised by a list of house group duties pinned on a notice-board: the messenger team and the keys team were mixed, but the hostess team listed nine girls, the chairs team four boys.

Special treatments

One particular feature of Gladstone was weekly separate assemblies for boys and girls. There had been complaints about the girls' behaviour, most of them (the deputy headmistress thought) from the men. The ladies had been 'a bit worried', but males were the 'most vociferous'. A Ladies Working Party was thus set up to deal specifically with girls' behaviour problems, and one of their recommendations was a girls' assembly, so that female staff could 'make an impact' on the girls. A year later the Ladies Working Party as such had become defunct, as it was increasingly felt by members that pupil behaviour towards teachers was more contingent on individual classrooms than on school policy. As the deputy head put it, 'To a great extent the kind of behaviour you got in a classroom depended on how you prepared, the kind of atmosphere you got in a classroom, in fact how the adult treated the adolescent.' In sociological terminology they had moved from a socialization to an interactionist perspective, or to the 'culture contact' idea (p. 164) — that pupils will be exhibiting particular strategies in line with how they see power exercised.

However, the separate assemblies survived, mainly because of the perceived success of the girls' assembly. The two were indeed very different, linked to the original impetus for their conception. The girls' assemblies generally had a theme, and were organized by the girls themselves, from different classes, under a keen female member of staff. Ironically to me, the first girls' assembly I witnessed had the theme 'Man', and contained 'Far across the ocean', sung by a male singer, and a reading from D.H. Lawrence. Other assemblies had focused on drugs, Penwood Forge Mill ('the girls were thrilled to bits, because the boys never do anything like that') and one on seal culling which had escalated into a visit to the school by the BBC to stage a programme on it. Boys' assemblies were more 'straightforward', with pupil participation replaced by staff exhortations about rule-keeping. The girls' assemblies were also used as a control device, as the head said, 'It's the morning when uniform, this sort of thing, can be checked on more easily, problems in the girls' toilets can be checked on more readily, and so on.' The deputy headmistress usually spoke after the theme, — whether or not to 'sermonize' depended on the girls' behaviour before or during the assembly. Sometimes it would be to encourage the girls' aspirations, to exhort them to see further than Scrapton.

The success of the girls' assemblies seemed to lie in the girls' involvement and the feeling that they were receiving special concern: the increasing number of interested teachers taking part in the themes meant greater attention; even the 'sermonizing' was directed specifically at them; they were being treated seriously, talked to with old-fashioned respect — 'Ladies, move along please.' Certainly behaviour was noticeably 'better' than in mixed assemblies. My wenches automatically rejected the assemblies as 'boring', but the rules of their group style did not, as we have seen, permit much enthusiasm, particularly for anything initiated by top stream girls. If they talked, it was at their normal pitch, as they rarely made any symbolic concessions such as whispering, but generally they, too, were quiet, and did not cause any problems to participating staff.

Special attention for girls also emerged on the sports side. Often in mixed schools, the boys' football results have greater prestige than the girls' netball matches, reflecting the far greater importance attached to masculine sport in society and the media generally. However, the head of girls' P.E. had instigated 'quite a strong reward system' for girls, including special sportswear and certificates for team members, and medals for good performances. The boys were doing something similar, but again 'not to the same extent'. (The wenches did not participate in team sport any more than they did in assembly, and this reward system did not have much impact on them.) The boys had a parallel 'special treatment' angle in the Air Training Corps, which had no equivalent for girls; the only permanent extra-curricular activity for both sexes was the Christian Union.

The relationship of school ideology with the social area and intake of children is clear from the school's position on extra-curricular activities, and is worth examining at this point. The head explained the failure to develop this side as due to the 'twilight shades of the area', or 'the amount of responsibility as we see it that many youngsters have in their homes' (which would presumably apply more to girls). There was also 'the general lack of feeling for the school that we perceive'; most staff travelled away from Scrapton at the end of the day, 'and it requires a certain dedication to remain behind and show enthusiasm when youngsters are not enthusiastic'. But a teacher commented:

> I would like to see some changes in curriculum, to have a more
> outgoing curriculum towards the community, things like this.
> And there's a lot of pupils in this school who do things on their
> own, in their spare time and they do them very well indeed, and
> the school ignores it, and everything that's done well, an
> impression to me, the school tends to play down — we're an
> academic type of school, over-academic possibly for the type of
> kids we've got.

There was a Parents' Association, but although the parents would
prefer a Parent-Teachers Association, the head explained that 'if we
called it that, then they would expect far more cooperation from
teachers than the staff are, I think, prepared to give.' In no way was
Gladstone a community school. The mutually reinforcing cycle of
non-involvement by all parties, whether teachers, parents or pupils,
meant an emphasis on the selectively instrumental role of the school:
academic success, and its corollary, convergent good behaviour. Community service was done mainly by low stream pupils, or was chosen
by 'more able' children as an alternative to physics. The aim, unsurpri-
singly, was not to foster any radical intervention in the community, but
to provide a range of (usually sex-typed) activities to promote individual responsibility; the function would again seem to be a reproductive one, both of sex roles and social roles.

What overall messages or rules are then conveyed about appropriate gender-related behaviour by these aspects of the official and hidden
curriculum? What begins to emerge is that aspects of sex roles will be
emphasized if they are useful to the school's goals, others played down
if not. There are basic administrative conveniences of the division of
labour and allocation of responsibilities, whether to staff or to pupils.
Drawing attention to the sex of a pupil is acceptable in our society in a
way that drawing attention to other characteristics is not: a teacher not
knowing names can at least specify 'you two girls' in a way he or she
could not say 'you two blacks'. Communicating knowledge of sex-
related differences enhances the impression of the teacher 'knowing the
score' about his pupils. Where it increases involvement and thus
control, special attention can be given to one sex — in Gladstone in the
form of girls' assemblies and sports rewards. Practices such as sending
the girls out first — 'Ladies at the back can go' — would have the dual
control function of establishing the girls as 'ladies' (with all the

behavioural implications) and of installing into the boys the notion of proper respect.

The aspects of sex roles being accepted in Gladstone are the non-powerful, non-threatening ones: for girls it would be the domestic, caring role, or the 'maturity' attached to the restricting role of being 'ladies'. Maturity leading to more apparent sexuality or physicality, and thus increased bargaining power, would however be played down. Men teachers might be put at a disadvantage; women teachers might be upstaged. The two aspects of 'ladylikeness' and sexuality are seen then as mutually exclusive, and conversely, to be unladylike is to be by implication immoral; a girl fighting, or even watching others fight, was instantly labelled as 'common'. Only in the school records of the girls did the crime of 'brazen deceit' appear; the boys might receive the imputation 'lovable rascal'.

It is not enough, then, to say that the school reproduces sexual divisions; it has its own institutional interpretation and usage of that division, in accordance with particular problems of social reproduction — the need for differences in academic achievement — and of control. Each teacher has the same combined problem in the classroom; we must now turn to definitions of the 'good pupil' to see how these expectations impinge on sex roles.

Teacher Definitions of the Good Pupil

To locate the 'normality' from which deviations are noticed, teachers were given a questionnaire which was adapted from a sex role stereotype investigation by Broverman et al (1970). Subjects there were divided into three groups and asked to indicate on a questionnaire the attributes describing a 'healthy, mature, socially competent' a) adult — sex unspecified, b) man, or c) woman. The researchers found not only a double standard of mental health operating, with different attributes characterizing men and women, but also that concepts of a 'healthy male' did not differ significantly from those of a 'healthy adult', whereas 'healthy' women were perceived as significantly less healthy by adult standards:

> Acceptance of an adjustment notion of health, then, places women in the conflictual position of having to decide whether to exhibit those positive characteristics considered desirable for men and adults, and thus have their 'femininity' questioned,

that is be deviant in terms of being a woman; or to behave in the prescribed feminine manner, accept second-class adult status and possibly live a lie to boot.

To see whether double standards also operated in teacher expectations, a similar format was constructed, using 44 bi-polar items such as 'not at all aggressive — very aggressive' or 'very gentle — very rough' (all items already being tested as sex-stereotypical) (See Figure 3, p. 223). Teachers were told 'You are asked to think of fourth or fifth year pupils in your school, and then indicate on each item the pole towards which a well-adjusted, reasonably successful pupil would be closer'. For one third of the teachers the word pupil was replaced by boy, for the remaining third, girl. If the findings were in line with Broverman's for clinicians and patients, I expected there would be divergent definitions of well-adjusted pupils for boys and girls, and that the teachers' concept of the 'healthy' pupil would be parallel to that for 'boy' but not for 'girl'. Girls would then suffer the same dilemma as female patients, having to choose between being an unfeminine but favoured good pupil or being of feminine low status. A further consideration was whether the joint responses would verge more towards the masculine pole for each item or the feminine, and thus what the implications were for boys' orientations as well as girls'.

The results were far more complex than hypothesized. First, teachers had fewer sex differentiated expectations than surmized. For three-quarters of the items, similar characteristics were seen to be possessed by 'good' boys and girls, or in some cases no significant results were achieved because teachers themselves were not agreed. However, it is interesting to examine those items which *were* sex differentiated. The successful, well-adjusted girl would be gentler, more interested in her own appearance, cry more easily, be less active, quieter, dislike maths and science more, and, interestingly, be more competitive than either boys or pupils in general. The successful boy, on the other hand, would be less emotional than the girl, more ambitious, enjoy art and literature less and be more inclined to think himself superior to girls. With the exception of competitiveness, we can see girls and boys in these traits fulfilling the 'good pupil' role according to conventional sex stereotypes. Presumably the girl to be successful has to be even more competitive than boys, to balance less assertive female traits or expectations (as would apply to successful females in many professions). Alternatively, competitiveness would accord with girls' greater individuality, noted in previous discussions.

Successful girls were seen as more independent than were successful boys, although the differences just fell short of statistical significance. The other stereotyped traits do match teachers' perceptions elicited in the interview, particularly girls' greater emotionality, passivity and interest in appearance.

These traits, then, are used to explain behaviour — whether conformist or problematic — and are also associated with academic success. It would seem that good or bad pupils are seen to operate from the same basic sex stereotypical traits, but maybe give expression to them differently. With 'good' girls, concern with appearance might lead to neat work and immaculate uniform; with the 'deviant' girl, it might lead to expressions of femininity which infringe dress rules or teacher-pupil interaction. It is not (as thought for healthy patients) that girls might have to deviate a good deal from the 'good female' role to accord with, in this case, a generalized 'good pupil' role. Girls' greater gentleness and competitiveness, liking for art and literature, interest in appearance, are more greatly valued by teachers; conversely, boys' lesser emotionality, greater ambition and activity are held in higher esteem. The perfect pupil would presumably be androgynous, selecting aspects of both sex roles.

An examination of the items showing agreement among the three groups throws more light on this (see Table 4). If the attributes of the good pupil are listed in the order in which they incline towards either a feminine or masculine pole, we find at first sight roughly equal numbers of male-valued and female-valued items. Yet there are differences in the import of the traits esteemed: the female-valued items are more likely to be those relating to control in the classroom: cooperation, responsibility, maturity, lack of aggressiveness or disruptiveness. The male-valued items are those relating to achievement — confidence, logic, career-orientation. This accords with the twin tasks of the teacher in the classroom, to maintain group order while promoting individual learning — and the 'good pupil' has the seemingly difficult task of exhibiting female 'stereotypical' traits of conformity together with the masculine attributes of purposeful attainment.

However, the female-valued items receive higher 'scores' from teachers, so that summing divergences from the mid-point (the sex undifferentiated point) we could arrive at a crude 'femininity' score of 135, against a masculinity score of 56.8. Put another way, the traits valued by teachers in the good pupil are more stereotypical of females than they are of males. Teachers seem more concerned about classroom order than pupil achievement, although many of the items can of

Table 4 *Teacher stereotype questionnaire (items undifferentiated by sex of pupil)*

	The good pupil is more likely to be:	Average amount of distance from mid-point to sex stereotypical pole	
	helpful	11.7	
	motivated	11.4	
	not disruptive	11.3	
	responsible	11.2	
	not aggressive	11.1	
Female — valued Items	hardworking	10.5	
	conscientious	10.2	
	doing maximum work	9.6	
	neat	9.2	
	interested in the opposite sex	8.6	
	aware of feelings of others	8.3	
	mature	7.2	
	conformist	5.7	
	never using harsh language	3.7	
	talkative	3.7	
	home-oriented	0.8	
	placid	0.8	'femininity' score = 135
	blunt	0.7	'masculinity' score = 56.8
	feelings not easily hurt	0.9	
	oriented towards the peer group	1.1	
	objective	1.2	
	not expressing tender feelings	1.6	
Male — valued Items	easily able to separate feelings from ideas	1.9	
	dominant	2.7	
	keen on sport	3.0	
	never conceited about appearance	3.7	
	not easily influenced	3.9	
	acting as a leader	3.9	
	career oriented	4.6	
	adventurous	4.7	
	independent	6.2	
	self-confident	8.8	
	logical	8.8	

course contribute to both: the hardworking, conscientious pupil is unlikely to be a behaviour problem.

Of interest is the finding that the items with a low 'sex stereotypical' score (where the teachers were inclined to mark the mid-point) tend to be those associated with the individual feelings of the pupil. With the clinicians, these separated 'normal' males and females quite distinctively; the teachers seem less concerned or observant of this. There are obvious explanations: clinicians by definition are concerned with the individual's expression of states such as anxiety or happiness; the teacher has multiple concerns, a more diffuse role, and perhaps thirty clients. The clinician operates on a one-to-one basis and therefore is in a position to be sensitive to inner thoughts. But it is indicative that the only 'emotion' item given a high score is 'aware of the feelings of others': we could interpret this, cynically, as implying that it is immaterial what the good pupil is feeling personally, as long as he or she empathizes with the teacher. The question of control seems paramount.

A contrast with an interview question caused me some puzzlement initially. I had faced teachers with the 'forced choice' situation 'If you had to teach only boys or only girls, which would you choose?' As with an earlier study (Davies 1973), a consistently large proportion (in Gladstone 71 per cent) of teachers of both sexes said that if they had to choose, they would teach the boys. If the good pupil exhibits more female traits, why do teachers prefer boys? The answer seems to lie, again, not in generalized 'sex stereotypicality' from pupils, but in selected traits. The good pupil displays certain female attributes conducive to classroom order and progress. Girls en masse, on the other hand, can exhibit a whole range of other female traits which can cause the teacher problems, and many of these relate to the 'feelings' and 'emotions' dimension examined above. Girls are rejected, we recall, because of their 'tantrums', their 'surly, catty nature', because they are 'devious little bitches', 'vindictive' towards each other. They are malicious, and 'destructive little madams'. Those minority teachers who prefer girls do so because they *like* the emotional side: girls are better at 'dealing with emotion and human values' (RE teacher); girls are 'more sensitive, respond to crafts' (art teacher). A few teachers appreciated the fact that the girls came to them with (personal) problems.

The bulk of teachers, however, appreciated 'outer' rather than 'inner' qualities. Boys were 'more forthcoming', 'full of ideas', made 'a better oral contribution', were 'livelier' and 'more enthusiastic'. They were, it is true, 'cheeky' and 'boisterous', but this contrasted with the girls 'sitting like puddings'. In any case, they 'saw reason quicker', were 'easier to control' and, of course, 'didn't bear grudges'. The deficiency of adjective stereotype questionnaires is that they cannot probe the meanings attached by teachers to concepts such as 'conformity' or 'motivation'. It appears that it is not enough for a pupil to be conformist; pupils should show outward manifestations of it — eagerness, enthusiasm, acceptance of teacher authority. This would again relate to the teacher predicament of dealing with large groups: one needs instant feedback on effectiveness, and this, it would appear, boys are more prepared to give.

A strange reversal emerges: it is in fact the boys who are more sycophantic, more ready to enter and conclude the negotiations, and ignore the contradictions which bothered the girls. Literature on managerial styles suggests men succeed partly because socialization into group or team considerations, rather than privatized concerns, means that they can be aware of and use people in their work and friendship groups, but also be tolerant of weakness (Hennig and Jardim, 1976). Women managers are more likely to be concerned about day-to-day competence, and to take matters on principle, thus being intolerant of hypocrisy or inefficiency. This has been noted already in the wenches' response. Male managers apparently recognize the need to work out team strategies to win, and the need for a leader or coach. We may find here both a clue to, and a critique of the 'correspondence principle' — that the social relations of schooling correspond to the social relations of the workplace. The acceptance of hierarchies and tolerance of authority may be, paradoxically, more salient for male pupils and workers than for female, in spite of the former's outward themes of toughness and independence. A distinctive attitude towards supervisory authority was noted in Jephcott's early study *Married Women Working* (1962), where women rejected 'democratic leadership' in favour of 'an efficient organizer whose skilful management was their direct gain and who would be considerate and flexible in meeting their individual needs'.

The socialization literature indicating girls as being more oriented towards adult approval (p. 139) is not necessarily undermined by this: we need again to explore motivations for, and styles of conformity. Girls may conform more because of individual self-image, or avoidance of adult disapproval; boys may conform more because of this socialization into group orientations. Boys may 'take' deviance imputations better because they can take them as representatives of a team, whereas girls, as noted, take them 'personally'. It is not for nothing that teachers find interactions with boys more 'clear cut'; even though at one level boys are breaking rules, perpetrating fouls, at a deeper level they are committed to the spirit of the game. They will be stringently, but fairly refereed, and (as we shall see later) avoid the final red card of being sent off, or suspended. There is no guarantee that girls are even on the pitch, let alone playing the same game. I was reminded of Northrop Frye:

> The boys for the most part, resisted the educational process openly ... the girls, on the other hand, were far more docile; they tended to be obedient and do as they were told. It was many years before I realised that docility was by far the most effective form of resistance. (Frye, 1971)

What worried the teachers was not being made aware of what pupils were thinking, until perhaps it was too late: 'The girls are inhibited, I don't *know* them'; the boys 'seem to make you feel more at ease'; 'I feel more comfortable dealing with a lad'. You could, as noted, tease a boy and be able to gauge the response.

I thus found contradictions in the teachers' assessments of girls, and was also reminded of the Schools Council findings on teachers' perceptions of West Indian pupils, which it is worth quoting in full:

> The following observations have been made in informal conversation by teachers, none of whom could be accused of prejudice or malice.... It has been suggested, for example, that West Indian children are both unusually demanding of teachers' attention and, at the same time, indifferent to the good opinion of their teachers. It has been suggested that they are arrogant and yet have a low opinion of themselves. They have natural 'rhythm' and exceptional physical coordination and yet they are clumsy. At school they exhibit a lack of enthusiasm, while managing to be exceptionally exuberant and keen. They are silent, inarticulate and they talk too much. Their parents impose too severe a discipline on them, are over-indulgent and are completely indifferent. It is impossible to get their parents involved in the affairs of the school, yet they interfere too much. A strong, simple Christian faith apparently dominates households where children are never shown any standards.
> (Schools Council, 1970)

Similarly, the following observations were made by Gladstone teachers: girls were apathetic yet aggressive; they accepted everything you said but they argued too much; they were less easy to put down but they were more submissive; they ended up in tears for every little bruise while managing to be more placid; they were more frivolous yet they thought more deeply. A possible reason for stereotypical thinking, whether of race or gender, and especially for contradictory stereotypes,

72

is simple ignorance — for the teachers, it was better the evil you know. 'Girls clam up — they might like school but they never say anything.' If girls say nothing they are thus sulking, or bearing grudges; if they say something they are 'aggressive with the mouth'. Their not knowing the girls as well as the boys increases the possibility of labels being applied: one teacher specifically thought that labels 'stuck' more on girls than on boys, that they would come up from the lower school tagged a 'right little madam' and hence not be given a chance. Given the semantics of female labels, one can understand the greater permanence; in the staffroom of the lower school I indeed heard girls being referred to as 'cows', 'bitches' or 'madams'; these are already adult labels which give few avenues for 'settling down', in contrast to the 'right lad' or 'real rascal' used for boys. Again the extremes are explained, for girls' maturity either makes them seem more conformist or suspiciously adult and female.

One might expect the sex of the teacher to make a difference here, yet females as much as males preferred the boys for their outward traits. Female teachers may be able, as one said, to 'outbitch' the girls, but they would prefer not to have to. Only three items on the stereotype questionnaire were differentiated by the sex of the teacher: males were more likely than females to see good pupils as less interested or conceited about their appearance, and more likely to see good pupils as more logical. Would these relate to sex-linked concerns of teachers themselves — females with appearance, males with logic? Yet these were the only traits where statistically significant differences emerge: the overriding concerns of teachers occur regardless of their own gender characteristics.

Another explanation of the paradox of teachers preferring boys while anticipating female traits, is linked to that of different *initial* expectations. In classroom observation one day I noted that only the boys were searched when attempting to find the culprits for stink bombs. Aggression would be deviant from either sex, but, as we saw, aggression from girls was noticed far more. Not only that, but it would be interpreted differently: 'Boys are very ready to stand up for themselves, they don't like to be made to look stupid, made to look girlish in any way, they'll fight to prove that, whereas the girls, it tends to be a lot of bitchiness — she *says* that I'm so-and-so, and I'm not standing for that — and then there's a fight.' Boys' defence of identity is thus called 'standing up for themselves', while girls' is 'bitchiness' (and note the coupling of stupidity and girlishness). With girls not being expected to fight, such behaviour will receive a more adverse label.

Different, but unrealized preconceptions arise also over work: 'I would expect the girls to adopt a better attitude, but I don't think they do' (MT), and over dress. The deputy headmistress said: 'Boys have always been notoriously more untidy than girls, but the girls are getting as untidy as the boys, I feel. I still feel the girl ought to set the standards on the whole — I think a girl who's untidy looks appalling.' Preference for boys was explained by one male teacher in these terms:

> 'In some ways I'm old-fashioned, always put the other sex on a pedestal — hate to see them do anything to lower their image. Whereas I expect the boy to be like me. Affects me far more to have to punish a girl.'

Therefore, for many teachers girls are a disappointment. They should be setting standards in work, behaviour and dress in accordance with school and cultural images, but instead they can behave like the boys. At least with the boys 'you know where you are.' A double-bind emerges for the girls: teachers may prefer boys, but if girls act like boys they will disappoint and confuse the teachers. Girls would have to select particular male traits of extrovert, team-based resilience without the accompanying aggressiveness or untidiness, to become favoured; even then their behaviour may be interpreted differently. A further double-bind arises because pupils are expected to produce some 'female' traits, yet if girls produce too many of these they are labelled 'emotional' or 'little madams', or their docility is viewed with suspicion for what it might conceal.

The stereotype questionnaire indicated no lack of problems for boys either. Good lads would.have to display 'female' qualities of being neat, conscientious or gentle, which may run counter to masculine concerns. This was the dilemma highlighted by Willis, which made the 'lads' reject the 'cissy' image of the 'earoles' in favour of their own reiteration of working class themes of toughness and excitement. If, as the psychologists maintain, personality formation is a search for consistency, it is unsurprising that some boys will prefer the coherence of a 'masculine' culture, some girls the consistency of a totally feminine image. An offshoot from this enquiry came from the questionnaire being given to a control group of 34 teachers, all from different schools. There were few significant differences, but they are worth attention. Gladstone teachers saw their good pupils as more conformist and less likely to use harsh language. Other teachers noted their good pupils as more confident, less emotional and more interested in the opposite sex than did Gladstone teachers. It would be unwise to draw any conclusions from these few items, but they might support the idea that a particular school would have an identifiable ideology for its pupils (as with Rutter's school 'ethos' (p. 214)) which would impinge on sex roles at certain points.

In Gladstone we have seen a preference for the controlled converger, asexual except where particular sex role leanings support school and classroom order. There are some instances of apparently different standards of normality operating for the sexes, but also an indication of many similar rules by which a good pupil, irrespective of sex, is defined. However, the multi-dimensionality of this pupil means that girls may be more likely to infringe rules on some dimensions, boys on others; and teachers will 'prefer' boys' infringements.

School Treatment of Deviance

In looking at the whole process of 'becoming deviant', the first step has now been taken of establishing rules of normality by which deviance is defined at a broad institutional or collective level. Next, we should examine whether the deviance is processed differently, once recognized. The overwhelming impression from both teacher and pupil interviews was that boys are treated more harshly, or conversely, that girls 'get away with' more. In this respect Gladstone appears no different from any other researched school where boys are subject to more negative sanctions. The three major areas for differential treatment emerging here are the linked ones of physical punishment, referral and the relationship between the male teacher and the female pupil: these will be reconnoitered at the institutional and then the classroom level.

The school treatment questionnaire asked teachers to specify possible school reactions to a set of six hypothetical offences by pupils in their fourth or fifth year. For each item the sex of the offender was reversed for half the teachers — for example 'Robert (Sharon) is frequently late for school, although he (she) lives only a short walk away. What treatment will he (she) receive?' In addition to lateness, the areas were uniform; graffiti; bullying; smoking; and misbehaviour in assembly, thus covering a range of infractions (see Figure 2, p. 221). The hypothesis was that identical behaviour from different sex pupils would provoke identifiably different responses from the institution; instead there seemed initially a greater range of possibilities *within* each sex than between boys and girls. Even using broad categories, anything between five and twelve diverse types of sanction were mentioned for each item. For the repeated lateness, for example, where the official school policy was short detention, and where the majority of teachers mentioned this, there were also teachers who thought the pupil might be caned, get lines, be let off with a caution, have parents contacted, and (for girls) be referred to the group tutor, the deputy headmistress or the education welfare officer.

Uniform received an even bigger range of treatments, from 'finding the reason' through to suspension. Many teachers outlined for both sexes the career pattern of warning — sent home to change — letter to parents, although being sent home to change was twice as frequently mentioned if the pupil was described as a female. This would go with the earlier suggestion of higher dress standards assumed for girls, of their being expected to set an example. Removal of the evidence was the obvious treatment for graffiti, but for boys teachers were equally likely to mention caning. This was thought possible by a few teachers for girls, but eight other categories were specified for them, including lines, essay writing, 'dirty jobs' round the school, and once more, referral to the group tutor or deputy headmistress.

The crime of bullying found boys three times more likely to be automatically caned, while the majority of mentions for girls involved referral to a member of the hierarchy (as if this were punishment enough). The boys, of course, would have to go to senior staff for their canings, but it is indicative that teachers knew that caning would be the result, while for girls the fact of their referral seemed the extent of their vision. Smoking was the only offence for which physical punishment was predicted almost equally for the sexes. However, two teachers who were allocated the girl's name, mentioned (complained?) that she would *not* be caned, and even those disagreeing wrote 'possibly caned' rather than the bald 'caned' for boys. Offences in assembly meant boys getting punishments such as detentions or lines, with referral being the inevitable result for girls. Predictions were throughout often qualified by the recognition that it depended on the staff member involved.

Yet in spite of the resulting range of options envisaged, certain patterns do emerge. Instant verbal admonitions and allocations of detentions or lines seem equally likely for both sexes. Caning, we have seen, is far more likely for boys; for girls this is replaced by referral to senior staff, or by a greater range of possible sanctions. (That such referral is not unique to Gladstone is clear from the similar cases cited in a recent union guide for teachers — NAS/UWT, 1979.) Girls also seem to more likely to have their homes involved in some way, through letters being sent, or (as accords with school records) by suspension. This has important implications. The relative lack of consensus among staff about what happens to girls implies less knowledge or grass roots control over their treatment (and there may be parallels here with lack of knowledge of them in the classroom) and hence a more detached view. For pupils 'the reason for it is lost on the way' (FT). Even the group tutor resented having to pass problems on, and would like to have had the authority to cane the girls himself: 'Discipline in my group is my job; it isn't to hand it on to someone else, and the boys know that if they're caught doing a certain thing, Mr V will cane them. The girls know that Mr V can't. And I get more trouble with girls than boys.' Another implication lies in the length of the deviance processing: it may *appear* that boys are treated more severely because of corporal punishment, but the extended procedure of referrals upward through the hierarchy, or to parents, may in fact mean a longer deviant career for girls.

A relevant example is worth relating here. On the last day of lessons before their examinations, about a dozen fifth year girls were caught with chalking all over their skirts, having inscribed messages such as 'goodbye teacher'. After being made to stand in silence for an hour, the girls were all sent home with letters to their parents, excluded from school, and not permitted to return until their examinations. One parent was so disturbed, he came up to the school later with his daughter, and on being reminded that this offence would remain on the record card, was so infuriated he 'clouted' his daughter across the head all the way down the stairs. One has to examine why this apparently victimless crime of skirt-chalking received such extortionate and escalatory treatment. One reason would relate to the violation of the female image: 'they looked an unholy mess ... they looked a sight' (deputy headmistress). The other reason would be their temporary control over the school 'ethos': 'The school was literally having a good giggle, a good laugh, and you could feel the atmosphere, the temperature rise.' The punitive measures resulting from this combined threat to school ideology were, however, seen by the head as successful, and the deputy head's version of events was in fact recounted to demonstrate how contacting parents was a greater punishment than having the cane. She was aware that pupils were 'literally afraid of what might happen to them' when parents were called in, and was cognisant therefore of the apparent value of the implementation, or threat, of such a referral. This relates to the analysis of the wenches' experience of violence, which argued that the comparative tameness of two strokes of the cane may be ineffectual. Teachers, too, felt that because only the 'extreme' cases were caned, those were the girls to whom it was going to be 'water off a duck's back anyway'.

Reasons why girls were not caned as frequently included this perceived ineffectiveness, and hence preference for other indirect measures, and traditional views of the female, which made physical contact take on a different meaning. As two male teachers said, 'It possibly makes a girl look smaller than a boy to receive the cane', and 'What may be effective with an individual boy or a group of boys . . . is often a physical sense of an acceptance of corporal punishment, which is a *different* attitude to a girl's acceptance of it.' (It is interesting that the last teacher specifies 'or a group of boys' — this would seem to support the notion of a male team acceptance of punishment.) Another view was that equalizing caning would maybe generate more problems than were current, as the girls would 'kick against it', given their ideas about what were 'suitable' punishments. A female teacher said: 'They would probably see an increase in caning as an attack against them, as taking something away from them really.'

In sum, the directly causal view expressed by some teachers that the girls not having the cane (getting away with more) was the reason they caused more trouble, has to be treated with some caution. First, there is a distinction between girls not having the cane in a single-sex school, and girls not having it in a mixed school. The latter is a direct source of sex distinction, according with the traditional notions of the 'toughening' of the male and the 'gentling' of the female. As recorded in chapter 7, schools using more institutionalized violence towards boys tended to generate more delinquency and disruptive behaviour; the preference in Gladstone for 'ladyfying' the girls may be a source of conformity rather than deviance, as they respect their 'privilege' and behave accordingly. Secondly, the added complication of the cane being available for girls in Gladstone but rarely used, in some ways highlights the sex distinction rather than minimizing it. Girls would have to be really 'hard' cases (that is, masculine) before receiving the cane, the inference being of a deviation from the female norm as well as the pupil norm. To neutralize the effect, girls adopt a tough 'it doesn't hurt, it doesn't bother me' stance, thus further confirming the masculine image and increasing the likelihood of secondary deviance because of the contradictory problems caused. Thirdly, the alternatives to corporal punishment must be borne in mind. If no punitive action is taken, then girls may well sense increased power — and contempt — as we noted sometimes with the wenches; if, however, more public attempts at depersonalization are made, deviant labels may be just as efficiently applied. A male teacher asserted, 'Girls do react more to a verbal telling off — I'm not naive enough to believe that it shatters their lives, I do believe that it can upset them more than it would a boy.' In Gladstone, canings were conducted in private, so that pupils had a chance to compose their features before returning to the pitch; verbal harangues were more often *'pour encourager les autres'* in the stands. Thus these rituals would be doubly stigmatizing for girls: they 'showed them up' in front of peers and other teachers, and, because of their 'taking it personally', would disturb them more than they would the boys. Lengthy public humiliation, referrals to senior staff, contacting the home may in the end prove to be 'harsher' punishments than the 'short sharp shock' beloved of some juvenile crime prevention attempts and some Gladstone teachers.

Classroom Processing

Teachers themselves, however, were divided about the use of practices such as the cane, for either sex, and we must turn to individual classrooms and teacher styles to unpack further the issue of divergent treatment. A similar technique of presenting different sex/behaviour pairings to teachers was used to ask them this time what they would do personally in certain instances of rule-violation — for example 'You go over to tell Angela (Martin) off, and as you return to the front, she (he) mimics you under her (his) breath. What do you do?' (See Figure 2, p. 221) Patterns were once more complicated by the even wider range of reactions by teachers to the same offence — anything from ignoring it to having the pupil suspended. An additional complexity was that some teachers appeared to have stock responses to any occurrence, whereas others would vary their desist techniques. Yet others would refuse to hypothesize for certain items, on the claim that 'This never happens in my classroom.'

Each offence, then, shows a subjective reaction. For pupil talk, clearly teacher talk was the usual response for both sexes of pupil, in the form of a reprimand or a specific power-reminding technique such as sarcasm or making the pupil stand up. Boys were more likely to be moved within the classroom; only for girls, and by male teachers, was a talking to at the end of the lesson mentioned. For the mild pupil insolence of mimicry, similar ranges of responses were foreseen, including the use of humour, lines, removal, or simply ignoring the offence. Only for boys was physical punishment mentioned; girls were more likely to be referred to other staff. For a more serious rudeness (here telling the teacher to 'get stuffed') which would be more difficult to ignore without endangering control, these patterns are repeated and even more clearly sex differentiated: boys would get a 'clip', 'clout' or 'smack'; girls, especially by men teachers, would be referred up the hierarchy.

A fight between same-sex pupils would provoke the instant recourse of separating them, whether boys or girls. Only for girls was a delay in subsequent verbal discussion mentioned, only for boys a physical retribution. Girls may also prompt a reminder of deviance from their sex role, implicitly or explicitly. For example:

> FT: Keep both in. After lesson give talk on etiquette and tell them why such behaviour is not tolerated in society.
> FT: *Ladies* don't fight! 'We're not ladies'. 'Then it's time you were'. Separate them.

This last quotation indicates an added dimension to girls' resistance to such socialization.

For a cross-sex pupil offence — this time verbal insult using offensive language — more support for a sex role ideology is apparent. This would be quite explicit sometimes, with the boy being told 'That's no way to treat a lady!' (FT) or the girl being warned 'Young ladies do not use such language' (FT) or 'Such language should not come from a "nice" girl' (FT). For the boy, then, the offence would be the violation of cross-sex rules; for girls the violation is of her own norms of femininity. Both sexes might be requested to apologize, although one (male) teacher would 'ask Linda to apologize to her colleagues in the class' — the inference being that she had offended the sensibilities of all of them by her deviation from the norm. A far more frequent concern for teachers receiving boys' names was that such language would be an offence to authority rather than to the girl:

> FT: Wouldn't expect this to happen. Pupils have too much respect *for staff*.
> MT: Tell him to keep his insults for *outside my class*.
> FT: Not in *school time*, dear.
> FT: Tell him to watch his language and refrain from saying it *in my presence*. (My italics throughout)

There appears a sneaking suspicion that the girl may not actually deserve the apology, as the following responses show:

FT: Usually the girl starts the trouble.

FT: If Linda has equally offended, possibly give both extra work.

FT: Tell them (sic) not to use such language in class.

The final, work-related offence of not doing homework provoked teachers into sex-undifferentiated exhortations and reminders of importance, into detentions and referrals; however, only for the boys did these include specific associations with getting jobs. For girls, the reasons were the more immediate 'getting a good grade', 'passing the exam', or 'the need to succeed'. While not according with the finding that getting a good job is equally important to both sexes, it matches some teachers' assertions in the interview that finding employment is more salient for boys than for girls, as they are going to be the 'providers' or 'breadwinners'. Otherwise the necessity for current achievement made the responses from the teachers show symmetrical patterns in the way pupils were processed.

As remarked already, the first result to note is the individuality of teachers in their interpretations of pupil action and the effectiveness of their own response to it. Nevertheless, summarizing the mentions in each category of reaction does reveal patterned divergences which parallel institutional practices as a whole. Boys are more likely to receive an immediate 'clout' or to be referred for caning. This informal physical retaliation to boys is not part of official school policy as preferred by the head, but nonetheless is often seen as the most effective recourse by teachers, including females. The somewhat tortuous methods of the treatment questionnaires were administered on the assumption that teachers would not recognize or admit to differential treatment of the sexes, but an interview question in fact elicited this also, in a more direct fashion:

MT: You tend not to be so harsh with a girl as you would with a boy.

MT: I treat them fairly much the same ... I will perhaps use the force of my tongue more on a girl — I know it's wicked etc to use sarcasm, but it's never stopped me yet. (This teacher was also one who used surnames for boys and Christian names for girls.)

FT: I have hit boys and it's worked first time. I'd never hit a girl because I approach girls differently, right? There's easier ways with girls, hitting them wouldn't work at all in some cases ... I find talking to them, or trying to humour them,

perhaps, or just take an interest in them as a person works a
lot better than raising my voice or getting all hot-tempered.

FT: The boys now, they're silly little boys, and the girls are
young women ... and they're very nice, and very mature —
so you have to treat them differently. But if you do it subtly
enough they don't notice.

Some female teachers admitted 'slapping' or 'hitting' both sexes, but no
male teacher ever touched a girl, for 'obvious' reasons:

MT: With a lad, admittedly, I can always give him a quick
clip over the ear or something like that, you know, or get
hold of him round the scruff of his neck and say get on with
your work. I mean, obviously I couldn't do that with a girl.
Because the boys accept that anyway — I don't mean I'd do
anything to cause them pain or anything ... but because you
can do that with the lads.

It is questionable whether the lads do accept it, from what they said at
the pupil interview, but the point being made is that such treatment is
culturally available. A female teacher enlarged: 'Well, I mean male
members of staff find it difficult because they can't hit a girl, I mean
none of us is supposed to, but they can't because it's going to be even
more difficult if they do get into trouble, they might shout — I won't
say they shout rape, but the fact that a man has handled a girl in some
way....'

In this we have the crux of the distinction: a female teacher hitting
a boy is acceptable, or has maternal/familial connotations; a male
teacher hitting a girl is unacceptable because of sexual connotations. To
explain why a male teacher is *not* seen as acting *in loco parentis* we have
to look to the 'sexualizing' of women and girls (referred to in chapter
7), which leads to girls being incarcerated for 'being in need of care and
attention'; we must remember the dual standards by which joint, and
by definition identical, activities by males and females are seen as
immoral and shocking for women, non-important or even aggrandiz-
ing for men. It seemed earlier that the school selected out particular
aspects of sex roles suitable for its control and achievement functions;
here it appears that the female-as-sex-object ideology is one that the
school is unable to neutralize or ignore, even though it would be in its
interests to do so. The girl would 'have her mother or father up to the
school' immediately, as soon as she was 'handled' by a male teacher.
The objectifying of women (that any interaction must be sexual) may

be in the interests of patriarchy, but it is yet another contradiction which the school has to cope with. Pupils should have equal rights; but the concept of female as property to be protected is here used by the girls as a powerful source of resistance.

> *MT:* I suppose I find it more difficult to deal with girls' behaviour — it's difficult in that they tend to *know* that as a male you're going to have more problems dealing with them than a woman teacher would, I mean, I think . . . with girls they tend to play on the fact that they're a girl . . . I get the temptation to strangle them! I think they can see that and they know that I'm powerless.

We begin to realize the inadequacy of looking at just one side of the deviance processing, and have finally to abandon the concept of 'differential treatment' in favour of 'differences in negotiation'. The sexist image of man-the-hunter-and-seducer is not one the male in school can happily pursue. As a female teacher put it, 'I feel very sorry for the men that have to teach the girls, you know, they don't really stand a chance, because they can't really do anything if they start being cheeky or messing about because their reputation stands to be lost.'

Even over-concern has its danger: 'There's nobody as hard on a girl as a woman is. And there's nobody can show sympathy when she needs it, as a woman. Because it can be misconstrued if it comes from a man.' (FT) Another dilemma arises: girls, especially, seem to want personal concern and interaction, yet men have to be wary of this. If they cannot touch them, and they cannot be concerned about them, it is unsurprising that boys are preferred for classroom encounters. The only 'safe' male teacher role is the familial one of 'uncle' or 'grandfather', which one of the group tutors claimed to have perfected: 'I can get through to them by talking. Matter of fact, they look on me as some sort of uncle.' On another occasion he reported calming down one particular 'stroppy' girl by 'doing the grandfather thing'. Amongst the wenches, however, these roles were equally problematic for their self-esteem. Terri said 'I don't like him. I won't go over there half the time [to the support unit] 'cos I don't like him. Treats me like a kid of five. 'I treat you like an uncle, don't I?' I says, 'ugh' — he thinks he's our uncle, shows me up.'

Earlier on, pupils were seen to be in a double-bind because of expected pupil roles; here we see male teachers in an equally difficult position *vis-à-vis* girls. If they negotiate with them as boys, they face outrage because of violations against sex role expectations; if they admit the girls as representatives of an adult feminine ideology they undermine their own control; if they relegate them to the status of small children they become personally unacceptable. It is no coincidence that the teachers who most 'brutalized' the boys also had the most problems with the girls, as for example the group tutor who had the highest caning record and who would like to have had the authority to cane the girls. Those who are limited to a stylized 'masculine' authority role can call up few alternatives for girls. In contrast, those teachers who attempted to individualize the encounters according to situation and character had the fewest problems, for reasons which include the question of sex differentials. Pupils perceiving a teacher who would be aware of them as 'girls' or 'boys' *before* individuals, are quick to capitalize on this. A misunderstood incident had prompted a male teacher to threaten to keep a lower school class in. They had complained to Mrs K, who suggested two of them go to explain and apologize: 'Immediately one of the boys piped up "Oh Miss, let two of the wenches go, not a lad and a girl, and don't send a lad, let two of the wenches go, he'll be all right then". Which I thought was really telling. I'm not saying it's particularly him who treats girls . . . but that does happen, and the kids certainly feel that to a certain extent.'

Deference to the female sex role can, of course, be conducive to school control at certain points, and the relationship between boys and female teachers was an example. Boys were thought to 'have more respect' for female staff:

> *FT:* A girl will get away with a helluva lot . . . simply because they're females. But I think that works for a woman teacher too — suppose you had hit a boy, I don't think he'd go back for a woman teacher, I don't think I've ever known that happen, because you've always got that you are a female, and the boy knows that.

> *FT:* I think generally women teachers have — or can have — an easier ride than men, because boys, if they are going to be aggressive to a man, where they don't feel it's necessary to be aggressive to a woman perhaps.

It was felt that boys did not have to 'prove their masculinity' towards women; on the contrary, they saw them as matriarchal rather than combative forces. The school was anxious to foster this 'respect': the caning book censured 'gross rudeness to female staff' or 'misbehaviour during a lesson particularly to lady members of staff'.

However, other areas of the female sex role deriving from sex object 'ploys' were frowned on, particularly female strategies such as 'turning on the waterworks' or 'fluttering the eyelashes'. An interesting staffroom conversation resulted from an enquiry by me about Kath's younger sister Jenny. The deputy headmaster liked her because she was 'innocent' — she would 'bat her eyelids' at him, but she did not mean it in the 'deliberate feminine sense'. This led on to a discussion of girls 'smiling'. Mr N related how periodically he would find himself saying to a girl after he had reprimanded her, 'come on, you wouldn't get a boy smiling like that.' The boys would understand the implication and be amused — they would be a poof with such a smile — but the girl would flush and be embarassed. Mr N thus implies to the girls that he is too old to be taken in by such ploys; he also felt it was 'not fair', that some male teachers did not know how to cope with it. In that he felt it was only semi-conscious on the part of the girls, he would often deliberately draw attention to sex role behaviour in this way in the classroom, or would make the boys go out first for a change; he attempted, by always using their Christian name, to undermine what he saw as the 'brutalization' of boys. A young female teacher suggested that the boys might 'smile' in the same way at her, but that it was easier to cope with, that they were not really having to establish their maleness and would anyway be wary of displaying feeling because of the 'poof' label.

All this underlines the difference in meaning between male teacher/ female pupil and female teacher/male pupil relationships. In sum, whereas female teaching roles tend to be matriarchal, men cannot escape the possibility that their cross-sex interactions might be sexualized. Physical contact with a girl might be misconstrued; and girls can if necessary use time-honoured female strategies to gain immunity. Hence the preference for referral of the girl if real problems are caused. On the questionnaire, girls were far more likely than boys to be sent to senior staff for specific classroom misbehaviour, but this discrepancy was caused by a disportionate number of mentions from male teachers receiving girls' names. A typical supporting example from the interview confessed: 'If a girl starts being a nuisance, I'm afraid I'm very often lost. Tend to refer them to one of the women staff, I'm afraid. Side step the problem.' Although the official policy for referral was progressively up the chain of command, in practice for girls the tendency was to send them direct to the deputy headmistress, bypassing any other male teachers. This was a source of annoyance for her; but it was part of teacher and school perception of girls' sex role distinctiveness — that girls are best dealt with by women. Women can be both empathetic and tough; men can be neither without some risk.

That escalations in deviance can result from referral to others has become clear; what is also noteworthy is that, even kept in the classroom, girls' treatment seems far more likely to be delayed than does boys'. Both male and female teachers would specifically mention waiting until the end of the lesson or after school to talk to, or admonish girls; this rider was omitted for boys. This would be related both to reluctance to force immediate confrontations (when it is perceived that girls 'take offence' more quickly) and to the view of girls' need for more personalized contacts using reasoning and discussion rather than impersonal or stereotyped punishments. This takes time, thought and energy. One female teacher said, 'If you impose on the girls in any way, if you draw attention to them, they don't like it at all, they somehow take it very-personally ... you have to be really wary, I have to think a lot more about how I'm going to deal with a girl.' Delaying the deviance processing can have a range of effects, as does referral; there is always the danger of it not happening by the time the end of the lesson comes round; as we saw, the wenches were quick to scorn teachers who in the end 'never said anything', or they were equally adept at simply leaving a lesson before the teacher had a chance to speak. The split-site nature of the school complicated end-of-day deferments, as teachers travelled between buildings and were not always in a position to check up. The other possibility is, once more, confirmation of deviant identity because of the long drawn out process. Instant and completed treatment gives the pupil a chance thereafter to demonstrate conformist behaviour; sitting 'under a cloud' may also make a pupil conform, but it may be equally likely to generate sentiments of 'may as well be hanged for a sheep as a lamb'.

Teacher Types

Although sex-typed patterns emerged in the way deviance was negotiated, this was complicated not only by stream membership but by the large range of policies or views held by individual members of staff. Teachers may share some consensus on the 'good pupil', but the means to achieving such a success vary enormously. Nowhere was this more clear than in the interview question which asked about projections for school policy. The first apparent broad division was into 'hard' and 'soft' liners, with the former wanting tougher discipline, as the following examples from male teachers show:

> I know what I want from a system — hard treatment. I will go to the person who will give the treatment I want. By that stage, no good being soft.

> At the beginning of the term pretend to smash hell out of them, tell them what the standards are going to be ... have the different years coming in separately in the morning and smash them one by one, just to show.

> I think in awkward cases, in the classroom itself if need be, the shopfloor teacher should be allowed to cane. On the spot ... I think a lot of these children, coming from this area, do expect more severe punishment. I'm certain they get it at home, and they expect it.

(As we saw from the wenches, the fact that they 'get it at home' in no way leads them to expect it at school; on the contrary it was the parents' right, but *not* the teachers'.)

> Kids in this particular culture expect corporal punishment. Respect stems from fear.

> Easy to say motivate them, all this load of rubbish.

> I think what they could do is these punishment rooms. Put a kid in there for a week, and he must go to that room, must be in solitary, must work, and that's it.

These extreme hardliners were all male teachers (both young and old) who seemed to see school, then, as a battlefield, with tactics (surprise early attacks), hand-to-hand combat (might is right) and prisoners of war (solitary confinement). The campaign areas are crucial for territorial advantage, as two more male teachers reveal:

> If you can control the corridors, that's where the power is ... if you can go down a corridor and pick out five kids doing something wrong, that's five different classes you've got that know Mr G has got this ... he's a bloke not to tangle with.

> A lot of the kids don't know who the head is, to start with. You know they don't know that he's a hard man, he doesn't strike me as a hard man, and I think it's important to play the game ... you can't just be an administrator.

In contrast to such 'territorials' were the 'communicators'. These were the teachers (equal numbers of men and women) who saw the major problems of the school as the size and split-size militating against getting to know the children well, and/or who wanted more adult, individual and humane treatment of pupils. They commented:

Children need to *be* somebody.

The large numbers — you don't find things out in time.

There's more to understanding kids than just listening to what they say ... you've got to make relationships with them.

So many people forget that kids are young people, they have the same emotions and hang-ups as we do.

A teacher noted how sixth formers seemed to 'change overnight' within six weeks, and related this to the change in treatment from the school: 'I always try to treat every class I take as potential adults ... I expect them to take certain degrees of responsibility within that age range ... then I will readjust my concept and my attitude towards individuals within that class according to how they do behave.' In other words, the teacher would treat children as cooperators *until proved otherwise*, rather than 'smash' them from the beginning, *expecting* deviance.

The core of the softliner communicators constituted a small group who saw themselves as 'heretics' as far as the local authority was concerned, but who realized they had made an impact 'by being ourselves — and refusing to get in confrontation situations, just refusing to play along.' These teachers 'wouldn't waste their time' on uniform harangues, and would not pick on the minutest thing to explode on'. As one put it, 'We had a thing about lads wearing earrings, now I mean, that's no big deal, it doesn't represent the end of Western civilisation; the way the school reacts, it does represent something very serious, very threatening, a lad comes in, and he's wearing an innocent earstud, suddenly he's a criminal.' They wanted the school to spend more time on personalized pupil contact, less on power confrontations and rule enforcement. Some teachers focused this particularly on the girls, who they felt did or would benefit from the pastoral side, from feeling able to discuss problems, from being permitted to dress in an adult manner.

Predictably, the teachers whom the wenches accepted all fell into the 'communicator' category; those they rejected were the extreme hardliners (and of course those softliners who broke others of their rules). Such rejection did not go unnoticed. A woman teacher said 'And it's not good for the kids actually ... they hate the people, and therefore they've got no conscience about how far they go behaviour-wise, they *want* to offend, in the end, which is, they want to get at these people, you know, they hate them so much, it's quite frightening.' This teacher in fact summed up the effect of the two different teacher approaches when she contrasted two different assemblies that had taken place both on very snowy mornings. Most of the staff, having to travel in, had not arrived, but the children had. On the first occasion, the deputy headmistress was in charge: she apologized for having to keep them in the hall until the teachers came, reminisced about a previous difficult occasion, asked them to sit quietly, permitting them to 'obviously whisper amongst yourselves', and sympathized with their being cold. 'The kids were marvellous for her, because the kids generally are, especially in a situation like that, a desperate situation, they really will behave.' On the second such occasion, the group tutors took control. They were on the stage, and incredibly to this teacher and to the children, attempted to 'gloss over the situation' and pretend everything was as normal. They tried to run a conventional assembly, talked about King George, did not tell or reassure the children what was going to happen or acknowledge the adverse situation. They insisted on silence: 'Every time a kid came to the door, it was, "right, no talking, there will be no talking".' In the end the children took control; they could not bear the charade, and the assembly hall 'erupted'.

I was reminded of Durkheim's view of social solidarity being best achieved by rational means, including a rational view of control, authority and punishment. We saw the girls especially needing to have 'reasons' for behaviour before they will conform. The territorials, however, want unquestioning obedience from the native troops. Yet many pupils, and in particular the wenches, lack the spirit of Empire, and take every situation on its merits. They elect their leaders; their political instincts undermine a totalitarian regime at every point.

The labelling process is therefore a reciprocal one. We saw the wenches interpreting teacher behaviour in the light of previous in-formation from peers or siblings; and teachers can very swiftly be categorized too on the basis of single events like the assembly just described. One teacher (liked by the wenches) commented on being pushed into different behavioural styles by different classes:

> One thing that's intrigued me, fascinated me over the years, that . . . the same teacher himself can get a different atmosphere with one class to what I get with another. I cannot analyze how it comes about. It may be some occasional remark, when I first

> take the class, puts both on the wrong footing, I just do not
> know. Some classes which I would have thought would be
> parallel classes react differently with me.... Going in in a bad
> temper, it's reflected in the way you've spoken to them, early
> on — 'he's a grumpy old soul' and that's established a mental
> set.

Hence the 'break them early' teachers, not sensitive to this instant
categorization, in fact damage their subsequent chances of election. The
advice to beginning teachers of 'start tough and soften up later' has
enormous dangers. The territorial may get unquestioning obedience,
but he may equally engender insurrection and pockets of resistance.
The communicator may have continuously to argue his or her manifes-
to, but s/he is at least open to negotiation. The existence of different
styles may, of course, be another source of contradiction for pupils, as
they move from a teacher who demands total silence to one who may
encourage discussion. If the teachers are free to interpret their roles, the
pupils are free to interpret their response; no longer can teachers claim
authority on the basis of role alone. What is more, the interpretations
can be contaminated, and there are problematic overlaps for teachers
too: a repressed class can 'let off steam' with the next, more relaxed
teacher. Conversely a style of intimate 'chat', which the wenches
perfected with one teacher, would equally, and to their delight, get
another teacher 'mad'.

Finally there is the classic discrepancy that a pupil labelled 'difficult' by one teacher will present no problem, even be enjoyed by
another. Examination of the final report cards for the bottom stream of
the fifth year showed some pupils of both sexes inviting a fair degree of
consensus from teachers, but others where it was hard to believe
teachers were referring to the same child. Could a pupil really 'work
well' for one teacher and be 'bone idle' for another, be 'inattentive' yet
'thoughtful and diligent'? Did Debbie really switch from being 'resentful' to being 'a pleasant pupil'? How could Donna be 'an interesting
personality', 'too easily influenced', providing 'satisfactory work' but
'needing more effort'? Clearly teachers have different concerns. One
might select an attribute such as 'good sense of humour but has to be
reminded to wear a tie', while another concentrates on work or effort.
As in the question of treatment of pupils, they have varying amounts of
range, with some teachers using recipe remarks throughout, such as
'works to the best of her ability', while others favoured the specific
'work has gained appreciative comments from senior citizens who he

visits'. A second variation is in the permanence teachers attach to pupil behaviour; while one asserts: 'I am fed up of telling him to stop his noisy disruptive behaviour in the classroom and around the school. He should now be behaving like a young man not a child. This behaviour won't be accepted when he joins the Army', another admits of the same boy 'behaviour good *as long as* interested and occupied' (my italics). For Sandra, the label may well become a self-fulfilling prophecy: 'Does not wear school uniform, attendance poor. A firm would not accept this, so may find difficulty obtaining or maintaining employment.' Whether Sandra finds a job may clearly depend more on her school record than on her actual responsive traits. The question of different behaviour with different members of staff may, however, be touched on by a teacher: 'Elaine is a child of two extremes — can be pleasant and polite, but equally can be sullen, resentful, obstinate. Happily, the former is the dominant characteristic.'

The fact that all teachers respond, discipline or label differently clearly affects pupils of both sexes; what we are concerned with here is the interaction between sex-linked behaviour and teacher scenarios for pupils. Contrast the interconnection of a girl's sex role projection with a softliner and a hardliner. Both might draw attention to it — we saw Mr N commenting on, and sensitizing a girl to her 'smiling', but by saying 'come off it' implying that it was not appreciated or necessary. Mr V, on the other hand, who had thought girls 'sulk more', would give a sex-typed deviance imputation: 'Oh, shut up girl, you've got a mouth like the Mersey Tunnel, shut it', followed by an expectation for another sort of sex-typed behaviour: 'And I look at the rest of the class, and I say that's it, she's going to sulk for the rest of the lesson, we've got peace and quiet.' The girl is in an impossible position. If she does not remain quiet for a period, she confirms that, first, the primary insult had some truth and should not provoke a hostile response, and, second, that quiet behaviour would indeed be 'sulking' and therefore is to be avoided. If she does remain quiet, she confirms both acceptance of the original imputation and her subsequent image of being a 'sulker'. It is no wonder pupils feel they 'hate' such teachers who force them into these dilemmas.

Implications

Whether a pupil accepts a 'deviant' label and is thus more likely to commit further acts of deviance to conform with that label is a phenomenon possibly influenced by gender, as detailed in chapter 7. The factors mentioned there are how often the label is applied; by whom; with whose agreement; and how publicly. This chapter's discussion of the way a school processes deviance has, in looking at rules and their enforcement, provided some refinements to the factors, especially if taken together with girls' perceptions. We would have to add, firstly, the length of time during which the label is applied. This may eventually make the label less publicly broadcast, and the stigmatization therefore less; on the other hand it may mean a larger number of people involved in the definition, and therefore more support for it. The question of how far teachers are 'significant others' also recurs; but the wenches' problem was that some teachers were not significant enough, and did not warrant respect — so this led to reactions *more* likely to generate adverse labels. Another refinement would be the extent to which a pupil took a deviance imputation 'personally', which was more likely for girls — not necessarily because of greater respect for the teacher's opinion as such, but because all interactions were seen as threats to, or confirmations of, personal identities rather than reminders of their adherence to the pupil role or of the extent of their participation in the classroom 'game'. A final complication was the degree to which teachers 'knew' their pupils: if teachers claim not to know girls so well, they would therefore seem more prone to stereotypical thinking about them than about the boys. Girls' deviant labels were linguistically more permanent and stigmatizing. 'Knowing' pupils required making relationships: and the balance, in this case, of territorials and communicators would affect the likelihood of behaviour categorizations and staffroom support for these. If girls are especially resistant to military forms of coercion, they are possibly likely to receive sex-typed deviance imputations, which simultaneously attempt to restore control and absolve the teacher by projecting responsibility onto deeply ingrained gender traits.

This chapter provides support for a labelling perspective on sex differences in pupil deviance, but only if we link this with wider culture contact. On the one hand, the teacher's task is to promote individual achievement while maintaining group control. This leads to a sexually relatively undifferentiated notion of the 'good pupil' in the classroom, as one who is able to display selective traits, some masculine, some feminine. On the other hand, teachers' own socialization, together with school ideology deriving from broader sex role assumptions, leads to diverse expectations, interpretations and treatment of the sexes. This means that deviance may be defined by different rules, or similar rules selectively applied. In addition, however, pupils are not passive victims of school and teacher ideology, but enter the school with learned strategies and definitions of the situation from which teacher practices are further derived. Teachers are not all-powerful labellers, but are themselves subjected to pupil projections of gender styles. Teachers are also extremely individualistic in their interpretations of pupil behaviour and school goals, and therefore can be subject to counter-labels by pupils. However, the overall joint impact is to reinforce particular aspects of gender behaviour: the 'conformist' girl is reinforced because she acts within the 'good pupil' role; the 'deviant' girl is also reinforced because of the deeper, more personalized, more 'moral' level at which her deviant career is defined and then lengthily processed. Boys' deviant or aggressive behaviour may be attenuated because it is more subject to instant aggressive treatment. But the complications we are adding to a basic labelling approach in order to include individuality and strategy points to the need for a further attempt now at a suitable explanatory model for deviant careers.

4   Scripts, Identity and Power

A wonderful exercise for concentrating the mind is to imagine that one is being interviewed on television and has precisely three minutes to say what one's view on pupil deviance is. While the great academic sport involves carefully undermining existing theories and thereby displaying critical, if negative acumen, television requires its personnel to come up with something recognizably positive or seemingly original. There is a great temptation merely to reiterate complexity; at this point, we would be demurring, socialization *could* explain girls' greater conformity, but only in conjunction with school treatment and labelling can it account for the 'extremes' of their behaviour; sub-cultural membership *could* account for different group styles, but the tenuous nature of this sub-culture needs a much more calculative, individualistic model; the sexual divisions required by a patriarchal economy *could* explain the school's reproducing certain sorts of gender behaviour, but they do not account for areas where the school or the pupils appear able to ignore these; nor does the notion of 'agents of the Ideological State Apparatus' do justice to the individuality of teachers in their negotiations with pupils, for we have found we must look at resistant teachers as well as resistant pupils. But by now the interviewer (and reader) would be becoming impatient, and demanding some conspicuous peg to hang their hat on. The task is to find a graphic way to absorb these complexities and to link micro and macro, the individual and the state.

To do this, I shall continue the television exercise and pirate the notion of 'scripts'. This is not new — the concept of scripts has been used to describe expressions of ethnicity (King, 1978), sexuality (Gagnon and Simon, 1974) and escapes from routine (Cohen and Taylor, 1976) — but it is an appropriate and flexible way to begin to describe pupil deviance. A 'script' I shall define here as the way an individual makes a statement about both their identity and their definition of the situation — for example 'There's no way I'm ever going to put up with that.' It is the result of a person formulating a certain interpretation, combination or selection of wider type-scripts; it is the momentary expression of what Cohen and Taylor call 'identity work'. A person's script — whether 'I always give as good as I get' or the alternative 'Arguing only causes more trouble' — indicates where that person stands in relation to what he or she perceives to be going on.

Personal scripts must be distinguished initially from societal type-scripts. The latter are the background expectancies attached to various statuses and memberships, whether of age, race, sex or class. The assignment of old people to non-productive leisure, women to the home, blacks to inner city ghettos and the titled to the stock exchange would be examples of the alignment of social 'types' to certain performances. The interaction of these type-scripts can be expressed as life chances, or as probabilities:

> Such perceived probabilities are best approached as multi-conditional: while most members of this society undoubtedly hold a very low probability that a bank president would be female, there is undoubtedly a still lower perceived probability assigned the type-script of a bank president being both female and black. (Harris, 1977)

One reason for the lower rate of deviance for women in society is the low probability or even absence of deviant type-scripts for them: 'It is of special interest to us that one consequence of the restriction of women to the private sphere is to make them less available for the public ascription of criminal and delinquent statuses.' (Hagan et al, 1979). It is not in the interests of male dominance, suggests Harris, to allow the development of deviant type-scripts for women, because women are needed not in prison, but at home so that men can work.

However, these probabilities for societal type-scripts do not impose absolute limits on individual script-writing. King (1978) describes variations in the selection of particular ethnic scripts for minority group Americans; she contrasts the man who accepts ethnicity as wholly limiting his life space and opportunities, with another whose ethnicity is only one script among a cosmopolitan repertoire, and who purposefully 'uses his blackness in American society'. Deviancy theory has to come to terms with the ever-changing facets of self, the borrowing, the anticipating of scripts on multiple dimensions. Although the sex role dimension is our concern here, this is only one of a range of structural factors which could be 'predictors' of script expression. Social class, geographical locality, occupation or education may be equally important. Kelly (1970) points out in his 'personal construct' theory that each of us not only has a unique range of constructs to view life and people, but that they are ordered on a different hierarchy of salience. Whether someone is male or female may stand at the top of one person's list; whether conventional or unconventional may head another's. Similarly, we appear to 'choose' which one of the structural factors and their accompanying type-scripts will assume the master script for us at any one time. Women do not *only* use sexual scripts, but may assert sexuality if that has potency for the particular situation.

A personal script, then, is a social construction of reality, a limit on our actions, which however, 'allows us to elevate routines, regularities and mere behavioural sequences in such a way that we can assert superiority over the everyday world' (Cohen and Taylor, 1976). 'My door is always open' boasts a lecturer or a headteacher; the fact that this may be patent nonsense, either literally or metaphorically, is immaterial — the person is saying 'I am an accessible friendly type who supports democracy and the breaking down of barriers' — and in the end believes it himself. A script is the imposition of our identity on the scene as we view it.

While using a now well-explored dramaturgical analogy, the concept of scripts avoids the pitfalls associated with role theory, for 'roles', defined usually in terms of 'sets of expectations attached to a social position', have connotations of being static, deterministic, implying a consensus view of society. A role 'incumbent' who 'occupies' a position does no justice to the flickering complexity of human interaction, the multiple realities which make up the hundreds of miniature dramas of our everyday lives. Scripts can perhaps best be seen as combination of Turner's 'role-making' and Goffman's or Berne's 'games': it is no linguistic accident that the word 'play' is used for both roles and games. Avoiding the over-tidiness, wholeness and inertia of 'The Role' or 'personality-type', scripts can cover the range of individual or group expression, from a whole scenario through to one-liners, while allowing for the reflexive self as audience when no-one else is there. Scripts can become a life long 'career' projection — 'I've always got on well with children'; or they can be temporary, as for example the 'face-saving' scripts often used by the pupils: 'I'm not bothered'; 'I don't care what they think of me.' The favourite 'we just had to laugh' script of the wenches would be difficult to encompass in terms of a single role; similarly the script for 'you don't say that to me' implies a whole sequence of possible dialogues and a pressure into stances from others in the way 'the role of resister' could not. The use of a television rather than just a stage metaphor will enable us to examine other projection skills and techniques we noticed in the wenches' 'accounts', such as recorded highlights and action replays.

A script analysis, then, allows for a range of interpretations of personal identity and social context, while indicating the importance of the joint team which pushes forward the passage of the play. A person's repertoire of acts and statuses originates in, and must be validated by the social group; but the concept of scripts differs from socialization in that it implies the individual's ability to write and re-write his or her own lines; to perform differently in different programmes, in public and in private; to experiment with different parts within the same play; to ad lib; to edit; to forget. An important aspect is the interpretation of the script by the audience. In the same way that teachers have to distinguish 'natural' laughter from 'subversive' laughter in their deviance imputations (Woods, 1976), they will also have to distinguish relatively unscripted 'talk' from what linguists call 'performative utterances', implying motives, intentionality, identity work. Keddie (1971) gives an interesting example of a teacher's differing interpretation of the same line 'Why should we do social science?' according to whether it was spoken by an A or C stream pupil, whether it was a 'genuine' question or a question identical to 'Why do anything? Why work?'

While there are parallels to the notion of 'strategy' which has been effectively used elsewhere (A. Hargreaves, 1978), I prefer script analysis because it allows for the concept of lines being written for others — as in the school's typescript for the good pupil — and also because it can cover the whole range of expression from throwaway one-liners to entire life scenarios. Strategy is sometimes too grand a word for the idle experimental bits of repartee through which pupils try out different possibilities for action or power, some to be instantly discarded, others to be polished and refined, and lovingly preserved for future use.

In that a script encompasses both objective and subjective worlds, a concept of deviant scripts can link micro and macro theory: 'Me background don't give me a chance' can be a commentary both on the objective reality of the deviant *vis-à-vis* the state and also a subjective self-justification for continuing deviant behaviour. Script analysis also highlights the significance of the actual language used, together with the accompanying body language of gesture and intonation. Of importance is how the articulation of a script does not just describe but further defines action. Repeatedly saying 'I am the sort of person who . . .' will condition behaviour far more than any physiological traits. The wenches asserting 'That's me all over' or 'I can't help it, I have to join in' provide not only a justification but a forecast of action.

Structural Type-scripts

Our task is to identify the various sources of personal scripts, the sex role differences in their expression, and the availability of deviant scripts. At the structural level, everyone is subject to the general framework of a gender type-script; and continuing the bias of this book, I shall use female type-scripts as a basis for illustration.

Under patriarchy, in spite of changes and ranges, the female role is defined explicitly as a relational one: female status derives from a woman's position *vis-à-vis* a man, whether as marriageable prospect, as wife, as property or as mother of his children. That 'mother' is not sufficient status on its own is clear from the low prestige and financial support still accorded to unmarried mothers. The spinster — the woman who has no official relationship with a man — is a term to evoke pity or disparagement, in a way bachelor is not. (We saw the girls avoiding both these non-relational female roles.) There is no masculine equivalent for the word 'mistress' with all its ownership connotations. Indeed, it was argued that the wenches' concerns and accounts, although on the surface varied, all derived at root from relationships; their identity could be established only by how others were seen to 'treat' them, whether teachers, boyfriends or parents. Even aggressiveness derived from this dependency, for the girls' strongest reactions were to threats to how they might be perceived by men, not insults to their intelligence, activity, prowess. As I taped their conversations, they would enquire, for example:

> *Julie:* Do you ever play this back to your husband? (LD: why?) Just wondered. Case he wondered, who's this girl carrying on.
> *Debbie:* Does he ever talk about some of we? Like, does he say, who's that?

The irony was that, although it was in my interests as objective listener for them not to care what I thought of them, their concern about what my husband thought confirmed my own mere intermediary status. Many female teachers in the school had to be acknowledged as women on their own, but — as we noted — the popular female teachers were those who revealed aspects of their relationships with husbands, who could share a joke about boyfriends. The wenches' favourite sub-plot of teasing Miss T about Mr H was done delicately, with much innuendo, and carefully scripted. 'But', they said to me, 'Debbie stirred it up too much.' She had taken the lines to the male teacher: 'That's your fancy bit, ain't it, Sir.' She had spoilt the play by confrontation, for confrontation was one of her favourite scripts at the time. Not only had Debbie infringed the stylistic cultural rules, but what she said was an insulting irrelevance: Mr H was not to be defined in terms of his relationship with Miss T, although the converse was valid.

Capitalism added to patriarchy defines the relational and secondary status of women still further, but in a changing economy also throws up contradictions. While patriarchal socialism could work within a collective or kibbutz system, the nuclear family with its sexual division of labour performs key functions for a capitalist economy, so that the resultant domestic, privatized type-script for women is a pervasive one. The scripts for 'inevitable romance' and 'fulfilling motherhood' are literally written and acted out by the media and advertizing daily; there are few female type-scripts that give alternative scenarios to love, marriage and producing children. Thus, in spite of their own family experiences, most of the wenches have no alternative long-term lines to the marital dialogue. How long Debbie will retain her 'You're better off on your own' script is a matter of conjecture. It is easier to embrace a romantic or 'magical' female script, in the same way that Cohen (1972) describes the working class boys' limited and 'magical' attempt to restore working class community.

Advanced industrial society also, however, benefits from having a certain number of women in the labour market. The passive female type-script generates less union activity and confrontation than with male workers; the masculine breadwinner role means that women make fewer wage demands for themselves. They form a useful low-paid subsidiary sector in productive industry, or their domestic lines can be easily translated into other caring and service roles supportive of the male labour market. The problem for capitalism of simultaneously maintaining domestic and wage labour scripts for women is managed by a fine series of balances. In war-time the patriotic script took precedence, and encouraged women into munitions factories and into agriculture; at present in a time of economic recession and a depressed labour market, we are seeing a re-emergence of the 'first-five-years-of-life' maternal deprivation tragedy, with politicians stressing the need for mothers to remain at home with young children to combat social evils such as juvenile crime. This script has the dual underlying function of easing closure of expensive nursery education and releasing jobs for male workers, thus alleviating to some extent the eventual threat to the system of massive unemployment. Current type-scripts promoting 'community care' have also been analyzed by the Equal Opportunities Commission as being, in fact, a euphemism for 'female responsibility' — it will be individual women who eventually take the burden of the old and the handicapped, not men or the state. Soviet Russia also has had to reintroduce family scripts, when women too enthusiastically learnt their employment and career lines after the revolution; not only were they not producing enough new workers, they were undermining the family unit now seen to be essential to state capitalism as much as to private sector capitalism.

Cultural Adaptations

Combinations of working and motherhood scripts for women therefore have particular temporal, social class, regional and ethnic variations. Driver, for example, attributes his controversial finding of West Indian girls doing better in school than West Indian boys to the traditional concentration of power, property and prestige in the hands of women — 'the unspoken assumption among many West Indian women that they, rather than their husbands and brothers, are the guardians of their family's good name and providers of its stable income' (Driver, 1980). While Scrapton women are not solely responsible for the family's subsistence, there is nonetheless a long tradition of married women working, often in heavy industry such as foundries, sometimes in what were termed 'dirty' or 'unpleasant' surroundings. The description of Scrapton as 'matriarchal' may be related to this female experience of heavy work, and also to a local scripting of the domestic dialogue. As noted, female type-scripts are only probabilities for action; not only can women extemporize around the themes, but they can, and do, create forceful and substantive parts for themselves within what might appear to be supporting roles. The domestic script is appropriated as a power scenario, where the woman is dominant, literally the producer — of children, food, and other services — and director of the whole play, as well as acting the key part. Daughters are understudies for the central role, looking after younger siblings, babysitting, or being kept away from school to care for new babies. The male may provide the financial backing for this drama, but the woman is central, simultaneously powerful in this role and progressively limited by its typecasting.

The women's collective drama group, provided by the extended family typical of Scrapton, is an even more influential and self-sufficient venture. It provides a pool of actors who can step in at short notice to 'help out'. While this gives opportunities for women to practise other work or leisure scripts, it means that their domestic part can never be completely filed away, but has to be reserved because of the need for reciprocal understudying elsewhere. It also means that the male has fewer opportunities or incentives to learn the domestic script: there will always be somebody from the agency to outshine him.

The male working class script, on the other hand, justifies or even celebrates manual labour in its themes of toughness or machismo (Miller, 1958; Willis, 1977). This may mean that physical action is as important as the lines men speak. The ritual aggression at football matches documented in Marsh's *The Rules of Disorder* (Marsh et al, 1978) demonstrates how carefully stage-managed this action may be; but the availability of a physical rather than a verbal retort means the possible transformation of self-projection into violence in and out of the home. The female reaction to violence can be manifold: there is avoidance; there is the 'weakness' script which portrays the woman as so fragile as to denigrate the man that strikes her (and neither of these two scripts is available to men); or there is the incorporation of reciprocal violence into the female scripts, as we saw in Scrapton. In the area round Gladstone, one has to fight, sometimes literally, for one's rights, for one's chap, for one's money, for one's prestige — and 'girls can fight much dirtier'. There are no Queensberry rules in female fighting scripts; the powerless can afford no such luxuries. As the Newsons discovered:

> When girls do fight, we might expect the exchange to be more vicious on average, especially in view of the fact that there are few socially prescribed rules for physical combat and its resolution between girls as opposed to between boys.
>
> (Newson et al, 1978)

The script is a largely improvised one.

Combat can be symbolic, too. Teachers had commented on the tendency of girls to 'fight for their rights' in school more than boys.

But pure or extreme patriarchy denies the female the right to exist meaningfully on her own — and, of course, those who have the fewest rights will be those most concerned to protect them. A defensive, even combative script may become part of the female repertoire. It will have to be balanced against the media script of romanticism and motherhood, and each girl will take elements of both in her final version or versions; but both can, however, be seen as the heritage of the 'suppression' which made Myrdal link together 'Women, servants, mules and other property' (1969). Outside the domestic sphere, these are primarily *reactive* scripts rather than initiating ones. There are few scripts to change the situation they are in, merely to manage it. A discussion lesson revealed the girls being scathing about Scrapton — 'there's nothing to do' — but it was not only that they did not envisage leaving it, they had no idea as to how it could be altered.

Individual Transformations

Feminine type-scripts, plus their local adaptations, give the girls a range of scripts to work from. They will in school form loose associations with other girls who operate on similar scripts to their own, and then consolidate and extend the range of available scripts, and the power of them *vis-à-vis* teachers and other groups. We noted the group styles and rules, the commenting on solo performances, the shared acting out, whether in pubs, discos or classrooms. We saw the need for repeat broadcasts by the girls of situations where they had triumphed, where the stage was littered with bodies. Joint scripts are clearly more powerful, in terms of pushing the action forward, or, like a Greek chorus, commenting on the plot; yet they may be less potent in terms of the promotion of individual identity or status. Because of individuation, each girl appears to work on a unique life script, with a unique combination of sources. Debbie casts herself as the 'black sheep of the family', tells of threats to 'have her put away', and announces finally and somewhat triumphantly 'I'm a crinimal' (sic). Hers was the ageing starlet role; she would have a cigarette 'to calm me nerves down'; she would claim, seriously, 'I'm dying. My life ain't worth living.' Her preference for a woman–of–mystery script to support this dramatic and deviant role meant the frequent reiteration of lines such as 'nobody understands me' or the dark 'you don't know me. They don't know the half of it.' One source of her 'crinimal' script is clear from the account of bringing her mother some daffodils from a Mothers Day service, at ten years old: 'Me mother swore blind that I'd pinched them off the garden.' Terri's mother, too, reminds her of a disruptive script (partially handed down from her brother): 'Our mum says, you ain't been in no trouble for ages.' Another source of scripts is the peer group: Kath explains the start of her school 'reputation' thus:

> I dunno, how did it start off' Mr C — we put the basket on the door and all the rubbish fell down on his head — we kept doing things like that, like the other kids used to do, so we just tried it, didn't we? The fifth year used to tell us what they used to do. When you mix outside.

Both Terri and Kath had in fact been coached in masculine scripts by their fathers — 'They've toughened us up' — but they also had feminine scripts as well, being fashion and boy conscious, and, Kath especially, not above a feminine wile towards male teachers. For Julie, the chosen school script had originally been written by an older sister: 'I've got one sister what's just left, and one what's left before . . ., the one what's left before, her used to be in trouble, and I'm like her.' She also sees parallels between her script and Debbie's with regard to boyfriends: 'Debbie and me, we're very similar to one another. Every chap we go out with, we can't stop long with them. We've got a different chap again after.' But in spite of this fancy-free characterization, her long-term life script is a traditional one. It contains a 'quiet' chap who will marry her not because she is pregnant, but because he 'thinks a lot on her'.

A proportion of the wenches, in fact, have in reserve a 'settling down' script. As Donna put it, 'My behaviour's been better in this fifth year than it has all the years, ain't it?', and Janet: 'I behave myself in school. Last year I was really bad. I've quietened down this year.' The recognition of the impending need to embrace a mainstream feminine script in order to consolidate a mature female image means a frequent casual abandoning of old lines. This change bewilders teachers sometimes, as when one asked Linda 'Why is it you can be so charming?', and she replied 'I've settled down, I have.' Sharpe had noted in one London school that it was common for girls to fight each other until 14 or 15, and still remain fashion conscious. In Gladstone, even 'rock hard' Rajinder, in a final conversation with me in the support unit (for swearing at a P.E. mistress with whom there had been a long history of physical aggression), reckoned that she had been worse in the three previous years than she was now. Having started off in the middle stream, and been demoted each year because (according to her) of her behaviour, she would work somewhat harder if she 'had her time over again'.

School Type-scripts

These personal scripts are constantly being rewritten to accommodate both institutional type-scripts and individual teacher scripts. The initial greater conformity of girls at school can be related to the overall dearth of deviant type-scripts for women in society, and also to the fact that the girl acceding to a 'suppressed' female role fits neatly into many aspects of the good pupil script at school (for example 'helpful', 'responsible', 'doing maximum work'). Conformity derives not so much from a positive allegiance, but from a negative, waiting type-script that requires females not so much to prove themselves, but to not disprove themselves; the conforming girl's impression management noted in chapter 2 was a maintenance script, not a risk-taking, innovatory one. The preferred school type-script for girls in Gladstone was the lady-of-the-manor part: mature, ladylike, but aware of domestic responsibilities. This articulates well overall with girls' concern for reputation and its symbolic courteous treatment. Boys have many more problems of maintaining character consistency against the good pupil type-script, and need the supporting cast of the sub-culture much more.

Yet girls can cause problems for teachers; their privatized scripts mean a preference for the 'viewers at home' role in the classroom, whereas the boys are more inclined to be the studio audience, 'fooling about' on occasion, but willing to participate in the live broadcast. (The school's valiant attempts to counteract female low status by special serialized weekly assemblies did not, as we saw, sufficiently rouse the wenches from their observer role, from true Brechtian 'alienated' theatre.) There are, anyway, few type-scripts for males displaying *private* emotion; yet girls may find it an effort to concede their personal scripts to the show. When teachers commented on girls being more 'vocal', 'more confident to express what they feel', it was to explain disruption, not participation.

For teachers, the problem of equal importance to anomie is what to do with a girl once she is disruptive. Just as there are fewer deviant type-scripts for women in society, the school suffers from a lack of appropriate deviant type-scripts for girls. Boys are expected to be naughty; and boys are expected to expect retaliatory treatment. Yet for girls the punishment structure is not there; and teachers have to fall back on a wider 'immorality' type-script, with, as we saw, particularly stigmatizing consequences. The 'deviant' school type-script for boys — naughty, rough, untidy — does not cause problems for the boys; it can be written into their own scripts without too much difficulty, and may even orchestrate well with masculine concerns. A similar type-script for girls, however, will necessitate either a divergent script from the culture of femininity (for example Rajinder the fighter) or an exaggerated and hostile insistence on the original feminine script (Lorraine persisted in wearing her leather coat round the school on the grounds that teacher obstinacy about hanging it up was because they were 'jealous', not really because it was untidy). As in fact the 'naughty, rough and untidy' type-script is mostly less available for girls, teachers will use the 'emotional and resentful' type-script; but just as roughness is punishable by more roughness, emotions are countered with more emotions, degenerating into the 'bitch and slut' type-script with all that that entails.

Just as we saw the high-ability type-script as sexually neutral, and the low ability lines as gender-biased, conformist pupil type-scripts may therefore be unisex, while deviant ones are sex-typed. Girls may comply more because their scripts harmonize with the good pupil role; when they do disrupt, their scripts do not fit any bad pupil type-script, and everyone must improvize. Boys may disrupt because there is a bad pupil script on hand for them, but in this scenario the school already has the best lines.

Individual Teacher Scripts

The pupils, then, have their personal life scripts drawn from localized adaptations of structural type-scripts; the school has its pupil type-scripts which, in a mixed school, are written in accordance with its sometimes contradictory but joint concerns, which are the transmission of social and sexual roles, and the maintenance of audience control. The fundamental dilemma is that in a school, the pupil participants are both actors and audience. The teacher, as actor-director, has to teach new lines, edit and expurgate others, while keeping the audience-cast amused and participating — even though some do not merit even a walk-on part in the great educational production of examinations, and will insist therefore on using their own lines.

The teachers will write scripts for themselves and the cast as they go along, in accordance with their own biographical interpretation of wider type-scripts and with particular teaching problems and pupil expressivity. The need for a range of scripts is acknowledged by many teachers:

> I have two fourth year classes, and I react completely differently with each class ... bend the rules for one particular class. (LD: Do most teachers have different rules for different classes?) Probably the ones that get on with them, the ones that have difficulty keep the same state of mind all the time. I treat it as a game in a way ... it's an acting game, and I pretend at being annoyed. I rarely get *really* annoyed ... it's fortunate because I can turn it on and off.

The distinction between fake anger and 'real' anger is recognized by teachers and pupils alike: 'I mean, if you cane a lad, you don't cane him with venom. I mean, sometimes I'm so angry I hand the cane to Mr N or somebody, I say, you'd better do it, I'll kill him.... You don't cane in fury; but you don't lay it on soft either.' Real, unscripted anger is far more awesome to pupils than the ritual, scripted, predictable annoyance. For some teachers the school type-script for staff of no unofficial hitting, and the lack of punishment structures for girls, is a source of strain: 'I know that one shouldn't (hit), but one has to behave as a responsible parent would, sometimes ... but then we haven't got any other way, half the time, a lot of it's frustration. And I think that years and years of self-restraint can twist you.'

We saw that the territorials tended to have undifferentiated 'control' scripts for encounters with pupils. They did not appreciate individual creativity, and I would often observe the attempt to desist by the put-down 'You're not special'. One teacher worried that the attention in the support unit made pupils, especially girls, feel 'too special'. Hardliners also were implied to have a penchant for 'catch 22' scripts: Kath was accused of starting the strike about school meals: 'They said, "we know it was you." I said "It warn't", they had me for answering back and chucked me out anyway.'

The communicators showed, as noted, a preference for 'relationships', that is, different dialogue according to perceptions of pupil needs and responses. A technical teacher who let the remedial class 'be a bit more bouncy' spoke, however, of the danger of mixing the channels:

> The only time it becomes a problem is if, say, you've got a lad
> finishing a job off with you, with the lower school class, now
> he's got his standard, which is a lot noisier, calling you and
> different things, shouting across the room which you wouldn't
> let the first years ever get away with, so they see him doing
> that, and they think, oh, we can do that.

He implies that scripts are easily photocopied for others' use. The
doubts of the hardliners about the support unit are understandable: it
did provide a very different setting. Only in this play for particularly
deviant characters was an all-adult cast apparent. Here was an attempt
to provide humanizing scripts: the actors drank coffee, had carpets,
were bombarded with 'please' and 'thankyou', and were treated as
responsible people. Withdrawn characters were given more lines to
say, in being persuaded to converse; a large girl in trousers, who always
wanted to be a boy, was encouraged to diet, to take an interest in her
appearance — in other words, was given a female script to practise.
Participants were assisted to work, but their productions were not
necessarily scrutinized, for they could choose to retain areas of privacy,
as we do in the outside world. Verbal exchanges were conversational
rather than the often necessarily artificial question and answer of the
normal classroom. An outside observer could have been forgiven for
assuming that the concern would be not how to get pupils out of the
unit, but how to get the rest of the school in. Arguably, however,
pupils would emerge even more deviant than when they entered; such
personal attention and humane interaction would make them less
willing to embrace the impersonal anonymity and artificiality of the
classroom.

Pupil Script Writing: The Sex Difference

When we examine the possible range of pupils' scripts — girls'
especially — the need for flexibility among teachers becomes even more
pressing. Because of the absence of adequate deviance-processing
scenarios for girls, the resistant girl, once rejecting the conformist
script, has perhaps a greater range of scripts to choose from, a greater
potentiality for power, than the boy. She can take over a male script.
As Terri said:

> The girls are stuck up, they don't want anything to do with you
> if you play up, so we had to mix with the boys, start playing up

with them — but they'd want to do things better, and you'd want to get the better of them, so I tried to be worse than them, 'cos they're always bragging — like we did this, we did that, so then we do it.

She can join in the overtly sexualizing scripts which might have seemed a male preserve: a female science teacher described her innocence in her early years of teaching with a class of boys:

I remember one day I was talking about the camera, and they were in hoots, and I mentioned holes, and exposure, and goodness knows what, my every word, and I also mentioned that I was hard up — I don't know where that came into it — and everything I said they took the wrong way, and I said 'I've never had a class like you before, what's that matter with you?' 'Er well, we ain't had a woman before, have we.'

In their uncertainty, the boys took refuge in rugby club humour, their shared worldly knowledge demonstrating maturity, superiority and group membership all at the same time. Yet girls can and do use similar suggestive scripts, with the wenches enjoying dirty jokes and innuendo in the classroom as much as the boys. A photography lesson (which must be twelve years after the previous example) displayed them all paralyzed with laughter from having to 'fiddle about' in the dark bag. 'Get in the bag!' says Debbie to Robert, with heavy *double entendre.*

Alternatively, a girl can take on an exaggerated feminine script, with the presentation of self being achieved through make-up, fashion, obvious talk about boyfriends, making up to any workmen in the school, even 'flirting' with male teachers. Similarly, Anyon denotes coy postures in American girls as the 'appropriation' of femininity, which can be used to resist, for example, the flow of work assignments. The extension of femininity to open sexuality was a more obvious form of resistance, in that it enabled girls to get attention, disrupt lessons, and even turn the boys against the male teachers (Anyon, 1983). In the UK, the 'culture of femininity' was the one noted by McRobbie (1978) as the basis to the counter-school culture, although in Gladstone it was certainly not the only female script available or used by the girls.

What is striking, in fact, is the number of scripts which stem from an originally low status position. Warner describes the 'female operator' as part of the underdog political style: 'shuffling, playing dumb, playing up and dissembling are so many manipulative strategies of rational actors in oppressive circumstances' (Warner et al, 1973). The 'low caste' approach was in evidence in school; it is interesting how well the orchestration of the girls' parts fits in with the 'accommodation attitudes' listed in comparisons between blacks and women (Hacker, 1969) — for example: 'deferential/flattering manner'; 'outwit white/ men folk'; 'supplicatory whining intonation of voice/rising inflection, smiles, laughs, downward glances'; 'careful study of points at which the dominant group is susceptible to influence.' The linkage between the various scripts for subordinacy is shown by this discussion of the politics of caste:

> The subordinate is more oriented towards the superordinate. Just as the student 'psychs out' the professor, and the child works his or her way around parental mood, so, too, the woman may be more oriented toward her husband than he is to her. The superordinate initiates more interactions, while the subordinate is typically more passive.... The superordinate is less likely to disclose information about him/herself than *vice versa*, so that information about oneself flows opposite to the flow of power. (Hochschild, 1973)

The 'disclosure of information' is especially relevant to our perceptions of girls' greater readiness for vocalization of their feelings. Further, Konopka noted that negative stereotypes of minority groups are always closely related to sexual behaviour, as seen from the ugly accusations made about Jews under the Nazi regime, the hidden fear about Negroes, and the parallel 'unnamed horror' that is present in talk about delinquency in girls (Konopka, 1966). With one of the few deviant type-scripts for girls being a sexual one, it is small wonder that a moral counter-script will be part of their repertoire.

Withdrawal, or indifference, is another common ploy in uneven contests. Ignoring the teachers altogether, refusing to acknowledge their lines, has enormous potential power. One teacher said, 'A girl will simply carry on until she's been told about three or four times, and when the message finally gets home, she will stop.' A withdrawal script with the exit line 'boring' is equally neutralizing. It is difficult for teachers to find a counter-script to anomie, when all attempts at joviality, coercion or enthusiasm fall into a silence. A culture of powerlessness will also generate 'helpless' scripts — we saw the 'injured innocence' of the wenches; the teachers observing their 'whining about it', 'turning on the waterworks', feeling 'you can't push them without them breaking down and crying or something ... you've lost'. In this way a loser script becomes a winner script in the end.

But in addition to these 'low caste' approaches, the girls could reverse the normal power roles by pulling out what can only be termed a 'mother' script, talking to the teachers as if they were small boys:

MT: Donna!
Donna: (back to the teacher, looking at some wedding photo-
  graphs, irritatedly shouts) *What?*
MT: I want to start.
Donna: (not moving) Well, *start* then.

A similar patronizing destruction of the teacher's lines was Linda's: 'He says, "you'll have to have the cane." I says, "I'll have to have the cane then, won't I?"' The implication is that they have more important issues to think about than these childish pursuits. With women teachers the script can be the confidante one, as we saw with the wenches advising teachers on boyfriends and make-up, or simply ordering them about — 'Miss, come here' — as if with equals or even subordinates.

Finally, there is some version of a tried and tested confrontation script, in its extreme form called 'turning out the language' or 'giving someone a mouthful'. 'Telling you what you can do' we saw as a preferred form with girls rather than boys, according to the teachers; and girls are 'aggressive with the mouth, language, volume, quantity of words rather than actual physical assaults'. The teacher's 'Mersey Tunnel' type-script for a girl is indicative of the perceptions of girls' vocal response. Because of the female 'style', the struggle for prestige tends to emerge in verbal aggression (in spite of the availability of a physical script if necessary). When status comes from what you are rather than what you do, language is the key weapon rather than action expressed in 'fooling about' or physical supremacy. A cookery teacher remarked 'Boys may tip up a bowl of water, or in fact throw it at one another, but you can deal with that, it isn't malicious.' Verbal confrontations are less valued by teachers, and, as noted, labelled 'bitchiness' or 'resentfulness'. In that language represents thought, they possibly suspect a greater permanence to girls' opposition than faced with a physical display that can be seen to start and stop. Hence the view that girls are less amenable to control; thus the preference for, and increased interaction with the boys, and in turn the greater 'resentment' of the girls. A cycle of resistance is set up. Tests for power become ritualized, habituated; the scripts become crystallized and hardened. The supreme victory for a girl and for her script is when she can report that a teacher is 'frightened' of her — and just through the use of language. Female power scripts are only countered by those who know the lines. As a teacher put it: 'That's why they (the girls) play up men more than they play up women. The men don't know how to deal with it. Being a bitch myself, I know exactly how to deal with it. Don't try beating me, I can do better!'

As outside school, the scripts are sometimes individual, sometimes directed and acted out jointly, and the joint scripts must also be explored for sex differences. The girls appeared to act together as *'agents provocateurs'* to force the teachers to write their own confrontation scripts for the entertainment value:

> MT: This particular group of girls, some of them were very intelligent, and they used this intelligence rather than for work, to play staff up, which they could do *quite* easily. Once you've got your back put up, there's not much you can do about it.
>
> FT: There'll be a few girls who've got together and almost consciously worked out a pattern of behaviour, you know, they try ever so hard to be difficult in a way, whereas the boys, just by their nature — wherever they are, in the classroom, in the corridor, out of school, the sort of boister-ous, tough image, you know.

This last teacher put her finger on a crucial difference in performances: the girls 'almost consciously' write special school scripts, the boys merely bring their lines in from the machismo programme on the other channel. Hence the predictability of boys, the admission that teachers feel more at ease with them. Willis may be correct when he locates the male counter-school culture firmly in shop-floor culture; but while the girls' counter-school 'culture' has derivative elements from the female working class culture, the contradictory nature of this culture itself, and the need for individuation of the girls, means a far greater range and a more creative working of themes. One 'difficult' girl, who if pressed too hard 'might explode' it was felt — in other words, who hinted she always had a confrontation script at the ready, was then described with her sister at a school production:

> The way she was speaking was *incredible* — she's normally got the Scrapton dialect accent, and she was speaking perfect English, and being so refined, such a lady in front of her sister — it was incredible, the change in her. I do feel that this minority of girls who are like this in the school really want to give off this tough image, and not being interested, when

they're outside live up to a totally different image, whereas the boys are more consistent.

It may be significant that the pupils talking in Woods (1976) of 'laughter' in school, who distinguished between 'mucking about' in school and 'acting your age' outside, were all girls. It has been argued before that context may be more important for females than for males, and the fluency with which girls appear to switch scripts may lend support to this.

It is not, however, that girls are any more 'superficial' in their responses, for the scripts may be deeply experienced while they are occurring. Another teacher located the sex difference not in the actual lines, but in the depth of the characterization:

> Boys might even say the same things, but they would say it in a different way, which might pass it off as a joke, rather than downright insolence. Tone of voice ... I was thinking of the remedial science group, there are girls and boys in that set who are equally capable of making what could be offensive remarks, but on the whole it would be the girls who would say it in an insolent and surly way, the boys would say it in a joking way, and I wouldn't mind so much.

One is reminded of King's remarks on the schools' differential interpretation of 'insolence' whether from boys or girls (p. 192). Here, the boys, by semi-joking, are not fully changing the direction of the play, merely temporarily providing comic relief. Theirs is a role distance, a natural break, rather than a different script; the girls would say the same lines 'for real', and by tone and body language convey the emotive meaning behind the words. These are Goffman's 'character contests', and the script is about honour, not just diversion: 'Honour can be engaged, namely the aspect of personal make-up that causes the individual dutifully to enjoin a character contest when his rights have been violated — a cause he must follow in the very degree that its likely costs appear to be high' (Goffman, 1969).

The range, unpredictability and in-depth playing of the girls' scripts as we saw caused problems for the teachers who had little flexibility in their own scripts, or had little experience or inclination to play opposite the female lead. A preferred male response was simply to write them out of the show:

> She's been the only pupil where I could easily have sloshed her one, but I never let myself get that involved, because I think,

well, they're not worth it, in the end I don't *care* about them . . .
to me they're just not important, if they want to rant and rave,
it suits me, and I do what I can to get them put out of my
classes.

The result was, as documented, that the girls tended to be sent to the
controllers. For the benefit of these new viewers, this entailed an action
replay of the foul for which the player had been sent off, with the result
(depending on who was editing the highlights) of confirming or
denying the deviance label. The girls, too, were not without their
supporting cast; bringing a parent up to the school was a real threat to
teachers. Donna, when she had problems at home, repeated *ad nauseam*
one morning that she would not be in community studies that
afternoon because 'I have to wait for me social worker.' She was
gratified, because she was now a person who 'owned' a social worker
— another character had been added to her list of *dramatis personae*.
Even I became written into the wenches' scripts; initially this was in the
role of first bystander, to be called on as referee if necessary; later they
cast me as their personal biographer, and were gratified to have an
additional and appreciative audience. The teachers claimed they behaved *better* in class when I was present; but how much of their script
was specially written for this recording will never be known.

Experimentation, Rehearsal and Crystallization

To summarize so far, we have seen pupil scripts located in basic social
type-scripts and in sub-cultural, localized responses to those type-
scripts, whether as the assignment of women to domestic labour or of
working class men to manual labour. Girls appear to have a wider-
ranging repertoire to draw on, particularly of female scripts designed to
enhance status and counter power. The school will also have certain
gender-related type-scripts for pupils, although teachers as individuals
have their own classroom scripts, and will vary in their range and
ability to improvize. It remains to ask how certain scripts can become
habituated or routine, and the character of an individual or institution
confirmed. The interaction of pupils' scripts and school scripts creates
new dialogues unique to the institution, and the importance of this at
the micro level should not be underestimated. A teacher describes the
difference between Gladstone and her Sheffield school:

Large comprehensive, bigger than this, same sort of area —
lower class industrial types, and the kids there were very

amenable, they were very nice, they had a great sense of humour, and they weren't well behaved, but — you could get on with them without a great deal of effort, they knew what was expected of them, and they largely conformed to what was expected. When I came here, it seemed to be the main game of everybody, including the top band fifth year, which really shook me, to have a battle with staff, you know, you stand there and they sit there, and you spend the entire lesson fighting each other.

A girl put it more briefly when she confided 'I don't understand why some of the girls are as cheeky as they are. They was cheeky at our old school, but not as cheeky as they are here. I was very shocked. I suppose it's the area.' As Eggleston (1979) observed from his ecological comparisons: 'Different schools, different areas and different regions produce different children from astonishingly similar social material.' Yet even within the same catchment area, schools can vary in preferred scenarios:

> *Kath:* Our school's worse for playing up and that, but going out with blacks, getting things, their school's worse . . . 'Cos their school's all clean — if we see a bright wall, it's gotta be drawed all over . . . they call playing up not working, we call playing up using our mouths, don't we, keep shouting in the classes.

I have been suggesting that the presence of territorials on the staff may encourage 'battles' to become a dominant script, and it is, of course, as easy for 'noise' or 'shouting' to become self-reinforcing and escalatory. Yet simply 'deviance amplification' models, useful though they are, are not enough; the problem with labelling theory is that it tends to portray processes as emanating from an identifiable 'act', or imply the absence of expectations or labels as neutral events. A script analysis shows how the *absence* of type-scripts is important, in that it permits individuals to write their own. It shows, too, how scripts can be learned, borrowed, plagiarized, 'photocopied' from others, or rehearsed alone, without need for identification by the powerful.

Stylistic differences between institutions are the cumulation of long and complex negotiation processes. Crystallization of a script occurs initially through individual rehearsal of a particular dialogue which probes opportunities. Walker and Adelman outline the function of 'joking' in this respect, in particular how a child is able to create and sustain an identity by projecting herself through a unique relationship with a teacher, not necessarily shared by other pupils in the class:

> What strikes us about the relationship between Colin and Karen is the way she seems to be constantly playing minor variations on the theme of him as likeable but inefficient. It is as though she is able to create an individual identity for herself out of the stream of classroom events by the use of fluent repartee to manage incidents in a way that keeps Colin within the image she has defined for him. She therefore creates an identity for herself, not as a public figure in the class, but through her ability to use talk to maintain her definition of the situation and so sustain a unique relationship with Colin. Her identity is dependent on her image of him and her ability to make it stick when she talks to him. (Walker and Adelman, 1976)

Such interdependency is not necessarily covered by labelling theory, and needs more recognition of personal *creative* exchange, even in 'ungrammatical' power relationships. Musgrove fears that sex and humour may take the power out of schools as social and educational systems: 'Jesters can make suggestions about dangerous and normally forbidden issues to their superiors; girls can often do likewise (when the superior is male)' (Musgrove, 1971). Semi-serious, experimental repartee to counter power may well become not just part of an individual's repertoire, but intrinsic to a particular relationship, and eventually coalesce to become a preferred style within an institution. The transformation of an experimental script to a routine one encompasses what Kelly calls 'repeating what seems promising':

> Behaviour is indeed a question posed in such a way as to commit man to the role and obligations of an experimenter. We shall not so much be asking *what makes* people behave in the way that they do, nor *how to get* them all to behave in the way that threatens no-one, but we shall ask, instead, how can *behaviour be employed* to seek the answers that stir human curiosity. And when we see behaviour that distresses us, we will spend less time wondering what conditioned it, and ask, instead, what is the experiment that is being performed, what hypotheses are being tested, how the outcomes are to be assessed, and whether it opens or closes the door to any man's further adventure. (Kelly, 1970)

The way in which the school may transform experimental behaviour into a type-script is an essential of any reproductive process. Writing on 'face-work', Goffman (1969) notes that 'regardless of whether a person takes a line, he will find that he has done so in effect', that the other participants will assume he has more or less wilfully taken a stand, and themselves act accordingly.

Labels are therefore not so much 'applied' and 'accepted' as experimented with. A final example of a girl's script will demonstrate how a deviant will not just 'live up to a label', but creatively transform the 'special treatment' into a power script for herself:

> *FT:* She goes to another class, and she expects that teacher to give her special treatment. 'I'm not doing this, I'm not doing that!' — she knows if she plays up enough, that teacher will ask to have her removed. She has enquired of me whether I was teaching her next year, and I said I didn't know, which I don't, and she said, 'Oh, I don't suppose you'd have me, would you?', implying that I would ask to have her removed. I mean, she's obviously got that in mind the whole time. She's carved herself out a reputation and she's almost belligerently looking for someone to ... she *wanted* me to say 'No, I wouldn't have you at any cost'. You know, I didn't answer her. If I said 'Oh no, I wouldn't', then by some strange chance I did have to teach her next year, then she'd have me from the word go, I wouldn't have a leg to stand on.

This girl had worked out a winner, a double-pincer: if the teacher showed willingless to teach her, she was condoning her deviance, revealing herself as 'saft'; if not, the girl could be hostile, expand the script to establish her reputation, show that she had been right all along. An interesting and strangely relevant finding from a study by Bannister was that when reading transcripts of children's recorded conversations back to the participants themselves, girls were able to recognize themselves much more easily and at a younger age than were boys (Bannister, 1977). It appears that girls are better able to identify their own individual style; the question of the creative appropriation or individualization of 'deviant' or 'conformist' labels seems especially salient for females. Teachers may be shifted into unique relational stances by the resultant script-writing of the *pupil*; the absence of deviant type-scripts for girls is linked to the lesser likelihood of identifying a 'normal deviant' in their case.

It has been documented (Wise, 1967) that girls tend to experiment with delinquency, but are less likely to persist. In Gladstone, girls experimenting with the (for them 'deviant') curriculum choice of metalwork were also less likely to persist. Every school would need micro-level examination of its reaction to script experimentation, of whether such is accorded positive or negative reinforcement. Kelly's point about 'opening the door to adventure' is an important if ironic one here: 'difficult' girls by their very creative power may especially confirm their subordinate position. For the school does not grant deviant scripts the status of structural resistance or identity work, but merely tags them inappropriate or immoral; by practising resistance skills in terms of relationships rather than curriculum, girls may deskill themselves occupationally.

Power: Long and Short Term

This last question, of life skills, can be clarified if we converge on the crucial issue which underlies the whole discussion of pupil scripts: that of power. Paradoxically, girls' scripts in school may be temporarily more powerful because they derive from the culture of powerlessness. Women have had centuries to perfect scripts to counter power, to protect their status against male dominance. They are practised martial arts experts — using the strength of the opponent to resist and overcome. If men treat them as helpless, then a script for helplessness will enable them to exert their will in other spheres. If they are relegated to the home, they will make that a locus of control. If they are handled as sex objects, they will use their virginity or sexuality to bargain with, making themselves 'cost' something, and will upgrade their value once more. Writing on female criminality, Adler (1975) thought:

> Women have been presented as childish, devious, indirect, petty, seductive, inappropriately domineering, and incomprehensibly manipulative. It is not difficult to see that, aside from total submission, these are the only options available to the weak in dealing with the strong.

Yet we have seen the importance, too, of 'joking relationships', in much the same way as anthropologists see jokes as the management of 'ungrammatical' identity relationships; there are many other strategies available than just 'weakness' scripts, as observed with the girls. Moves towards equality, but where women will simply have to compete with men, lose, and form a subsidiary class, may find women reviving the untouchable script. A bargaining model of sexual stratification is one that has been used showing how the resources and trading of income and sex between men and women change over time, with women in an advanced economy increasingly using income as a resource (Collins, 1971). Women may win power and value, alternatively, by stressing differences, establishing their own society; they may use sexuality, as in a brothel, or purity, as in a nunnery. As well as having different resources for bargaining, women apparently use very different bargaining strategies (Tedeschi, 1973). They are more concerned with presentation of self, and take cues from both the situation and the behaviour of other people to draw inferences about what conduct would look best in the eyes of others. They prefer accommodative solutions, and will respond more cooperatively to cooperation, but if others exploit them, or seek competitive advantage, they are more concerned with saving face, and hence react in such situations with greater retaliation and vindictiveness than men. This description accords well with the findings from the girls, and clearly underlines the need to examine power and exchange differentials in school.

If school is a testing ground for relationships as well as cognitive skills, in a mixed situation the girls experience a double but linked set of asymmetrical relationships: teacher/pupil and male/female. One cannot always distinguish the control war from the sex war in everyday negotiations in school, and they may be similarly orchestrated. It is no coincidence, for example, that the 'resentment' attributed to girls at school is also cited in the psychology of power as an accompanying stance of subordinate groups:

> A relationship is always vitiated in proportion to the degree of power present. Dominance is inseparable from pride or arrogance, while deference or compliance indicates weakness, if not servility, and is accompanied by resentment, conscious or unconscious.   (Sampson, 1966)

Boys, too, face power asymmetries in school, and will sometimes exhibit accommodative strategies in a similar way to girls; but evidence comparing mixed to single-sex schools shows boys in mixed schools having a higher opinion than do the girls both of their own sex's and their own individual capabilities (Hutt, 1979). 'Difficult' girls in school often experience three sets of asymmetries which would relegate them to a marginal group: teacher/pupil, male/female and high ability/low ability. For Donna and Rajinder one would add white/black. It is not surprising that they will exert all known 'wiles' to resist the teachers-as-dominators, plus many new variations of their own. Meeker established that rather than there being universal sex role differences, *status* was the vital factor to explain situations where sex differences did occur. In task behaviour, for example, differences are minimized when equal status, leadership and respect is positively and overtly established between the sexes (Meeker et al, 1971). The combination of historic and contemporary asymmetries in power and status proves to be the decisive factor in sex differences in script writing.

Although an increasing range of female scripts in the West can be linked to women's occupational emancipation, it is doubtful in the end whether one can welcome girls' deviance in school as either an advance for the women's liberation movement, or as a breakdown in sexual divisions; for it is no more a revolution than is boys' gang life described elsewhere. Just as working class boys may in the end confirm their position in the wage labour structure by rejecting the avenues to mobility the school offers, resistant girls may increasingly close off during their school careers any others options than factory work or the dole followed by early marriage. School becomes doubly irrelevant, both for marriage and job prospects; their range of potential scripts becomes in the end reduced. Sexual identity *may* be an avenue to social mobility and status, in terms of marrying upwards, or using the casting couch; but the girl refusing to take part in the educational production does not in general have access to many 'career' scripts which can permeate the boundaries of class and sex. Therefore one is not just examining the range of alternative scripts for pupils, but their efficacy in terms of future control over their own lives. A resistant script for a girl in school may be only a temporary source of power.

Scripts: The All-Purpose Tool

If we refer to the theoretical possibilities outlined earlier, and developed in chapter 7, scripts would seem a viable way to draw together the salient parts of these sometimes competing explanations. Biology on its own appears unconvincing, but biological features do give rise to, or act as justification for wide-spread type-scripts for males and females, which cannot be ignored and which must form part of the analysis. With regard to socialization, the notion of scripts can include the transmission of such type-scripts, but also provides for the strategic response of individuals and segments of society in the ingenious way they manipulate their lines and write counter-scripts. Similarly, it enhances the uniformity of sub-cultural theory by emphasizing the extemporization round the expression of cultural values. It can incorporate labelling theory in terms of the reinforcement of scripts — that is, how an actor is allowed or encouraged to rehearse his or her lines; but it extends labelling by the concept of appropriation, or of borrowing others' lines, thus accounting for both primary deviation and initial conformity. Finally it can supply the structural variables of sex, race and class which simultaneously constitute limits on the writing of day-to-day scenarios and provide opportunities for power negotiations. In that a script may be the codification of an ideology, and as such can be identified in specific school practices, it provides recognizable examples of structural forces or correspondences; yet the notion restores the creativity lacking in simple reproductive models, and can apply equally in socialist as in capitalist societies. Schools can therefore be examined in terms of the availability, the potency or the absence of scripts for individuals and sections of the pupil or teacher population, and the heritage traced.

In my enthusiasm for the idea, I seem to be presenting scripts as the sociological catch-all. Yet there is no compulsion to embrace the notion: the beauty (and the irony) of a script analysis is that it permits the reader to assemble hastily her or his own scripts for resistance.

5 Towards Independent Appraisal

The Times 'Misprint of the Year Award' went to *The Kent Messenger* for 'Sir Roger Manwood's Grammar School, founded in 1563, will go educational in September next year.' This book has taken the somewhat unusual step of approaching the analysis of pupil deviance not only from gender differences, but from the base-line of girls; it remains (after a synopsis) to 'go educational' and broaden the framework for application to any mix of pupils.

The root issue, it has been argued, is power; the tool for analysis is scripts. To edit the lowlights so far, a particular economic order will be associated with type-scripts which facilitate the learning, the performance and the acceptance of the interlocking roles which maintain that order. The inevitable asymmetries in power and status between these roles will provoke supportive scripts either to reinforce a power position, or to acquire status, or to cope with a less prestigious part. Both the type-scripts and the secondary tactical scripts will be assimilated within the home; the new actors interpret and re-write these, and add new scripts of their own to assert individual standing. Educational agencies also 'teach' both type-scripts and tactical scripts for these wider social roles, but being places themselves of asymmetrical power, engender their own type-scripts for the survival of the school economy. In turn this entails adaptive scripts for the management of identity by both teachers and pupils. These new tactical scripts will contain lines plagiarised from other learned adaptive scripts, whether the originals were to gain power on sex, class, race, age or any other social dimension. There will also be new and unique scripts written specially for the occasion and for the institution. The geometric progression by which one script demands another will mean a complex intermingling of tested recipe and innovation; the mass of contradiction forged in school life by divergent goals is itself a source of creative response. In each individual school, these scripts will be experimented with, adapted, crystallized or shelved, depending on the technical performance of the actors and the dialogue preferences of those in control.

In the specific case-study of Gladstone, we saw an androgynous good pupil type-script, although one not incongruous with the expected performance of the 'normal' female; yet if they were not going to conform, boys and girls were expected to 'deviate' in different ways from the good pupil script. The boys' deviant type-script was tightly orchestrated by the school, the girls' more open to improvization. The especial nature of classroom management, and the need for feedback, meant that the good pupil role was only partially coincidental with the 'needs' of the economy for certain roles. Few power type-scripts were available to either sex in terms of control of school or community. A preference for culture-contact models of socialization is expressed on p. 164, and the 'colonial' scenario is in fact an apt one for Gladstone. The school type-script for teachers was that of colonial administrator, using the ancient principle of divide and rule. District officers had their own jurisdiction, but could refer dissenters to regional capitals for justice. The girls had their own particular conformist and deviant type-scripts for the behavioural conduct of teachers, perceiving and playing on character contradictions in teachers' acting out of these parts.

Both pupils and teachers exhibited a range of tactical scripts to assert status within or above these basic dimensions. Teachers tended towards either warfare or infiltration techniques, with communicative styles being notably more successful in taming the natives. Both male and female pupils shared many tactical scripts because of their basically similar power position *vis-à-vis* teachers, although the girls' scripts tended to be stronger on vocalization and presentation of self, the boys' on physical action and team or chorus work. The overt negotiative and bargaining devices of the male were preferred by the colonial administrators; the girls had a more extensive repertoire to manage power differentials in school because of their access to tactical and subversive scripts from the female culture of powerlessness, their traditional accommodation to colonization by men.

Gender is, of course, by no means the only power asymmetry of importance. The detailing of pupils' scripts has highlighted the *variety* in power possibilities; and Marxist models reducing everything to social class would be similarly limited if they ignored other structural features which are perceived or appropriated by individuals. My preference in pursuing a final model would be for a more Weberian identification of rival status groups. The most appropriate in this tradition is Lenski's synthesis of functionalist and conflict perspectives which sees society as a series of 'distributive systems' for the allocation of power and privilege (Lenski, 1966). Lenski drew a series of adjacent boxes to demonstrate how a society may be stratified on a range of parallel dimensions, which may include class, ethnicity, property, sex, education, political power and wealth hierarchies. Each individual holds simultaneous membership in each 'system' of power, and the systems do not always correlate perfectly. (Examples of non-correlations in this country would be the West Indian doctor, or the female MP.) The weighting accorded to each of these dimensions in terms of the allocation of resources to an individual will vary between cultures and over time; the sex attribute which is a totally limiting factor in one culture may be secondary to an ethnic or class dimension in another. Social change can be explained not just by shifts in power within one dimension (with, for example, some occupational groups gaining ascendancy over others), but also by alterations in the weightings attached to the relative importance, of, say, wealth versus education. Struggles for power involve not only struggles between individuals and classes, but also competition between systems, and thus between different principles of distribution.

If we transfer Lenski's model to the micro society of the school (Table 5), we see that the weightings attached to ability, or gender, will again vary between institutions and over time. Just as Lenski could forecast the probability of an individual acquiring scarce resources by

Table 5 Systems of power in a hypothetical school

rank/role	ability	gender	social class	race
10	8	5	5	3
Head Deputy House heads Teachers	'intelligent' A ↑	A male	socio-economic class I II A III	A white
Prefects 6th form A				
5th form B		B female	IV	
1st form	B 'remedial'		V B	Asian West Indian B

plotting his (sic) position on all dimensions (and hence almost according him a 'score') one could plot a member's position on the school's various hierarchical distributive systems of rank/role, ability, gender, social class and race, and arrive at an institutionally derived 'status score'. While individual A scores highly on many dimensions, individual B does not. A is likely to be a 'well-behaved' pupil; B would be more likely to represent the wenches of this study. My argument is that a pupil who is accorded few official sources of power and privilege by the controlling agents will have to find other ways of establishing identity and efficacy. One of these is to stand the model on its head and *use* the lowly position as a source of control. We already have studies by Hargreaves (1967) and Lacey (1970) on polarization — the maintenance of 'low ability' cultures by pupils as a means of identification and group status; Willis (1977) has explained how social class styles come to be translated into school resistance; an ethnicity example would be the specific display of West Indian culture in school as a means of group signification and strength; and this study has revealed how the gender dimension can also be upturned to provide a powerful avenue for bargaining and exchange. 'Cultural capital' (the storing and manipulation of useful cultural knowledge) can be made from subordinate as well as dominant positions, if only temporarily. A child may bring into school the scripts deriving from his or her position in the various hierarchies of the distributive system of the society; how far these are reproduced by the school is linked with how far the school's distributive system 'corresponds' with that of society. In functional terms, the school may need to turn out fewer deviant girls because they 'fail' themselves later by remaining further down the occupational and property systems, but the struggles for ascendancy are no less immediate within the school's own allocation of scarce status resources.

An analysis is useful only insofar as it can be used by people to examine the basis of their actions. The implications for a school, therefore, need to be outlined so that the value of any such institutional introspection (and implicitly of the analysis) can be assessed. The model should have a set of questions to accompany it.

1 Pupils What type-scripts are available or distributed to pupils within the school? Are there internal contradictions implicit in their adoption, or tensions with outside school type-scripts? What sort of status passages or moral careers do they provide?

2 Teachers What type-scripts are available or distributed to teachers from the school administration? Are teachers aware of type-scripts written for them by pupils? What contradictions are generated by the divergent functions of the teacher within an agency which simultaneously attempts to make children more the same while making them more different?

3 Structure To what extent are pupil scripts a reflection of their position in the power systems both of school and wider society? Are there size or organizational factors in the school which generate large power differentials between its members? If legitimate opportunities for identity work are not available, will pupils have to write their own scripts for these? Are pupils who lack power on one dimension likely to appropriate a script from another dimension? Does the rehearsal of immediate power or face-saving lines in school militate against the acquisition of effective longer-term career scripts?

4 Interpretation How are pupil scripts assigned meanings by teachers? How do they become finalized, duplicated for the pupil's or for others' future use? How are pupil biographies rewritten by teachers in the light of new scripts? Conversely, are pupils given an opportunity to change their lines, to rewrite their own biographies, and will experimental attempts at new scripts be given credence by teachers, once an individual deviant type-script has been written for a pupil?

Ironically, although this study started from a query into gender and deviance, the message to teachers is not necessarily to look specifically at differences between boys and girls, but at differences in power. All power corrupts, but it is both absolute power and absolute powerlessness that corrupt absolutely. Schools are not socializing agencies, they are colonizing agencies. It is hardly surprising that there will be resistance to this colonization, especially when it acts in the interests only of the potential tribal leaders. Pupils who are denied dignity, humanity, a recognizable 'specialness' to themselves and others, will resort to power confrontations to restore a feeling of presence and avenge indignity.

This begins to sound self-evident, but I have been struck by several things during the course of this enquiry. One is how threatened some teachers appear to feel by the thought of treating pupils in their everyday exchanges as they would adults, and how they ignore the important social rules of courtesy, allowing others to save face, making another feel they are of interest. The seemingly desultory conversational exchanges which the girls had with favoured teachers in fact gave the girls important messages about adult status and worth. If a colleague asks us to repeat something, we do not immediately reprove them for not listening; if a guest is late, we do not threaten and bluster, but accept their excuse at face value. And if we can be so tolerant and understanding of adults who have the freedom to shun our company, it is curious that we can feel free to withhold such important social imperatives from those who are forced by compulsory education to witness our presence. Pupils can be doubly threatened in our schools: they are subject to non-adult encounters from those purporting to be adult models, and they cannot escape. To the teachers who reply 'Pupils behave like small children and must be treated accordingly', or 'Kids need discipline and boundaries', I would respond that we *all* need discipline and boundaries; but these should be seen to be logical, equitable, adult and designed for maximum welfare, rather than arbitrary, infantile, one-sided and designed to intimidate the majority.

Another striking feature has been the ingenuity which the officially powerless bring to bear to tolerate their situation. Discussion of the girls' tactical scripts has perhaps provided an antidote to some of the feminist literature portraying women as oppressed, exploited and even dehumanized. It is essential to spotlight the variety of creative and inventive possibilities in female response, to show women as alive and humorous, if one does not want to replace critiques of sex-typing with further objectified stereotypes. This is not to minimize or underplay questions of subordinacy in the economy, but to draw attention to the exploitable possibilities as well as the counter-productive strategies of resistance, in the search for real alternatives to any asymmetrical social or sexual divisions. Also, the uncovering of such diversity in pupil responses to power has demonstrated the need for examination of *all* aspects of pupil 'deviance', and not just the oppositional cultures which are the most obvious to teachers or the media, or even to researchers. Such deviance would include the boy 'deviant' from his gender type-script by choosing cookery, as well as the girl deviant from hers by fighting; it would include both 'anomic' and 'retreatist' responses, which may be favoured by girls particularly, but which preclude the learning of any long-term power scripts for control and change. Labelling theory's preoccupation with acts which are defined as deviant has drawn attention away from the equally important pupil deviance which can be safely ignored.

If schools are to do anything about the reduction of inequalities in power and prestige in society, then they will begin to do this only by a redistribution of power and prestige within themselves. As long as their function remains primarily to categorize, type-cast, examine and to fail a large percentage (in effect to ensure the real creation of possibilities only for a minority) then the bulk of school children will have little chance to exercise power for the creation of life-long possibilities. This study has confirmed that pupils very efficiently learn the temporary exercise of power and control, but this is a by-product rather than the professed aim of the institution. Rather than try to play down pupil deviance, the message is to incorporate it: to make decision-making, analysis of power, techniques of argument, the use of social control (in other words, basic political education) a central component of curriculum. Enabling pupils and teachers *together* to be aware of and analyze their own strategies and scripts, plus the immediate historical reasons for them, would not only tackle pupil deviance, but be a starting point for a similar assault on the structural world outside school.

Moreover, pupils must actively and officially arbitrate in the running of the institution. In the long term, of course, examinations *specifically designed* to eject large percentages of school children with nothing official to show for eleven years compulsion, will always be the major block to giving status and self-realization to all; but even if the school still decides its inmates' future, it could at least pay them the compliment of allowing them to decide their present. A beginning could be made, for example, by pupils themselves deciding the rules by which deviance is defined. This examination of sex differences in such deviance has underlined the varied resources for power and prestige that pupils have if status is *not* accorded by the school, but radical change in social or sexual divisions demands a collaborative rather than an antithetical dialogue. Similarly, immediate confrontation can be avoided by more efficient colonization; but peaceful independence requires in the end a handing over of responsibility. One pupil, one vote?

Part II
Review Section

6 Relevant Research on Pupil Deviance and Sex Roles

The review section begins with the unenviable task of attempting to summarize the existing field of knowledge about sex differences in pupil behaviour. It is, however, not a field, more an ecological sanctuary of variously sprouting and neglected branches. Information has admittedly to be gleaned from two major and very different sources: first comparative surveys of schools or local authorities, and secondly investigation into teachers' perceptions and interaction with pupils in classrooms. It becomes an exercise in creative landscape gardening to blend these two growth areas into something approaching a 'field'.

Comparative Surveys

The preliminary comment on past and current monitoring of pupil deviance must be that, although many of the surveys quoted below are quite large, the overall picture is a patchy and sometimes frustrating one. No two studies start with the same aims or appear to rest on the same assumptions. Clearly, surveys commissioned by bodies as disparate as, say, the Schools Council and The National Association of Schoolmasters (NAS) are likely to ask different questions and to have different concerns; and they will be distinct again from the investigations by individual academic researchers. Most do not, of course, set out with the specific intention of gender comparison, and sex differences have to be hunted for, or extracted from often unexplicated data. The only saving grace of the jumble of data that follows is that its very patchiness vindicates the need for more studies such as my own.

Language is a clue to researchers' assumptions about normality, and we might begin with the notion of pupil 'involvement' in school.

(Would we research convicts' 'involvement' in prison?) At primary level, most studies in Britain and the United States show girls demonstrating a more favourable orientation to school than do boys. They are happier, and exhibit a more positive feeling towards their school experience (Jackson, 1968); they show more ready compliance with authority (Kellmer-Pringle et al, 1966; Mitchell and Shepherd 1967). Girls continue at secondary level to like school more than boys, albeit with some reservations. The Schools Council (1968) survey found 15 year old boy leavers 'less identified with school life', although girl leavers tended to resent the restriction of school discipline and not being treated as adults even more than the boys. King's later (1973) and extensive sample of 72 secondary schools confirmed girls in mixed schools showing a higher level of 'pupil involvement' than boys.

It would not seem illogical, then, to deduce that a greater 'involvement' or 'identification' with school would lead to a less deviant response in the school's eyes. Accordingly, a 1973 Association of Education Committees/DES survey on violence, vandalism and indiscipline, involving a questionnaire to 100 LEAs, found three-quarters of the responding authorities believing that boys were more involved in misbehaviour than girls (Hansard, 1973). Two years later, the NAS sent questionnaires to all its members in primary, middle and secondary schools asking for the incidence of violent or disruptive behaviour during a three months period. Their report concluded that incidents were more frequent in secondary schools, and that, overall, violence and disruptive behaviour were more common among boys than among girls, with the peak age at 15 years plus (Lowenstein, 1975). One must remember that in questionnaires such as these, the headline-worthy incidents of indiscipline refer only to the pupils; teachers beating children is not counted as violence, any more than a teacher tearing up or defacing a child's work counts as vandalism. We have no research on sex differences in teacher violence, symbolic or otherwise.

Yet to continue with the pupil scene, the Pack Report on *Truancy and Indiscipline in Schools in Scotland* (1977) received information on the number of suspensions in a five year period:

> Such details as were given appeared to confirm *the generally held views* that boy offenders are in the great majority (although the number of girls in recent years is not insignificant), and that in the 14–16 age group is where the main problem lies. (My italics)

Boys were the more problematic in primary schools too. While listing factors within the home and the school which would contribute to indiscipline, the report makes no attempt to explain these sex differences. Indeed, some of the contributory factors they mention, such as earlier maturation, disenchantment by the non-academic groups, awareness of the inadequacy of existing sanctions, might seem at first glance to affect girls more than boys. The rest — high teacher turnover, pupil dislike for subjects, weakening of the guidance structure — would seem to apply to both sexes equally. Similarly, a potentially interesting study of pupils suspended from school in Sheffield over a twelve month period (Galloway, 1981) found a preponderance of boys (41 to 16), but then provided no further elaboration on this sex difference. Instead it probed all the predictable variables surrounding suspension such as family circumstances, catchment area, poor school attainment and clashes with a teacher; and then because 53 per cent of the secondary age suspended pupils came from only four of the LEA's 39 secondary schools, the study indicated the need for further exploration of the internal characteristics of schools. Yet if one sees a glaring sex difference as a key to unlocking a puzzling social phenomenon, then in this instance different practices by schools with regard to identifying suspension-worthy pupils would seem the place to begin, not end.

The need is to probe whether official school logging of 'indiscipline', and practices such as suspension accurately reflect the reality of pupil behaviour. It is possible that the 'generally held views' cited in the Pack Report predominate over actual instances. Heal's study of 600 pupils in the last year of primary/first year of secondary age range used a self-report 'misbehaviour' scale rather than official delinquency rates or school perceptions. The scale ranged from petty misdemeanours to more 'serious' activities — annoying people for fun, smoking and drinking. He found that while the school accounted for 10 per cent of the variance between children, the age, sex, social class and degree of involvement in 'unstructured leisure time activities' accounted *together* for only 12 per cent (Heal, 1978). Hence sex differences in behaviour were not so acute as might appear from punishment books. Likewise, in a study of third year boys and girls in three English comprehensive schools, Bellaby (1974) claimed hostility to school to be a predominantly working-class affair, and that it occurred about as frequently among girls as boys. The same proportion of girls thought that teachers were unsympathetic to their interests; the average 'seriousness' of their admitted acts of disobedience was only marginally less than that of the boys; and in fact more of them reported having stayed out of a lesson than boys. The possibility arises that gender alone might be less important in determining behaviour than the ideology of the school attended or its social class composition.

One of the most publicised studies to compare secondary schools is Rutter et al's *15,000 Hours* (1979) which demonstrated marked differences between schools in various outcomes. The authors noted that 'delinquency rates, *of course* were very much lower among girls than boys' (my italics), and therefore they excluded girls from the delinquency measures because of their small numbers. However, there were no major variations between all-boys' schools, all-girls' schools and mixed schools on any of the outcomes categorized as 'attendance', 'behaviour' and 'academic'. There was a trend, falling short of statistical significance, for better behaviour in girls' schools than boys' schools, and a similar non-significant trend for boys in mixed schools to be less delinquent than boys in single-sex schools. As in Bellaby, behaviour ratings were derived from pupils, not staff; but significant differences in behaviour between boys and girls in mixed schools were either not researched or were non-existent. It is interesting that there did not appear to be any substantial school effect on delinquency by girls, although there was for boys, in interaction with the child's family background and balance of academic intake of boys attending. The authors admitted they were unable to answer the question of why this should be.

While some of the above studies required figures from school staff, others used pupil questionnaires to chart behaviour. Definitions of 'disruptive' or 'conformist' behaviour will therefore depend on the questions asked, and to whom, making comparison between studies of questionable validity. 'Statistics' on indiscipline or misbehaviour are notoriously difficult to obtain (see chapter 8). However, one area of school non-conformity where records are kept and can be compared is that of truancy (though even here differences in definition and reporting techniques must be taken into account). The Pack Report had found a marked divergence between boys and girls in the extent of truancy in the first year of primary school, girls being absent much less than boys, but in the following years this difference virtually disappeared. Fifteen per cent of both boys and girls were at some time absent from school without adequate explanation during a six week period. The report does hint at different *reasons* for truancy for the sexes, however: it was surmised that girls were more likely to be kept at home by parents to ensure someone in the house, or, in contrast to the 'communal' truancy of boys, resorting to a 'sore head' to take a day off school spent alone at home, 'even' in bed. Tyerman, on the other hand, claimed in 1968 that 'all investigators agree that boys outnumber girls as truants, with ratios varying from 2:1 to 9:1'. The reasons cited for this difference were: that education officers and social workers are more reluctant to take official action against girls; girls are less aggressive than boys, and more willing because of their sex-typed upbringing to accept an unhappy situation; girls generally adjust more easily than boys to school and do better on school work. The author seems therefore to take a combined biological/social learning/labelling approach to explain his ratios. The variations in the quoted ratios, however, also need explaining. Official figures on truancy can be unreliable, and are generally understated. Parents may cover up; children may slip off after registration.

So perhaps the most revealing information again comes from self-report studies and schedules. A survey of pupils on Sheffield council estates found almost half the pupils admitting at least one truancy during the past year, and also found no overall differences according to sex (Mawby, 1977). A breakdown into age differences revealed girls more prone to absenteeism in their early years at school, but rather less likely later on. Social area (whether the estate was rated 'high', 'medium' or 'low' for criminal offences) also played a part for both sexes, and interacted with the effects of the particular school, although social class in itself was not significant. Answers on 'crimes' — thefts from individuals or from corporate victims, burglaries and vandalism — revealed boys tending to admit more offences than females. Because of his demonstrated link between neighbourhood, crime and truancy, Mawby asks for an examination of the sub-cultural stance on rule-breaking (which we shall look at in the next chapter). His findings are partially supported by Sharpe's study of Ealing schoolgirls: girls truanted as frequently if not more so than the boys, but whereas the boys often moved into delinquency, girls' truancy was not particularly associated with the delinquent behaviour. 'Their rejection of the monotony of school life and its imposed rules is not channelled into anything very anti-social' (Sharpe, 1976). The question of what pupils *do* when they play truant may be a decisive factor in explaining Rutter's finding that school has an effect on delinquency for boys but not for girls. What one needs to do is probe the meanings and motives attached to truancy, together with looking at the sub-culture and 'opportunity structures' of the neighbourhood, that is, the scope and encouragement to commit 'crime'.

Finally, there is the undecided question of whether pupil deviance in this country presents a static or a changing picture. Few local authorities have conducted their own fact-finding as to the incidence of disruptive behaviour in their area. LEAs can also be sensitive about adverse publicity; for example, Lancashire restricted the publication of a commissioned evaluation into its five disruptive units by Lancaster University in 1978 (Tattum, 1982). There might anyway emerge too many regional variations to permit generalization. While the Essex County Teachers' Association noted the increasingly disruptive influence of a minority of pupils (Essex CTA, 1975), the Chief Education Officer of ILEA claimed in 1978 to have 'no evidence that the incidence of bad behaviour in London schools is increasing; if anything the reverse appears to be true' (Tattum, 1982). It is possible that if there *are* perceived escalations in pupil disruption, this may be because of a disproportionate increase from the girls. The Berkshire Association of Secondary Headteachers (1975) documented an increasing number of disruptive children in the country's schools. Heads reported a monthly increase in each category of physical attacks on teachers, direct threats, serious acts of disobedience and refusal to accept the authority of the school, and they insisted that girls figured as often as boys. A report by the Staffordshire Education Committee noted a marked increase in the number of suspensions within the authority, but gave no breakdown for sex. Headteachers, however, were inclined to think that girls' behaviour was getting worse: while half thought that there had been no increase in the number of children generally involved in misbehaviour, only 30 per cent thought there had been no increase for girls. Twice as many heads thus thought there had been a general deterioration in female behaviour; this was seen to predominate in the 14+ age bracket. 'In this era of sex equality, they are unfortunately catching up with the boys,' (Staffordshire Education Committee, 1977).

Attitudes of Teachers

Although it is difficult to obtain 'hard' data on pupil behaviour, there is a body of cumulative studies on teacher perceptions of pupils, most of which appears to demonstrate that teachers view boys and girls differently within the same classroom context. There are two linked paths to explore here: whether the sexes do display different behaviour in class, and/or whether teachers are operating on expectations or rules for 'typical' behaviour for each sex. Kemer (1975), for example, asked junior high school teachers to select adjectives they felt would describe the good female and good male pupils; the resulting lists closely corresponded with current stereotypes about appropriate sex roles. The good male was active, adventurous, aggressive; the good female appreciative, calm, conscientious. It is interesting that the greater activity of boys as perceived by the teachers does not receive much empirical support from observational studies (Lobban, 1978); it may be that when teachers are forced to differentiate between the sexes for a researcher they fall back on cultural stereotypes rather than particular experiences.

Nonetheless there seems a strong indication that, at infant and junior levels at least, teachers show a preference for female rather than male pupils (Ingelby and Cooper, 1974; Good and Brophy, 1972). In the classic large-sample study in Britain by Douglas in 1968, teachers tended to see boys as less hard-working, less able to concentrate and less willing to submit to discipline than were girls, with this being true across social classes (see Douglas et al, 1968). Similarly, Hartley (1978) found infant teachers defining boys as untidier, more impatient, dirtier, lazier in general, rougher, noisier, more immature, more lacking in concentration. Such behaviour does not go with the stereotyped 'successful' pupil; it seems that teachers of this age group are not favouring girls as such, but the manifestations of 'feminine' type characteristics in their pupils. Another enquiry asked primary school teachers to react to descriptions of aggressive or dependent behaviour assigned to hypothetical male or female pupils: teachers clearly preferred dependent to aggressive behaviour, regardless of the sex of the child (Levitin and Chananie, 1972). It appears that the orientation towards the teacher herself may be critical. Davie et al's (1972) longitudinal study recounts more boys than girls rated as 'maladjusted' — more frequently showing aggressive or restless behaviour. Girls were more prone to thumb-sucking, nail-biting, to be miserable and tearful. 'Maladjustment' is clearly not a neutral, objective term; definitions by teachers may in effect be linked more to the extent of classroom disruption than to the actual psychological state of the child. Nearly three times as many boys as girls were reported to have shown 'anxiety for acceptance by other children', whereas more girls were 'anxious for adult acceptance' in school — and, one supposes, therefore more likely to accede to those adults.

The sex of the teacher might be thought to be crucial here (particularly in primary schools which are predominantly female staffed), and this issue must be disposed of. The convergence of the parent/teacher role might indeed make the term 'adult' acceptance more tricky, more synonymous with 'mother'. However, the overall evidence is that sex differences in teachers which are relevant to the classroom are fewer and less significant than sex differences in pupils. The former tend to be submerged within the 'teacher' role; and subject matter taught, for example, may be a more potent variable in teaching style (Gannaway, 1976). Good, Sikes and Brophy's (1973) research concluded that although female teachers' classes seemed more relaxed and discussion-oriented than male teachers' (which, in contrast, were more structured, more focused on content), overall 'there is no support for the hypothesis that teachers are biased towards students of their own sex'.

I have examined evidence on teacher judgments from all over Europe, where the sex ratio of teachers is often different from that in Britain or the United States, but the picture remains amazingly similar. Girls are perceived as being more 'integrative', boys more 'dominating'. The girls receive higher marks on behavioural ratings, and like school better (Zinnecker, 1978). An EEC survey cites judgements from teachers that girls are 'over-achievers' and more able to cope with school's expectations (Thomas and Albrecht-Heide, 1977). A typical picture is painted by Wall (1973), in his case particularly from longitudinal studies on France: 'Girls throughout seem to be more stable and better motivated than boys, less likely to be aggressive, more likely to be nervous and neurotic, less likely to be delinquent.' He takes a 'faulty learning' model of 'problem children', and thus fails to address himself to the question of why these differences should be manifested so regularly; once again, the form is to document the lower incidence of girls' problems and then concentrate on why boys cause trouble in classrooms, rather than using the difference as a fertile beginning for analyzing behavioural response.

The notion of greater appreciation by teachers of 'feminine' characteristics in pupils receives support from the accumulated evidence that teachers criticize boys more than girls in the classroom. Hartley found boys getting greater disapproval; in Douglas's survey, boys were subject to nearly twice as much criticism as girls. One study documented boys receiving eight to ten times as many 'prohibitory control messages' (Meyer and Thompson, 1963) — which I am assuming does mean 'tellings off'. Buswell's case study of a comprehensive school found the disruptive behaviour of boys sometimes took all the teacher's attention for the whole lesson, while the girls recived no interaction at all (Buswell, 1981). Moreover, when teachers criticize boys, they are more likely to use harsh or angry tones than when talking to a girl about an equivalent misdemeanour (Jackson and Lahaderne, 1977) — A case of 'speak roughly to your little boy and beat him when he sneezes'.

However, the picture is more complicated than pure 'prejudice' against boys; it is bound up with teacher perceptions of what the sexes 'expect'. Interviews with secondary teachers revealed 73 per cent believing that boys and girls behaved differently, with boys being more active; the majority also thought that male and female pupils expected different treatment. Girls expected to be treated in a more ladylike, genteel, caring fashion, with consideration of their feelings; boys on the other hand expected more sternness, a setting of limits, authority, and did not want mothering (Ricks and Pyke, 1973). It would be difficult to disentangle the chicken-and-egg riddle of whether pupils 'expect' different handling because teachers have always given it, or whether individual teachers are merely reacting each time to the demands of their pupils. The most one can say is that the process is likely to be reinforcing or self-perpetuating.

A further and significant complexity is that while boys receive more negative sanctions, they are also accorded more positive interactions, both at primary and secondary level (Spaulding, 1963; Jones, 1971). The motive for pupil criticism, it appears, can have different origins: boys tend to be censured for bad behaviour, but when girls are criticized it is more likely to be for lack of knowledge or skill. Good et al found that high-achieving boys received the most favourable teacher treatment, low achieving boys the least, while the response to girls was far less polarized. One could always toy with the idea that this is linked to psychological findings that females are less variable in intelligence scores than males, who have greater representation at both ends of the spectrum. Are teachers hyper-sensitive to the greater variations in boys' learning skills?

Rather than responding primarily to the *sex* of the pupil, it may be then that the teacher is reacting to specific displays of behaviour. Martin (1972) found boys *demanding* more attention; Serbin *et al* (1973) suggest that boys are criticized, not for being boys, but for being more aggressive. Given that aggressive girls are disapproved of even more (Levitin and Chananie, 1972), it could be predicted that such girls would encounter as much, if not more censure for their behaviour. From their own study, and from reviewing the evidence, Good et al conclude that there is little evidence of consistent teacher predisposition towards either of the sexes, and thus that teachers' differentiated response could be more readily understood as being due to the pupils themselves: 'Teachers are primarily *reactive* to the differential presses that boys and girls present' (Good, Sikes and Brophy, 1973).

Many of these studies are American; most concentrate on primary schooling. If differential teacher treatment is a reaction to differences in pupil socialization, then it is likely that this will be both culture-specific and age-specific. Fuller's study of a secondary school in the UK (1979) found that the clear-cut differences in orientations towards pupils were not nearly so visible. Teachers appeared to use a common pool of values by which to assess pupil characteristics, whether male or female; there was no evidence of separate standards. In the actual treatment of pupils in the classroom, there was however some small indication of a higher evaluation of the male, while the written school report material indicated the reverse.

The greater 'appreciation' of boys in the classroom confirms my earlier study of two mixed comprehensive schools (Davies, 1973). Here, 72 per cent of the teachers, both male and female, said that if they had to make a choice, they would prefer to teach boys. Boys were seen as more enthusiastic, quicker to grasp new concepts, better 'on the oral side'. They did show behaviour problems, being seen as restless, independent, noisy and careless, as in the primary school studies mentioned earlier; girls, in contrast, were regarded as more mature, more conformist, more obedient. Yet further investigation revealed a pervading suspicion about the girls' submissive and mature exterior. Boys' discipline problems were interpreted as of the 'boys-will-be-boys' variety, with story book terminology abounding — 'prank-playing', 'mischievous', 'naughty', but always 'owning up'. Girls, however, were 'devious', 'insolent', 'insidious' and 'resentful'. There is clearly a wealth of difference to a teacher between a pupil who is mischievous and one who is insolent; and it appears that teacher approval of dependency and non-aggressiveness of girls may be translated into suspicion at their secretiveness and sulkiness at the secondary level. Girls were more likely to 'bear grudges'. A typical remark was 'There are more behaviour problems with boys than with girls, but if the girls do cause problems behaviourally, they tend to create more serious trouble for themselves.' Thus where an average tally of behaviour problems might indicate greater conformity from the girls, this conformity might not be across the board, or consistent. Although empirical work exploring this aspect of pupil reaction has been lacking at the secondary level, the descriptive or journalistic material certainly supports the 'extremes' contention, as for example:

The problems [the girls] pose for school differ somewhat from those which result from the natural aggressiveness of adolescent boys. The disruption caused by girls stems mainly from emotional difficulties which are the result of unfavourable circumstances and experiences and they are generally more amenable to the guidance of teachers. However, cases of extreme disruption can occur, and because these have an intense emotional undertone, they are often difficult to manage and sometimes impossible to resolve.   (Parry, 1976)

A headmistress of a Stockport mixed comprehensive school reported that potential candidates for an exclusion unit were mostly girls, who 'tend to adopt a sullen attitude in class if disciplined, rather than boys who often will settle down to classwork if rebuked' (*The Daily Telegraph*, October, 1976).

Girls' behaviour problems, then, may appear to teachers to be more 'deep-seated' at secondary level. Fuller suggested from her observations that deliberately disruptive tactics in the classroom differed between the sexes. Boys were more 'transparent' — fighting, kicking, the noisy use of classroom equipment — and boys' disruptive behaviour brought a quicker response from the teachers than did the girls'. Presumably staff have more experience of this swift response being effective, or are practising 'avoidance of provocation' (Stebbins, 1970) with regard to the girls. It may be not that teachers are deliberately according more positive and negative interactions to the boys, but that they are simply giving girls less.

Now we have kicked the ball around the pitch and looked both at surveys and case-studies, the field of gender and deviance does resemble more a battleground than a completed painting-by-numbers landscape. Girls are more conformist, but on the other hand some are not; boys are more aggressive and idle, but secondary teachers prefer them and spend more time with them; and these trends depend on whom you ask, at what period and how you frame the questions. Yet it is these very contradictions in pupil deviance which make it a fascinating arena for study, and which engender the range of possibilities for explanation to be tackled in the next chapter.

7 *Possible Theoretical Explanations*

The search here is for explanations which would account not only for greater female conformity in school, but also for girls' deviance when it does occur, and why it is seen to take 'extreme' forms or to be increasing in incidence. While my own version has already been presented, this section may enable readers to attempt their own synthesis from the range of theories available. Hence the studies are not 'weighted' in order of perceived importance or centrality; the aim is more a composite picture within each area of enquiry.

There may be less of a divide than we imagine between theoretical research and teachers' impressions of the actual classroom encounter; the barrier may be partly linguistic. The basic similarity between 'common-sense' and 'theoretical' accounts is demonstrated here by examining five possible explanations for pupil deviance and testing them in terms of suitability in accounting for sex differences in such deviance. The perspectives inevitably have many overlaps, but are grouped here for convenience under the general headings of biology, socialization, sub-culture, labelling, and social structure.

Bad Genes: The Biological Imperative

This is the 'innate' explanation of deviance: failure to conform is linked to inherited personality dispositions or 'bad stock'. Much of the early theorizing on criminality centred on this pathological theme — prison inmates were examined for large heads or misshapen skulls, for low intelligence, and the linkage between the extra chromosome and a tendency towards aggression has been well researched. The eugenics movement in the US after the turn of the century was particularly interested in racial characteristics and criminality, seeking to justify compulsory sterilization of those immigrants and 'feeble-minded' who were likely to pollute the gene pool. It was accepted that low intelligence and low standards of morality were likely to go hand in hand. Blacks were, of course, the particular target in this instance — slaves, argued one theory, had to be inherently stupid for allowing themselves to be captured in the first place.

Although many 'defective' models of deviance have largely been discredited (one study in fact showed a prison population displaying a higher average IQ than the warders), two aspects remain of interest here: one is the possibility of linkage between 'morality' and physical or mental development; the other is the phenomenon that most theories of female criminality have, until comparatively recently, tended to remain fixed within a biological or physical framework.

If we take female conformity first of all, then simple 'bad stock' can be ruled out; there seems no reason why boys in a family should inherit this more than girls. More persuasive initially is the physiological explanation, that the facts of physical difference — in reproductive organs, hormones, size, potential strength — are translated into an inherited predisposition to react to the world in different ways. The maternal, caring function of the female explains her greater passivity, her docility and conservatism; differences in aggression would be linked to variations in hormonal endowments between the sexes. At school age, girls' faster maturational rate would parallel a more rapid growth of morality (according to theorists within the developmental school of psychology such as Kohlberg and Piaget) — although what constitutes 'morality' is of course a cultural rather than purely biological feature.

However convenient female physiology is in accounting for conformity, explaining female deviance from a biological perspective then becomes much more tortuous. The early attempts are great fun. Lombroso and Ferrero's 1895 study *The Female Offender* rests, for example, on atavistic theory: women reveal fewer signs of degeneration because they have evolved less then men, and because 'the immobility of the ovule compared to the zoosperm' results in conservatism. However, in spite of her rarity, the female criminal makes up for what she lacks in relative numbers by the excessive vileness and cruelty of her crimes. She was thought to have all the criminal qualities of the male, plus all the worst characteristics of women: cunning, spite and deceit. Although fanciful, such accounts are worth drawing attention to here, because modified versions of this type of biological or pathological thesis still survive (in literature and in teacher perceptions).

Pollak's *The Criminality of Women*, published in 1961, while recognizing social factors in female deviance, looks to concealment of menstruation, the physiology of sexual relations and to the menopause to explain
women's criminal predispositions. Women also have special opportunities for theft and murder, using their position in the home and family
to avoid discovery. Because they are repressed, they look for ways of
avenging themselves on the men whom they perceive to be the cause of
their inferior status, this vengeance taking the form of false accusation,
perjury, assult, even arson and murder. The time of menstruation
especially confirms inferiority, and is linked to criminal activity. Pollak
was very much influenced by Freudian analysis, and he posited an
association between the menstrual cycle, the ultimate failure to become
a man (it being assumed that all women subconsciously desire to
become men) and sexual guilt. The menopause on the other hand is
associated with loss of womanhood which induces depression, irritabil-
ity and consequently crime. (For anyone wanting more entertainment
along these lines, Smart's (1976) book *Women, Crime and Criminology:
A Feminist Critique* provides an excellent review.)

These 'female iceberg' theorists dispute then that women are more
conformist, and suggest that they are only too deviant, but in a
different, or more successfully concealed manner. Yet little of this
description would appear to help explain differences in pupil deviance
outlined in the previous chapter. For the major part of their school
career, girls would have little opportunity to practise deception
through their sexual role; nor would their offences be committed in the
privacy of the home; nor are they necessarily or continuously more
repressed than boys, given the preference for girls by primary school
teachers. The menopause clearly does not apply; and their higher
achievement at primary level would not seem to support Lombroso's
theory of less advanced evolution.

Another way round the women-are-more-conformist-but-some-
aren't dilemma is to employ instincts (the forerunner of hormones).
Thomas's (1907) classic notion was of the 'four wishes', which are
expressed as the biological instincts anger, fear, love and the will to
gain power. These were not perceived to be equal in quality or quantity
for men and women, as Thomas believed that women had more
varieties of love in their nervous systems. He referred especially to the
maternal instinct which women are assumed to feel in response not
only to their own children but also to sick or helpless adults (particularly men). This additional and intense need to give and feel love led
women into crime, in particular sexual offences like prostitution. The

concept of 'instincts' is, of course, convenient for explaining any type of non-conformist behaviour; either the instinct does not seem to be present and therefore the individual is 'unnatural', as for example the mother who shows no love for her child; or the instinct is present, only in too great a quantity, which has to find an outlet — if necessary a deviant one, as in rape or prostitution. As with religious belief, the fact that there is no way of measuring these instincts seems only to lend support to the proof for their existence.

Apparently more scientific is the attempt to show that there is some biological or psychic imbalance present in women when they commit criminal offences. In Cowie, Cowie and Slater's (1968) study *Delinquency in Girls*, variables are identified which would distinguish the delinquent (or potentially delinquent) and the non-delinquent (or normal) girl. In particular they looked for signs of 'defective' intelligence, abnormal central nervous function and impaired physical health. However, the value-laden, moralistic concept of 'normality' is revealed in this passage about a group of 'delinquent' girls:

> The main impression one forms on seeing a group of these girls is that of lack of grace or beauty; in technical jargon, they tend to be of dysplastic physique ... most of these girls have no real awareness of themselves as individuals. They have no long-term aspirations, no dominating interests and are content to drift along on a diet of pop music, pep pills and parties, using sex as their credit card.

The book relies on an implicit notion of the 'normal' girl, who is by nature more 'immune' to delinquency, less affected by social circumstances than boys. This explains why sex differences in delinquency have remained fairly steady, in spite of greater 'permissiveness'. Yet the identification of factors behind 'normal' or 'natural' sex differences is hampered unless we recognize the social construction and cultural interpretation of concepts such as 'grace' or 'aspiration'. In the detection of 'dysplastic physique' one is reminded of Lombroso's search for atavistic features like misshapen skulls or very thick black hair; the high moral reproach about 'using sex' ignores how 'good' girls may use their virginity to bargain with as well.

Mistrust of female sexuality also seems to underpin socio-biological explanations of female passivity. An example of this is in the classic text *Childhood and Adolescence* (1962), where Hadfield takes a view of woman as combined cow-and-virago, deriving his 'insights' from child and animal observations. He sees male sexuality as forceful and aggressive, female sexuality as receptive and of necessity seductive:

> There are basic emotional differences between the sexes ... I have seen a heifer tenderly licking the neck of a bull for a long period but he remained passive and couldn't care less! *That is why* the female adolescent is equipped with the will to seduce. Sexual play depending on this relationship is very common. You often see an adolescent boy bullying a girl and twisting her arm while she cries to him 'Stop!' But as soon as he stops she starts to provoke him again. He likes bullying to show his strength; she likes to be mastered. *Both conform to their sexual natures.* (My italics)

Such preconceptions about the 'female mode of personality' form the starting point for the pathological argument. The premise is that female delinquents must be far more 'abnormal' than their male counterparts, because delinquency among girls is such a perversion of, or rebellion against their *natural* female roles which stress passivity, conservatism and attractiveness to men. In small-scale studies, the concentration has been to identify these abnormal characteristics — educational retardation, poor homes, ungainly or masculine appearance, psychiatric disorders (see for example Konopka, 1966). The theorizing remains at the same stage of development as characterized 'knowledge' of male criminality thirty or more years previously.

Attacks on the biological determinist explanation for women's roles are now to be found throughout the feminist and anthropological literature. In order to tackle the anatomy-is-destiny position with regard to deviance, it is worth rehearsing some of the relevant arguments from the fields of anthropology, clinical psychology and sociology.

From anthropology it is argued that physiological explanations for behaviour confuse sex and gender roles. Because there is a biological and chromosonal base to sexual differentiation, it is being assumed, without evidence, that there must be an equally immutable biological basis for gender differences in the way that men and women act out their roles in particular cultures. Thence appears the evolutionary argument, that men were the hunters, women the carers or gatherers; but it is difficult to see why biases associated with man's earliest adaptations should remain with us today. Biological factors clearly make certain social arrangements highly likely, and insofar as woman is defined in a maternal or domestic role, her 'universal subordination' can be accounted for. Women confined to the domestic sphere will not have access to the sorts of authority and prestige that are the prerogative of men; the exercise of autonomy or aggression for them will be seen as illegitimate. Yet although women often perform similar roles and exhibit similar orientations in many cultures, there is enough documentation from anthropologists like Margaret Mead on societies where roles are apparently reversed, or at least undifferentiated, to show that there is nothing universal about sex roles or personalities which would point to an immutable biological cause. Mead comments on the element of wish fulfilment in the assumption of a natural correlation between femininity and nurturance:

> We have assumed that because it is convenient for a mother to wish to care for her child, this is a trait with which women have been more generously endowed by a careful teleological process of evolution. We have assumed that because men have hunted, an activity requiring enterprise, bravery and initiative, they have been endowed with these useful attitudes as part of their sex-temperament. (Mead, 1966)

Yet just such signs of wish fulfilment will be seen to emerge later in teacher ideologies for pupils.

Secondly, whereas in most people agreement does in fact exist between sex and gender roles, clinical research on individuals who show contradictions — such as hermaphrodites or intersexuals — again questions the inevitability of the linkage. In one study, nineteen patients who had been brought up in a way that contradicted the sex of their chromatin pattern were reported to have developed a satisfactory gender identity. Another thirty-one had gender identities in contrast to the sex of their hormones and also to their secondary sexual body development. Apparently the upbringing of a child as male or female can be successfully changed only before the age of eighteen months to two years, coinciding with the learning of language. The social factors of rearing appear to override biological development. Such researchers suggest:

> An individual's gender role and orientation as boy or girl, man or woman, does not have an innate preformed instinctive basis as some theorists have maintained. Instead the evidence supports the view that psychological sex is undifferentiated at birth — a sexual neutrality one might say — and that the individual

becomes psychologically differentiated as masculine or feminine in the course of the many experiences of growing up.
(Hampson and Hampson, 1965)

In addition, our learning will subsequently influence our physiology.
Recent studies of human hormones have indicated that hormone levels
(which are supposed to govern behaviour) are themselves highly
sensitive to changes in social environment. Stressful contexts apparently lead to a decrease in testosterone (Kreuz et al, 1972) (or as a sign
hanging in the office of one the Watergate aides was supposed to have
read: if you have them by the balls their hearts and minds will follow.)
    We must also here consider carefully menstruation and the current
publicity given to pre-menstrual tension. The latter has been used
successfully to obtain lighter sentences for women who were more
prone to commit offences during this time. While not denying the
existence of either severe menstrual pain or PMT for some individuals,
it is hard to countenance it as a fundamental *cause* of criminal or deviant
behaviour. Again, it is linked to culture and learning. Paige (1969), for
example, found that the pain of menstrual cramps was markedly higher
for Catholics and Jews than for Protestants. The cultural significance
attached to menstruation or the menopause is not considered by writers
associating these with crime; yet this varies widely. In some religions
and cultures, menstruation in particular is a way of excluding women
from many activities; so attitudes *towards* biology seem as important as
the 'basic' biology itself.
    Hence a third area of critique is the sociological one — the argu-
ment that biological explanations of behaviour fail to take into account
the socio-economic, political and legal context in which actions occur.
Such structural features affect sex role expectations as well as deviance.
Critics of the 'cultural deprivation' thesis have long attacked the
'middle class' norms by which other class life styles or orientations are
defined as 'deficit' or 'deprived'; yet, similarly, biological determinism
seems to go hand in hand with an uncritical acceptance of the 'natural'
male or female, and hence with normative standards of femininity or
masculinity. With girl delinquents especially, the projection is as
deprived and inadequate, failing to achieve 'normal' passivity or
appropriate sexuality. Deviants are not considered to be social critics,
rebels, or members of a counter-culture, but instead attention is drawn
to biological anomalies or psychologically 'sick' individuals. The
approach therefore ignores the motivation of deviants, the possibility
of an individual or collective rational response to a problem. 'Innate'

explanations are unable to account for contemporary or historical change, or for cross-cultural differences, except on a long-term, 'evolutionary' level. One would need, as did Durkheim with suicide, to address oneself to the question of why more 'abnormal' or 'sick' individuals are produced at different times or locations. We are no nearer to explaining any increase in girls' disruption in school.

At the classroom level, these contextual and reactive issues are very important. While mentioning physical features such as different matur-ational rates between the sexes, teachers in my study school did not see these in isolation. Girls' earlier maturity led to greater conscientious-ness, but also presented problems. The chain of reasoning was that because girls mature physically earlier, they look and feel older; their circle of friends (especially boyfriends) tends to be older, and they are more vain about their appearance. By the fourth and fifth year, and sometimes younger, they will have a social life outside school based on 'adult' values and concerns; they are not 'girls' but 'young ladies'. Greater maturity may mean a lower boredom threshhold; and girls engaged, or thinking of engagement, would especially be likely to see school as irrelevant and child-like. Teachers of course realized that 'maturity' was a relative phenomenon, linked to treatment received and social norms about relationships. There was some feeling that girls were 'basically' more emotional and more prone to express their emotions: 'Part of their disruption is expressing what they feel.' But there is no way of knowing whether girls actually 'feel' more than boys, or are merely more inclined to give vent to feelings. The two conditions may be inseparable anyway, if one accepts the view that not just the expression of emotion but the appropriate emotions themselves are culturally learned.

Purely biological explanations thus ignore people's interpretative capacity, the ability to regulate behaviour through culture and power, through symbolic forms like language. As Adler (1975) points out, displays of aggression and production of oestrogen depend on whether a threat is from a dominant or subordinate person. The human capacity for abstraction and symbol formation extends the range of 'size' to include factors only remotely related to actual mass — wealth, lineage, social connections, skill, intelligence. These may be perceived as 'big' and accorded dominance. What tends to be overlooked in studies showing different levels or amounts of anything between the sexes, whether hormones or personality traits, is that there is more variation *within* a sex than there is *between* the sexes. The most one can say is that human behaviour is organized by the *interaction* of any biological propensities with culturally specific expectations or symbols that coordinate actions and decide the means of survival. Ecological studies show increasingly that behavioural possibilities are rich and variable, with new patterns of behaviour emerging when confronted with new environments. What distinguishes humans from animals is the ability to *overcome* physical limitations. Whether we fly or not depends not on the possession of wings, but on human invention and individual ability to afford it; a similar combination of cultural construction and economic position might equally be of greater importance in deviance than is basic biology.

The Bad Home: Socialization and Control Perspectives

The suspicion by teachers that there is something in the 'home background' which triggers off pupil deviance is a natural one. When accounting for sex differences in such deviance, the obvious related area of concern is that of socialization in terms of sex role learning. That in virtually every culture boys and girls are brought up differently from each other is now well enough documented. While advanced societies appear complex and relatively flexible in the transmission of roles and statuses, sex role distinctions still constitute the basic primary division. We always need to establish (for example on the telephone) the sex of the person we are talking to before knowing how to interact with them; a frisson runs through us when we realise we have made a mistake. 'What a lovely little boy', people would cry of my neutral looking nine-month old daughter, being covered in confusion when I disabused them. One lady continued inexorably, 'What's his name?' 'Anna', I replied, firmly. 'That's a funny name for a boy', she reproved. We also hate to have our first impressions of others challenged, and this is especially true of gender impressions. We have already begun, in effect, to treat them accordingly, and such differential treatment begins from the cradle.

If we then examine this socialization process in western societies, it is possible to list out the accumulated body of evidence that parents encourage boys to be ambitious, outward-going, tenacious, adventurous, noisy and curious. Girls are taught to be docile, kind, cheerful, domesticated, quiet and clean. 'Traditionally the little girl, and later the woman, are confined to a low level of dirt, disorder and physical aggression', comments Adler (1975). Sex role learning is of course relational, rather than the single internalization of one role. Hargreaves

(1976b) found young children having efficiently aborbed sex role stereotypes to the extent that they could project likely behaviour for *both* roles. When he asked primary children to write about the opposite sex they produced comments like 'girls don't like to play rugby because they are frightened they might hurt themselves'; 'girls are sisseys, boys aren't they're brave'; and 'boys are very sexcy to me and Natalie and they play pooling up dresis (sic).' But children could not only write about the opposite sex, they could also complete projection tests *as if* they were a child of the opposite sex, and produce remarkably stereotyped responses.

Let us then select two aspects of this sex role socialization that seem to have particular relevance for deviancy study: aggression and conformity.

Aggression

Looking at referrals to child guidance clinics, one finds that boys are more often referred for aggressive, destructive and competitive behaviour, girls (if at all) for personality problems — for example, excessive fears and worries, shyness, timidity, lack of self-confidence, and feelings of inferiority (reports Chesler in *Women and Madness* (1972)). Other studies show that although women display less overt aggression, they reveal more anxiety about it, and more hidden hostility: 'These findings suggest that women are at least as aggressive as men, but society forces them to control or channel this aggression, and the consequence of this is an increase in apprehension and anxiety concerning aggression' (King, 1974). Such societal 'forces' start early: in their longitudinal study of children, the Newsons document that girls were reported by their mothers to display more aggression at home than boys; but seven year old girls who quarrelled with friends did so by shouting at them, in contrast to boys who were more likely to settle disputes by physical force. The Newsons comment that this is related to a 'cultural understanding that it is neither seemly nor safe to allow little girls to brawl in public places' (Newson and Newson, 1976). Definitions of 'aggression' — whether it is verbal or physical — would seem to be important here; there is also the possibility that mothers perceive more aggression in girls because they would be more sensitive to inappropriate outbreaks.

Hence whether or not there is any endocrine reason for the sex differences in display of aggression, it would appear that social learning and identification at least direct the 'correct' expression of personality characteristics. It is significant that it has been found possible to predict degrees of adult aggression from that displayed by boys, but not from that displayed by girls. Dependent girls, on the other hand, tend to become dependent women, but dependent boys do not become dependent men (Kagan and Moss, 1962). Socialization therefore seems to be a continued, varied but forceful process, so that tomboy or cissy characteristics may be sanctioned at an early age but the 'appropriate' sex role expression will occur from later learning. As children grow older, there will clearly be more urgency attached to manifestations of the 'correct' gender role. Girls are usually expected to be non-violent, and would be discouraged from fighting or using weapons. Even when women do commit violent crimes, their gender role and socialization is reflected. With homicides, for example, women have been found to kill relatives or lovers, using a kitchen implement such as a knife — a domestic tool with which they are familiar. In robberies they appear to play 'secondary, supportive roles' (Hoffmann-Bustamente, 1973).

Conformity

In parallel with the expectation for controlled aggression is the pressure towards greater conformity from girls. Our concern here would be compliance with 'morality'. The Eppels' standard study of adolescent attitudes (1966) found that girls have a fairer image of adults than do boys, better relations with adults, condemn dishonesty more, accept moral codes more, approve more than boys of manners and self-control, and approve rather more of accepting orders. They seem to have acquired, in Eysenck's term, a more efficient 'inner policeman' (policewoman?) to help control atavistic impulses.

It is difficult to determine, however, whether the greater conformity of girls results from some internalized conscience or is merely extemporized avoidance of social disapproval (if indeed there is a distinction). According to Kohlberg (1967) girls reach a 'good girl' stage earlier in their development than boys reach the equivalent, and stay there longer. He suggests that they have to distinguish between 'prestige of goodness' and 'prestige of power', and since little power is allocated to women, the only alternative is to be a 'good girl'. This would sound a calculating sort of 'goodness', an almost rational weighing up of the alternatives. Morris (1965) tested attitudes towards non-conformity, and claims from her findings that there is more shame felt by girls than by boys when they are questioned about having been in trouble with the police. They were more reluctant to admit to their deviant behaviour even though it had been officially recorded and in certain cases was common knowledge among the respondents' peers. They were also more critical than the boys of delinquency in general. Whether the girls 'really' felt more guilty or disapproving, or rather whether they were responding in an interview to what they saw as the expectations of conformity, is difficult to assess (self-report studies where the respondents remain anonymous appear to show few such sex differences (Campbell, 1977). Either way, the response observed by Morris would seem to demonstrate the bombardment experienced by girls towards a conformist personal front.

The question would be how and why such pressure is exercised. We could usefully discuss here the issue of control over children and examine the contribution of control or deterrence theory.

Control theory

This starts from the premise that people are neither innately evil nor good, but neutral; left alone they would not recognize any moral boundaries. 'Men are born free to break the law and will refrain from doing so only if special circumstances permit' (Box, 1981). Socialization therefore is extremely problematic and fragile, rather than an automatic transmission to the next generation. Individuals' preparedness to surrender the possibility of diversity depends on three aspects: the attachments they form, the commitments they develop and the beliefs they accept. It is not *faulty* socialization that leads to deviance, but the *absence* of informal controls, the concomitant lack of attachments to adults, the failure to develop adequate 'social bonding'. Conversely, conformity is made possible by social arrangements (like jobs) by which individuals can acquire goods, prospects and reputations. But the deviant is one who has not been aided in his or her calculations about the price of conformity. 'Deviants are people who have nothing to lose.' There is variation, then, in the extent to which people believe they should obey the rules of society, or which ones they should obey; a sense of injustice would serve as an experience which prevents the development of an adequate social bond in the first place. 'Delinquency is not caused by beliefs that require delinquency, but it rather made possible by the absence of (effective) beliefs that forbid delinquency' (Hirschi, 1969).

The immediate question is, therefore, not why are some particular children delinquent or deviant, but why are we not *all* deviant? The answer is Hobbesian — we would be if we could — but most of us are deterred from deviant activity by attachment to conventional institutions (like work and marriage) and the rewards they offer, combined with controls exerted by family and community. The explanation for sex differences in deviance would be that girls are socialized more efficiently and earlier into the development of these attachments and beliefs. Some recent researchers have thus successfully tested the hypothesis that there is an inverse relationship between informal (for example, parental) and formal (for example, police) social controls, and women are more frequently the subject of informal social controls, men of formal. Both mothers and fathers control their daughters more than their sons, and mothers control their daughters even more than their fathers do (Hagan et al, 1979). Their data indicate that delinquency is perceived as 'fun' by adolescents, but more fun for boys than it is for girls (in that the taste for risk is socially acquired); and it is the relationship between mothers and daughters that denies delinquency as a fun and liberating pursuit for girls. It is adolescent boys who disproportionately are allowed this outlet, at least to the point of encountering the police. Hagan et al thus tackle Wrong's (1961) attack on the 'oversocialized concept of man', and suggest that perhaps part of the problem was that these determinist perspectives focused nearly exclusively on men, and if their own findings were generalized, there may be reason to assume that women *are* oversocialized, or more specifically over-controlled. 'Thus we have argued that in the world of crime and delinquency, as in the world of work, women are denied full access to the public sphere through a socialization sequence that moves from mother to daughter in a cycle that is self-renewing.'

British material would seem to support this suggestion of greater control of girls. While the Newsons' study in fact found few examples of different treatment according to sex in the early years of children's lives, their work on seven year olds discovered many more variations in behaviour and in parental response than was visible at four. Boys who stayed indoors for example were characterized as 'shy'; no such characterization of indoor girls was given. Mothers expected their sons to be 'little rascals', their daughters to be 'little angels'. Boys thus grew up viewing rule-breaking as part of 'being a man', girls saw rule-keeping as part of 'being a woman' (Newson and Newson, 1976).

Seven year old girls were much less likely to play in the street or roam outside. The mothers of these girls were more likely than mothers of boys to fetch their children from school, suggesting that girls may be more closely supervised than boys. Further, mothers of girls were more likely to intervene when their daughters became involved in unsuitable friendships.

We could profitably digress a little here to look more closely at the different meanings for boys and girls that the relationship with the mother has. For girls, there is the possibility of direct modelling on the female role which has no parallel possibilities for boys. In many cultures, and typically in the west, the father is absent for a large part of the child's day. Boys have to define masculinity in terms of 'non-feminine'; they are thus more dependent on the peer group for consolidation and testing of their masculine role, while girls are able to proceed by positive and direct imitation, or some process of osmosis. It will be interesting, of course, to gauge the effects of large-scale unemployment on this situation — although the other relevant current employment trend, that of the increase in working mothers, would not seem to affect role modelling, as children are typically left with (female) nursery staff or women child-minders. Thus while both sexes initially 'identify' with the mother/female, boys have to shift to a broader, culturally-defined masculine role, rather than learning through a personal relationship. That this 'bond' for girls can override later experiences is suggested in McRobbie and Garber's work on female sub-cultures: 'There is nothing to suggest that participation in a 'Mod' sub-culture sharply loosened bonds between mothers and daughers, or significantly undermined the girls' self-conception and orientation towards marriage and the family' (McRobbie and Garber, 1975).

Those searching for common variables in girl delinquents or maladjusted girls also pick on the importance of the mother-daughter relationship. Campbell (1977), in comparing girls from a local assessment centre with a control group from a nearby secondary modern school, found only two significant differences between the groups with regard to home background and communications in the family: the presence of the father in the home and the degree to which the mother 'understood' the girl. 'One finding is the crucial importance of the mother. There is certainly a very clear relationship between the lack of a positive emotional bond between mother and daughter and the daughter's involvement in delinquent activities.' The concept of 'bonding' is of course a basic tenet of control theory. Another side of the 'trouble' spectrum, represented in 'disordered' children sent to community homes, has also evinced environmental theories of home background. In his analysis of the 'extreme' children found in Aycliffe, Hoghughi (1978) noted that fights between girls and their parents, especially mothers, were more frequent than is the case with boys; that the preponderance of non-accidental injuries were caused by mothers to daughters; that the incidence of mental and physical illness among girls' mothers was greater than in boys' mothers; and that girls' mothers were generally more 'uncooperative'. Hoghughi is aware of the *interactive* nature of all this: 'If mothers present problems, then daughters are more likely to suffer than sons; alternatively, if daughters present problems, then mothers are more likely to react adversely than fathers.' This would seem to lend support to the notion of role modelling for daughters, and to mothers reliving their lives through their daughters, what has been termed the 'intimate oppression' of girls. So the strong mother-daughter attachment may contribute generally to the greater control of girls, but a breakdown in this relationship may be a factor in the development of more alienated, anomic behaviour.

The question remains of why this bonding, or lack of it, should be so important for females. We seem to have to extend social learning to include 'anticipatory' socialization. In analysing Canadian delinquents, West takes a persuasive economic argument, implying the 'calculational assessments in favour of conformity' that are part of control theory:

> Females are not expected to be economically self-sufficient in our culture, and so are not subject to the same pressure for economic acquisition. Females are more likely to remain firmly within their families, and after becoming mothers, are usually very attached to their offspring. An economic base of support is guaranteed by male partners, or welfare; crime becomes less attractive. (West, 1979)

Informal social control would account for females being less willing to engage in risk-taking activities. We saw delinquency as 'fun', but a type of fun infrequently allowed to females, in that it anticipates a range of activities, some criminal, some conventional, that are more open to men than women. Delinquency involves a chance to pursue publicly some of the pleasures that are symbolic of adult male status outside the family. This view of socialization seems to support the view that the family acts to reproduce or confirm the existing sexual division of labour; even delinquency in males would be a reflection of anticipated roles and statuses rather than a rejection of, or an inadequacy in parental socialization. This is not necessarily contradictory to the control theory view that deviants are people who have nothing to lose, who lack commitments forbidding delinquency; for even self-interest has to find its expression in contemporary local styles and opportunities. But women are more restricted in their access to the public arena; for them there need be less discontinuity between the parental home and their own home and children, because work or even leisure may be only a temporary diversion in the cyclical process of socialization.

Socialization and school

The basic learning of a sex role, together with its appropriate personality and cultural displays, would thus explain the following phenomena for girls: less aggression both to teachers and other pupils; greater attachment to adults, because of mother-daughter bonding; more avoidance of breaking school rules, owing to the desire to appear 'good'; acceptance of school life as not too incongruent with present or future styles; acceptance of the individualism of school effort, because of the 'privatized' domestic role within the family; acceptance of indoor, sedentary pursuits; and acceptance of school as 'educative', in the same way that the woman socializes the family. The 'extremes' exhibited in girls' behaviour are accounted for by the fact that a girl is 'normally' better socialized, or more controlled, and circumstances need to be much more adverse before she will become a trouble-maker, or exhibit 'abnormal' traits. Explanations for girls who cause trouble would revolve around the theme of breakdown. Included here would be the notion of 'faulty' socialization: in the same way that boys are seen to be affected, factors such as broken homes, inadequate parental education, lack of communication, would evoke for girls a deficit model of upbringing. Secondly, there might be an inadequacy in the mother-daughter relationship; instead of, or in addition to the above, there would have been a breakdown particularly in this female bond, so that attachments to this role within society have not been properly formed. Thirdly, there would be the implication of inefficient learning of the female sex role, so that difficult girls are in fact more like boys, and therefore cause similar amounts and types of trouble. Variants on such a theme would be permission to be the tomboy; the learning of cross-sex traits because of the presence or influence of elder brothers; ideologies of equality from parents; and working mothers who not only are absent for much of the real identification and modelling, but also confuse the differentiation between male 'instrumental' and female 'expressive' roles.

But as the reader may wearily note, this chapter, or even this section shows no signs of ending here. There have inevitably been a range of critiques of socialization or role learning models to explain behaviour. That they may ignore the political and economic antecedents to child-rearing techniques is an issue more fully discussed in the last section. I want here to highlight the related difficulty of fully explaining individual and social class variation and change. Recent large-scale surveys of adolescent sex role stereotypes and attitudes to work and ability show that attitudes were less stereotyped in 1978 than in 1973; that females, especially, were becoming less traditional, particularly in higher socio-economic classes; and that there is a disparity between the views of boys and girls, so that some interesting negotiations must be taking place about accepted sex roles (Ditkoff, 1979; Sampson, 1979). The permanence implied by the first-five-years-of-life approach, and by the notion of a consensus on 'accepted' sex roles, gives little scope for the *interaction* of class and sex in deciding eventual role behaviour. When examining teachers' ratings of infants, for example, Brandis and Bernstein (1974) found that the effect of the sex of the child upon the teacher's ratings was greater in the middle class area than in the working class area. They thought the more favourable ratings of girls in the middle class area may have some connection with the more restricted socialization of girls, as reported by these mothers; yet girls in the middle class area were, by the end of the second year, rated *more* independent than the boys. The reasons for this would generate another great range of hypotheses, but we will leave it here just to demonstrate the complexities.

We also have to be careful about assuming that if parents 'encourage' certain traits in children, these will become permanently internalized. There is even doubt thrown now on the reliability of previous sex differences reported in personality (regardless of whether these are seen to derive from biology or socialization). They appear in some studies and not in others. Maccoby and Jacklin (1974) conclude, for example, that girls do not generally seem to be more motivated towards 'social' behaviour, nor less motivated towards 'instrumental' behaviour than boys. 'Existing empirical studies do not show girls to be reliably more sensitive to social cues, more dependent, more affiliative, more nurturant, more altruistic or more empathetic.' A further complication is the relationship between 'personality' as measured by verbal tests, and actual interpersonal behaviour: many tests seem to predict behaviour for men *but not for women*. McGuire comments:

> This finding of lower correlations for women than for men is not peculiar to the personality-influencibility area. Part of the lore of labourers in the experimental-personality vineyard is that if one wants to find strong relationships between personality variables and behaviour measures in college sophomores, one is wise to use male rather than female subjects.
>
> (McGuire, 1968)

The context in which social action occurs might thus be even more significant for girls than for boys. To return to aggression, there are clearly circumstances (such as war, or threat to offspring) when females may be just as aggressive as males. A study of the transmission of aggression through imitation of aggressive models shows that although girls imitated physical aggressiveness less than boys, there were no sex differences in verbal aggression (Bandura et al, 1961). Later, Bandura (1965) reported that sex differences in physical aggression could also be removed if additional incentives to imitate aggressive behaviour were offered to the youngsters. Similar findings were revealed in the now classic experiment by Leventhal et al (1968) where subjects had to teach another person (in reality a confederate) a concept using mild electric shocks as feedback to that person on his progress. The subjects were then told that strong shocks after an error produced faster learning. No differences were found between the sexes in the average intensity of the shock employed. All these findings seem to indicate that when females are directly or indirectly given permission to show aggression they will do so. Socialization seems at best to have a tenuous hold on future behaviours, and not be a 'determinant' of role conformity.

Reporting on American delinquents, Wise (1967) takes a thesis of 'role convergence':

> Far from being negligible in volume, middle class female delinquency closely resembles male delinquency in the number of youths taking part ... the fact that middle class boys and girls engage in similar kinds of delinquency indicates, perhaps, that they are not strongly influenced by traditional sex roles ... a change is occurring in expectations, associated with the social roles of middle class girls.

British material would even dispute whether this 'convergence' is only a middle class phenomenon. The adolescent 'fighting crews' in Robins and Cohen's *Knuckle Sandwich* (1978) are also increasingly female — what had been a male preserve, and an index of male sexual dominance, opened up to the opposite sex. The authors, however, attribute this not so much to the crew itself as to the advent of Bruce Lee; on the one hand he could be idolized, but on the other 'his films demonstrated that the so-called weaker sex could master a technique which meant they could fight on equal terms with boys — and win. Even if his girl fans didn't in practice follow the way of the dragon, Bruce Lee *ratified their entry* into the precincts of the fighting crew' (my italics). One lad was so badly beaten up by a group of girls he had to be taken to hospital. The presence of aggression would seem to hinge less on genetics, or even role internalization, than on situational interpretation of whether such behaviour is either permitted or likely to be successful. Like biological explanations, socialization theories underplay the meanings attached to particular contexts, the interpretative capacity of human beings, and also the motivation and purposeful activity of individuals. If they can, or it is in their interest to act within what they have acquired as appropriate sex roles, well and good; if not, the 'commitments' to beliefs will be temporarily or permanently shelved. Matza's concept of 'drift' might be better in starting to describe young people's orientation to contemporary values and typifications, even assuming there were a consensus on these.

At the school level, then, there are some issues raised about applying socialization theories to explain conformity and deviance. One is the abdication of responsibility that goes with acceptance of determinism, in the same way that Bernstein's identification of restricted and elaborated language codes absolved teachers from the responsibility for pupil failure. Differential treatment would be justified in terms of what pupils 'expected', or there can be the reification of 'society' or 'the family' which 'forces' pupils into sex-typed or deviant responses. Secondly, there is the complication of possibly different sex role socialization according to social class, which is particularly salient in discussing the school's preparation for women's work roles. Thirdly, like biological models, social learning theories give less emphasis to the meanings of particular contexts, different teachers, subjects or relationships. The fleeting nature of the 1000 a day interactions in the classroom (Jackson, 1968), the constant interpretive work of teachers and pupils in defining and managing the 'multiple realities' of school life, is reduced to a search for patterns in previous learning, or at best some generalized description of the 'interaction' between home and school. There can be sociological reductionism as well as psychological reductionism.

To incorporate control theory, and to avoid determinism, we need then a model of socialization which allows the individual some strategic choice. For preference, I turn to 'acculturation', although this is perhaps a clumsy term, intended to oppose 'enculturation'. It was forged to describe colonial contact between cultures, and has connotations of adaption and accommodation rather than conversion. If we use it with regard to the way children learn from adults, it enables us to recognize the former as active and decisive participants (rather than empty vessels to be filled, or objects of repression or domination). In admitting that even very young children have acquired competences and cultures of their own, we begin to see socialization as a two-way process, even if there is naturally a differential in power between those attempting to socialize and those supposedly at the 'receiving' end. Investigating the cultures of children is no mean feat, for the sociologist cannot, even on good days, pass herself off as a five-year old, or penetrate the culture; but accepting socialization as culture *contact* rather than *transmission* will give the flexibility needed to account for social change and will enable respect to be shown for the crucial and continuous interpretive work done by children and young people when they are 'being socialized'.

The Bad Set: Sub-cultural Studies

However 'well' designed and 'well' socialized the individual is, no-one would deny the impact of peers, contemporaries and associates on our immediate behaviour. Our genes and our socialization are of course geared to making us social animals, able to respond and contribute to the group for our own and for its survival. 'Getting in with the wrong set' is a teachers' way of claiming an adverse effect from that social imperative; and indeed sub-cultural studies have had a long tradition in deviancy exploration. Many of these have taken as their point of departure the 'psychogenic' assumption that all human action — not just delinquent — is a continuous series of efforts to solve problems. 'The crucial condition for the emergence of new cultural forms is the existence, in effective interaction with each other, of a number of actors with similar problems of adjustment' (Cohen, 1955). In contrast to the previous explanations, the sub-cultural approach will see conduct as conditioned by the fact of group membership, rather than stemming from innate or internalized personality traits and role styles; it is also able to see the rules governing action as at least partly created by the group itself rather than imposed on individuals by outside, or by 'society'. The study of a particular sub-culture is undertaken to discover the origins and effects of the unique set of prescriptions for action which mark off a grouping of people as distinctive, with these prescriptions having been variously termed 'norms', 'values', 'rules', 'focal concerns' and 'themes'.

As in most sociology, there is a dearth of studies specifically on female sub-cultures, which makes gender comparisons difficult. There is a variety of reasons for such a neglect. Clearly the sex ratio of the researchers determines the sex-ratio of the cultures they are able to penetrate. More criminality and delinquency is also male, and therefore the concern from the corrective tradition in sociology is to discover what particular aspects of group membership are likely to facilitate a rule-breaking response: female sub-cultures like the Women's Institute would not have the same impact or interest. Male sub-cultures are more visible, taking the shape of 'gangs', in contrast to women's groups which would be more privatized (McRobbie's 'teeny boppers', for example, gathering in each other's houses — which accords with Murdock and Phelps' (1973) distinction between 'street' and 'pop' cultures, with the former being more open to boys, the latter equally available, but more subscribed to by girls). One view is that women's sub-cultures are a direct reflection of male ones (girl cheer-leaders at male sports), or females are individually or marginally involved in male sub-cultures rather than forming self-sufficient groups of their own. Finally, there is the simple observation that women do not form sub-cultures as much as men. Girls' predilection for older boyfriends means that socially they can go into pubs, be bought drinks; they can occupy their leisure time, unlike the comparative age group of boys who have to hang around the streets 'doing nothing' (Corrigan, 1979). The existing 'opportunity structures' for group activity would be more limited. As noted in the previous section, parents control girls' spare time more closely; also girls may have to assume an apprenticeship for domestic labour which begins at home, with confining and time-consuming tasks.

Here then appears another neat solution on the surface: girls are less deviant in school because they are less used to being conditioned by group membership, and/or their sub-cultures (where they do exist) will have different constraints and concerns than boys'. To test this hypothesis, we could start by looking at the theories regarding the origins of deviant sub-cultures, in particular 'strain' theories of motiva-tion. These build on Durkheim's concept of 'anomie' — that society simultaneously exhorts all its members to aim for a common goal (such as wealth) and blocks off avenues to its attainment for the majority. This disparity between goals and actual means to those goals causes problems, which people have various strategies or safety valves to cope with. The reaction may be into forms of deviance, criminal or retreatist perhaps, depending on the availability of such sub-cultural groups. In their theory of delinquency, Cloward and Ohlin (1961) propose in this way that the economic system operates a system of closure just when adolescents have formed a set of economic and material aspirations which the larger society endorses as legitimate and encourages them to hold. The result of this experience of chronic imbalance between expectation and reality is a collective alienation which frees those adolescents most at risk to develop a countervailing authority to the state: the delinquent gang. (The notion of 'freeing' adolescents to break the law has parallels with the control theory proposition of 'the absence of effective beliefs to forbid delinquency'.) Albert Cohen, similarly, talks of 'status frustration', the systematic nurturing of aspirations to succeed, particularly in schools, among pupils who are socially dis-advantaged in the class of origin, and culturally disadvantaged by their upbringing in competing for 'status' resources. In evolving a collective delinquent response they both hit back at the system which has branded them as failures, and create a different status contest on terms more available to them.

The great strength of strain theories is that they link delinquency with the serious social and economic inequalities endemic in the structure in a way which appears to account for the nature and distribution of adolescent deviance. That official statistics demonstrate delinquency as being a predominantly male, lower class phenomenon has long been a crucial plank of the strain theory school. Within this framework, girls' lesser involvement in recorded delinquency is accounted for by their having fewer 'structural' problems than boys. Their future monetary and status position will depend on association with a male rather than direct participation in the economy, with its perceived blocked opportunities. Although women form nearly 40 per cent of the workforce, and over 46 per cent of females work for wages, their jobs are concentrated in the unskilled sector, or reproduce elements of domestic labour — serving men as bosses, or catering. Hence the view that 'women are judged, then, not on their occupation-al status but on their femininity. They are assessed in terms of their sexual desirability ... and their femininity is defined by their relation to consumption (appearance, taste, fashion awareness, clothes, chil-dren's appearance, home) (Brake, 1980). I might demand evidence that judging women primarily on 'sexual desirability' is a universal feature, and not confined to Brake himself, but the trend for even the latest mobility studies (for example, Halsey, et al, 1980) to be concerned exclusively with male workers, lends some support to the notion of women's invisibility in the occupational status hierarchy.

The nature of female deviance when it does occur, can again be explained within a 'strain' framework: the implication is that particular acts are related to, or rather the outcome of the frustration of primary success goals. Thus boys 'naturally' commit offences against property, and girls are involved in sexual delinquency. Girls' 'focal concerns' would be sexual and marital rather than occupational/financial. Women are related to the economic system through men; therefore sex, and their ability to bargain with it, becomes their major interest. Female delinquency follows the same lines. 'Promiscuous' behaviour is then much more akin to the 'negativistic, anti-utilitarian' theft-and-vandalism syndrome described by Cohen (1955), which rejects both legitimate means and ends. The sex difference in whether the delinquency was collective or individual would then be explained by the nature of the delinquent act. However, this does not for our purposes directly ascertain the likelihood of sub-cultural formations in school, and moreover neglects the double standards involved in the definition of and apprehension of 'promiscuity'.

We need to look particularly at the adolescent world, and unpack the possible linkages with both role theory and control theory. Girls are exposed to the same structured inequalities as boys, and would be aware of the same goals, particularly in school. At the same time, they have to manage the same 'dangerous passage' from parental care to work and back into a new family. Powell and Clarke (1975) suggest, however, that girls stand in a *differential* relation to the *same* set of major institutions. Whereas male sub-cultures inhabit the weak points between home/school and work, girls' 'space' for sub-cultural activity is not marginal, but more tightly structured than that available to boys. The family of origin exerts a more permanent hold; the reproduction of the girl as wife/mother is reinforced in other institutional spheres, in school and leisure, in media pressure towards consumable femininity. Girls' leisure activities and any sub-cultural groupings hinge therefore on particular definitions of femininity — whether 'steadies', disco groups or even 'scrubbers'; and this activity and group allegiance may itself offer a 'career' element. Support for the idea of leisure as a career for working class girls comes from Gill's *Luke Street* descriptions. Here the girls felt only a limited attraction to Casey's pub where the boys gathered. They preferred to go to the town dance halls, where there was a possibility of meeting someone away from the area. 'Their ambitions were to fulfil their roles of wife and mother *away* from Luke Street' (Gill, 1978).

In terms then of joint perceptions of school, work and the future, the convenient answer for girls' lesser participation in deviance and deviant sub-cultures is therefore that 'blocked opportunities' are not so apparent for them. They may indeed eventually stand in the same relation to the means of production as the boys, and be deprived of financial rewards, but marriage as a career initially holds the possibility of upward mobility. They can afford to be more optimistic; they are aware of different avenues to success and status through their relationship with a yet unknown man. Pahl's exploration of school leavers' anticipation of their future lives revealed that girls saw themselves facing the same problems as boys, but that these were more wide-ranging than simply the concern about employment which dominated the boys' lives:

> The inevitability of becoming a housewife, of facing birth and motherhood and of facing the death of her parents, and also her husband, at a relatively early age, made the difficulties about money and about employment just another facet of life's struggle ... somehow the girls had the rich tapestry of life as a source of satisfaction. The boys were more dependent on their work. (Pahl, 1978)

The 'richness' of the tapestry is, of course, contingent at least partially on social class; working class girls may, as Sharpe found, prefer being girls because they do not have to go out to work. The 'strain' theory needs refining, in that further differentials in socio-economic conditions have to be taken into account, particularly the badly paid and unsatisfying jobs available to women.

> Work is then not seen as attractive, but as an unfortunate necessity of life, and therefore the apparent opportunity to avoid it seems one of the advantages of being a woman ... if girls accept that their life will be fulfilling by having a husband and bearing his children, then this does provide a tangible goal, and one that can be reached without too many qualifications and training. (Sharpe, 1976)

Girls are in fact, she says, responding in a realistic and rational way to a social structure over which they have little individual control. One might hypothesize then that oppositional sub-cultures would be more likely to form amongst *middle* class girls at school (for middle class girls are apparently just as delinquent as middle class boys); on the other hand, middle class girls would have the twin possibilities of occupational success *and* marital success, and would be even less likely to feel frustrated than any social class of boy. An apt instance was the story a woman told me of her headmistress confiding in her when she was in the sixth: 'It doesn't matter if you don't go to university, Jane, because you're pretty; but Susan — Susan *must*.'

Femininity then, might be an *alternative* to labour power; although of course in many female occupations femininity, or even direct sexuality, is *part* of what they are selling:

> In other wage labour, women take their femininity with them in terms of the *value* of their labour as 'servers' ... they serve 'consumers' in hospitals, canteens etc. As clerical workers they serve men and the company ... In yet other jobs female sexuality as sexuality in display is part of the use value of the commodity labour power itself. For some secretaries, receptionists, boutique assistants, it is essential to be attractively feminine as well as to serve.   (Bland et al, 1978)

Mitchell, in *Psychoanalysis and Feminism* expresses this even more strongly: 'Women do literally sell their bodies — if not as prostitutes, then to the publicity industries, modelling and so on — much as men and women sell their labour power' (1975). So we have McRobbie reporting her girls as seeing the chance of getting jobs in the local department store as more dependent on appearance and voice than on qualifications — even if they had them. Any hostility towards school for working class girls at least, might then be construed as stemming from the perception of school goals as irrelevant, rather than from frustration at being denied them.

In spite, then, of class variations in actual job opportunity, the possibility of status through marriage or femininity (whether in or out of work) would seem a pervasive phenomenon for girls. If we now direct the cumulative logic of all the above 'strain' type arguments specifically to the school, girls' lesser involvement in oppositional sub-cultures would be explained by the school not being responsible for their collective experience of 'status frustration'. Hargreaves (1967) and Lacey's (1970) classic studies of male pupil sub-cultures built directly on the 'strain' thesis, showing how streaming practices and the simultaneous holding out of goals and denial of success to certain groups in the institution became a causal factor in the formation of 'delinquescent' sub-cultures, whose members then gained status through the holding of values directly and deliberately polarized away from the school values. For girls, however, school would not necessarily be perceived as an institution to cause failure, in that it would not have much perceptible influence on marriage chances. They do not take an O level in femininity; they can afford to sit back and wait it out. Status can be gained in ways that are different from, but not directly oppositional to educational aims; even in the bottom stream they would be able to foresee alternative means to success. Problems they did have would not be solved by *collective* hostility towards the school; for concerns about personal relationships, of managing sexuality, of solving the contradictions of being attractive and yet not experienced, would have to be solved individually in the long term, and not through sub-cultural inversion of school values.

Girls' deviance when it did occur could, in fact, be accounted for within the same model. It would be a reaction formation to being denied academic success in the same way as for boys; or a reaction against being denied femininity by the imposition of 'masculine' uniform, or against the concentration in the school ethos on academic and sporting success rather than proficiency in personal relationships. Another explanatory contribution might come from the debate about the *sources* of sub-cultural values. Are youth sub-cultures Cohen's 'malicious, negatavistic, non-utilitarian counter-cultures', that is, a recoil against middle class values, or do they borrow and act out concerns from the parent working class community? Under the second derivation, delinquency, rather than being a reaction to or product of deprivation and anomie, is a celebration of long-standing traditional concerns of working class culture; thus Miller (1958) identified certain 'focal concerns' of male lower class culture in the 1950s — toughness, smartness, excitement, autonomy, themes of trouble and fate. Downes uses the concept of 'dissociation' to describe the response to the middle class dominated contexts of school, work and recreation:

> 'The working-class boy ... who has been hampered in school by his attachment to working-class values, reacts to 'failure' not by frustration, reaction-formation etc, but by the reaffirmation of the working-class value system.' (Downes, 1966)

The disenchantment provokes an emphasis on purely 'leisure' goals, sedulously fostered by commercial 'teenage' culture. Such themes are taken up in Willis' more recent work, where the lads, rejecting the imposition of prolonged childhood, turn to the adult male world as a source of material for resistance. Smoking, drinking, 'having a laff', take on symbolic importance in the search for solutions to cultural and educational domination. Thus the idea of 'borrowing' from a parent culture might again illuminate girls' different styles of deviance in school; their 'anticipatory socialization', turning to a female working class culture, would not represent such an oppositional stance in school terms. But there are problems identifying the 'focal concerns' of female class cultures, even if generalizations were possible. Presumably there would not be the distinction between mental and manual (masculine) labour which made Willis' lads classify academic boys as cissies or poofs. 'Expressivity' for females would not be found in toughness; the socialization literature would suggest 'dependence' rather than 'autonomy' as a focal concern. 'Excitement' for them would stem from romance, from the building of a home, from giving birth to children; there would be little need to create excitement in the immediate environment. Various contradictions *are* built into female working class life: being sexually attractive but not promiscuous; managing the transition from girl to wife to mother while maintaining femininity; acting out a subservient role yet having to be 'caring', with the responsibility that that implies; being financially dependent, yet often working to maintain the family. These contradictions might however be solved by the centrality of the home as the female domain, by regarding work as pin-money, by seeing no discontinuity between the wife and mother roles in the same way (according to Chetwynd, 1976) that men do. But there is a desperate need for more field research to locate long-term female cultural solutions to contradictions and inequalities.

School sub-cultures

What we can do is turn to specific material on pupil groupings in school to apply the above framework directly. Again, I shall deliberately start from the perspective of female association. What is amazing about much of the writing from boys' only groups is the way authors suffer temporary amnesia about the partial nature of their original sample, and move on to make generalizations about 'kids', 'pupils' and 'working class youth'; it is as if girls were by definition subsumed under boys, or were somehow outside 'youth'. Alternatively, girls are occasionally referred to, but only, it seems, in their importance as a foil, a backcloth to the boys' activities:

> The lads usually take the initiative in conversation and are the ones who make suggestive comments. The girls respond with giggles and talk amongst themselves. Where girls do make comments they are of the serious, caring or human kind. It is left to the lads to make the jokes, the hard comments, the abrasive summations and to create a spectacle to be appreciated by the girls. The girls are clearly dominated, but they collude in their own domination.   (Willis, 1977)

The last sentence is reminscent of Hadfield's description of girls liking to be bullied: it is difficult to assess whether the generalized and sexist picture painted by Willis is an accurate portrayal of the lads' sexism, or is merely a representation of his own bias in observation. And if the boys do desperately need to impress the girls so much, who is really 'dominated' in this instance? Willis speaks of the lads 'partially creating' identities for the girls; nowhere is it suggested that the girls may 'partially create' identities for the lads. *Learning to Labour* was hailed as radical and innovative, and became the sacred text for many a conference; yet a clue to the inherently conservative sexism in Willis' interpretations is the way he periodically claims all sorts of astonishing things to be 'profoundly masculine' — the use of humour, taking the initiative, the ethos of the factory, doing unexpected or amusing things, and even 'the disposition to naturally take the active comple- ment to the appreciative passive'. Again the pressing need is demons- trated for empirical work on females which will 'bring women back in', and counter the absurd and arrogant notion that it is only males who are interesting, amusing and active.

Yet if we do look at what work there is on female groupings in school, there is no immediate clear-cut picture which we can set alongside, or counterpose to the boys' scene. First, girls' groupings appear to be smaller and 'more intimate' than boys' (Blyth, 1960; Murdock and Phelps, 1973) — and not infrequently simply a pair of friends. (The 'best friend' thesis also appears in the literature about adolescent female association outside school, as, for example, in Ward (1970) and McRobbie (1978)). Secondly, there does not appear to be much of the inverse polarization noted in studies of boys' schools — a replication of Hargreaves' study conducted in a girls' school found that the lower streams were actually *more* committed to the school norms than the higher streams, and had less of a non-academic 'counter-culture' as expressed in distinctive forms of dress and values (Brown, 1972). In the Lacey and Hargreaves accounts, ability and commitment to school norms went together, while sexual precocity, trendiness, opposition and low performance were linked. However, in this girls' school, and in Douglas' (1968) study, early maturity, extreme fashion consciousness and high ability were associated. Studies in girls-only 'academic' schools appear to demonstrate few clear-cut divisions: Delamont's was in an upper middle class private girls' school, where she found the pupils almost obsessively concerned with being quiet, being good at school, and getting teachers to like them. She comments:

> The broadly based curriculum and flexible 'sets' mean that the girls are not rigidly separated into arts and science specialists or into 'A' or 'B' streamers, but mix freely. As a result the informal friendship groups or cliques which exist are not mutually hostile, as are those described by Hargreaves and Lacey. Instead all the girls in each age group are friendly and form small groups on the basis of common hobbies or interests, rather than polarizing into hostile sub-cultures.
>
> (Delamont, 1976)

Similarly, Lambart's (1976) study of an urban grammar school for girls found that a 'deviant' clique of girls was in fact associated with reasonably good standards of academic work. In this school there was 'crypto-streaming' in the form of setting, but the informal structures of the class were related to social class and junior school attended as well as level of achievement and subject groups. An intricate web of orientations towards school, towards fellow pupils and towards teachers emerges here, which would coincide with Coleman's early findings in the United States (1961) that the structure of girls' peer networks was much more elaborate and complex than boys', which seemed to be organized almost entirely round sport.

In a different setting entirely, a mixed middle school, Meyenn also found that while distinct groups of same-sex friends were a vital part of the girls' lives (and while the girls were involved in constant manoeuvres to keep the groups intact in the face of school organizational shuffles), it was difficult to place these groups on a pro-anti school continuum. Each group did exhibit a relatively consistent culture, albeit with common features and interests across all groups; the difference lay in orientation to school. The 'P.E. girls' were noted for continuous attempts to get round school rules, and there was much cooperation in helping each other cope with academic aspects of school life. The 'nice girls' accepted school authority and, although cooperating in homework, were not concerned to break or bend school rules. The 'quiet girls', in the bottom sets for most things, had elaborate mechanisms to make this situation tolerable, to 'make it more fun if you're not clever'. Despite this inversion, they do not fit the picture in the literature of 'anti-school' groups; they caused no trouble, and they said they were happy at school. The 'science lab girls' were the only ones to take on the school's definition of 'learning' and 'individual competence', and did not help each other in tests. 'Breaking friends' was common in all groups, but only with the P.E. girls, quite successful academically, did fighting become physical; there was an indication of the girls' dominance over the boys in the area of fighting. Variations occurred in commitment to elements of 'teenage culture', but unlike Sugarman's (1967) study, it was the most pro-school and the most publicly anti-school group that were chiefly involved in this, specifically in terms of dress, jewellery and make-up. These two groups again were the ones most able to create space for themselves to avoid school rules.

The 'adolescent culture' is a theme which recurs in Ball's study of Beachside Comprehensive (1981). In this coeducational and distinctly banded school, Ball identified both male and female anti-school groups in the second band, groups who had more interaction with each other than they did with same-sex groups who might exhibit pro-school tendencies. The fashion/pop culture spread across both bands for the girls, but Ball noted identifiable differences in expression, with the lower bands more 'extreme' in their fashion allegiance, their colour choices, their heel heights. Items denoting loyalty to various pop groups were also confined to the lower bands. While the top band girls appeared to *combine* teenage culture and school values, for lower band girls it provided an *alternative* avenue for status, freedom and sophistication. Prestige for them also seemed to be gained in the same way as boys by the traditional inversion of school values — cheeking teachers, smoking, leaving the school at lunchtime. However, as with Lacey, the presence of pro- and anti-school sub-cultures did not mean that all pupils could be slotted into them, and there were some girls specifically who Ball termed 'ambivalent' — being anti-school in attitudes but not in behaviour. Deprivation of status in the academic sphere does not automatically lead to active resistance or sub-cultural display.

Is it then to social class that we must return in accounting for really oppositional sub-cultures? McRobbie, like Willis, uses a class analysis to explain not only girls' initial allocation to a stream, but also their continued response to schooling. The 'Mill Lane' girls, aged 14–16 and living on a Birmingham council estate, saw themselves as 'naturally' occupying an antagonistic relationship with the middle class girls at school, referring to them as the 'swots' or 'snobs'. They were at once competitive with them and contemptuous of their application, diligence and conscientiousness. They looked down on their lack of fashion-consciousness, their taste in boys. These girls perceived school treating them 'like dirt'; thus their own success, as in Willis, hinged on the ability to work the system and transform the school into the sphere, *par excellence*, for developing their social life, fancying boys, learning the latest dance, having a smoke together in the lavatories and playing up the teachers. However, it would seem that these activities are again not merely a 'polarization' of school values, a reaction formation *directly* traceable to school, or to the school streaming system. McRobbie argues that they spring from a 'class instinct' which finds expression by rejecting the official school ideology for girls and replacing it with a *more* feminine, even sexual one. The source of 'norms and values' is not just institutional:

> Marriage, family life, fashion and beauty all contribute massively to the feminine anti-school culture, and, in doing so, nicely illustrate the contradictions in so-called oppositional activities. Are the girls in the end not simply doing what is required of them — and if this *is* the case, then could it not be convincingly argued that it is their own culture which itself is the most effective agent of social control for girls, pushing them into compliance with that role which a whole range of institutions in capitalist society also, but less effectively, directs them towards?
>
> (McRobbie, 1978)

The notion of a culture, however derived, 'pushing' actors into a role is much in line with the more deterministic accounts of sub-cultures. McRobbie's version is perhaps more subtle, in that the girls appear to 'choose' this style as an oppositional expression; even so, there appears little room for individual deviation within the 'feminine' anti-school culture.

Yet while peer relationships and the social aspects of schooling are highly important to girls, this is not the same as saying that girls are necessarily *members* of a peer group to the extent that the group takes over, or that classroom life can be explained by supposing that it is determined by *external* constraints and pressures. A micro study, again in a secondary modern school, throws doubt on the whole notion of a 'culture' of norms and values which colours pupils' whole school experience. Furlong prefers the term 'interaction set' to describe the rather more fluid groupings of pupils which are contingent on particular classroom situations, and definitions of those situations. With his girls (mostly West Indian) there was not always agreement on the assessment of a lesson, or of a teacher; a girl would come to a lesson one day and work hard, while the next day she would take part in a common definition of that lesson and 'bunk it' completely. He asks:

> Why is it that even with teachers who are assessed as 'able to teach', some lessons are more 'successful' than others? . . . What can be said . . . is that 'how to define the situation' is a constant problem for these girls and one that demands continual negotiation. Unlike the successful grammar school pupil who knows how to look at his (sic) school experience, these girls constantly have to make sense of frustrating and often confusing situations. (Furlong, 1976)

Furlong argues therefore that action cannot be understood in terms of 'friendship groups', for these are not the same as interaction sets where membership can vary from minute to minute. His critique of Hargreaves and Lacey revolves around the contention that interaction does not just happen, it is 'constructed' by individuals, and circumstances such as different lessons offering different opportunities for personal achievement will change the meaning of classroom situations for pupils. There is no *consistent* culture for a group of friends; even the most delinquent pupils will be well behaved in certain circumstances. Furlong disputes the 'pressure' on group members to conform, the presenting of culture as an external reality. Such externalization misses the point that participants have to build up their respective codes of conduct as they go along, interpreting each other's actions and redefining the situation. The notion of a group culture oversimplifies pupil behaviour, making it appear more stable and rigid than it is. Furlong views culture rather as that which you have to 'know' to be able to behave appropriately in constantly changing circumstances.

In an unusual comparative study of grammar school girls and secondary modern girls, Llewellyn (1980) found that in spite of the apparent polarization between the top streams of the secondary modern and the non-examination groups,

> there was very little contact, friendship or solidarity between the non-exam girls, even though to outsiders (other girls,

teachers) they appeared to go around in a tightly knit gang. The composition of this group was constantly changing (partly due to truancy and non-attendance), and friendship and loyalty links were virtually non-existent. This was manifested very clearly in the spatial arrangements of lessons, where girls sat apart, separated and isolated from each other, a fact which contrasted vividly with the frenetic seating arrangements of the grammar school girls. As a result of this separation ... the girls' resistance to their lessons and teachers was either individualized and personalized: day dreaming, filing and painting nails, writing initials on desks and books; or invisible: they 'skived' off school. These patterns of behaviour make interesting comparisons with the anti-school model of groups of pupils (boys!) challenging *en masse* the teacher's authority.

These sometimes divergent accounts of the impact and consistency of girls' sub-cultures might be less discrepant if we look carefully at the variables involved. Two key interacting issues would seem to be the presence of boys, and the perceived width of the social class/ability range. In all-girls schools, being clever, attractive and good at sport are not incompatible; in a mixed school there may be more pressure to test and maintain sex role identity. In his comparative study of secondary schools, King comments:

Thus schools vary in the degree to which the sexes are taught separately, but there is no related sex difference in involvement level. In particular schools it could be seen that reduction in sex differentiation may have actually enhanced sexual identity. When girls in one school were allowed to do metalwork, they all chose to make pieces of personal jewellery.   (King, 1973)

Is it a coincidence that four of the studies I have just reviewed where the fashion/teenage culture element is either not mentioned or seen as not central to the girls, were carried out in all-girls schools? In those in mixed schools this comes out very clearly, whether middle or secondary level. There is a parallel here to the argument cited earlier that official ideologies of sex equality in a society may only serve to strengthen pressures towards maintaining 'natural' distinctions between the sexes.

Also, fluid groupings, or groups which have much in common as well as some distinct features, may well be more the pattern in unstreamed schools, or schools of more homogenous 'ability' or social class background. It is paradoxically in comprehensive schools, or at least comprehensive schools which differentiate sharply between their pupils, that 'oppositional' cultures may start to emerge, as identified by Ball and by McRobbie. The need for this culture to be traced back to a wider class and gender culture is obvious from the different expressive styles exhibited by Willis's 'lads', Hargreaves' 'delinquescent sub-culture' and McRobbie's 'Mill Lane' girls. The secondary modern schools examined by Brown and Furlong were, it is true, streamed; but assuming a more homogeneous social class intake, and less of an obvious contrast in the types of jobs and futures the school was preparing the girls for (eventually home-based orientations), then the need for a semi-permanent 'counter-school culture' is less strong. Instead, the girls' culture will reflect aspects of their particular socialization, *in interaction with* school demands, rather than in opposition to them. The reason that Furlong arrived at interaction sets may not be, as he supposed, that Hargreaves and Lacey were misguided, but that his own subjects were *girls*; one might want to return to role learning and home-centred, privatized cultures to account for why they sometimes acted in groups, sometimes individually. Meyenn comments on the 'fluidity' of his groups in the sense that no leaders emerged, unlike Whyte's Street Corner Boys, or Willis's lads. He hypothesizes that equality of status is a feature of girls' peer groups, this being related to a 'caring', 'supportive' role for women in society. 'The girls' peer groups may act as a particular kind of socializing agency within capitalist society that produces women who find it difficult or prefer not to compete with men.' The exception to this, his science lab girls, who were more individual and competitive, would perhaps already be anticipating different, less stereotyped family and occupational roles. The interaction of culture and sub-culture seems crucial: while sub-cultures may be short-lived, they 'may limit and confirm predictable social destinies ... or may open up and present a wider range of possibilities'.

This 'opening up of possibilities' is nowhere more clearly demonstrated than in Fuller's (1980) account of black girls in a London comprehensive school. Here a recognizable sub-culture did emerge in a group of eight girls of West Indian origin, but, surprisingly, it was one derived from a *positive* acceptance of being both black and female. 'Its particular flavour stemmed from their critical rejection of the meanings with which those categorizations are commonly endowed.' Their anger and frustration at labelling was not directed against themselves or others, but channelled into school achievement and the acquisition of educational qualifications. They worked hard; and yet they managed to give all the appearances of not doing so, and, without being seriously confrontational, behaved in ways exasperating to teachers. This 'smokescreen' for their peers was part of a 'strategic' political stand in relation to other people, including whites generally and white authority in school specifically. They were 'relatively sophisticated in judging who did and did not matter in their pursuit of academic qualifications'. Yet friendship choices extended to other black but 'non-academic' girls in the school, rather than high aspiring white girls. This choice of friends underlined the central importance of both their sex and their ethnicity in the girls' identity.

It would seem essential therefore, in any anthropological research on the presence and impact of pupil groupings, to identify whether the school is grammar, secondary modern or comprehensive; whether single sex girls, boys or mixed; and whether streamed or unstreamed. Each one of these eighteen possibilities, multiplied again by the ethnicity variable, would seem to have different implications for pupil response, to allow for a different interaction between previous cultural socialization and immediate definition of the situation.

If we now draw together the strands in this sections, we see that less 'status frustration' could explain fewer female oppositional cultures. In school we do find that, although there are of course groupings of girls, they appear more fluid, less polarized, less stratified and less predictable than in the reports of boys' school sub-cultures. Three major points of consideration emerge: the first is the relationship between proferred school careers and the 'careers' (whether work or leisure) out of school, and the question of whether 'strain' (perhaps because of the rigidity of streaming) elicits the need for group solutions and support; the second, linked to this, is whether in mixed schools pupils may want to maintain and display a sexual identity by reference to the cultural norms of a same-sex group; and the third is the likelihood that, unless the social class or racial base of the school is particularly divisive, girls may overall be less dependent on the group to determine day-to-day behaviour than are boys, and, as suggested in the socialization section, be more reactive to social context.

However, the variety and range of girls' oppositional stances that has emerged from the above studies and from my own search for the culture of the 'wenches' does show the power possibilities for females. Woods, in a recent supposed critique of Willis's study, points out that while we know the boys' attitudes towards the girls we do not know the girls' attitudes towards the boys. Yet, he claims, 'the chances are that they will be subordinate, for girls are exposed to a general culture of femininity which fosters passivity and subservience' (Woods, 1983). This section has demonstrated that Woods' own, yet typical, stereotype of a 'general culture of femininity' may be a gross misrepresentation of the richness, subtlety and power of girls' groupings in school.

A Bad Name: Labelling Theory

Teachers are in the business of making judgments on people; so notions of 'give a dog a bad name', or 'living up to a reputation' would be commonplace in describing the effects of the labels they apply. But we need at the outset to distinguish the more psychologistic 'self-fulfilling prophecy' approach from the branch of interpretive sociology that has come to be known as labelling theory. The former refers precisely to the phenomenon that our beliefs about another are likely to make us act towards them in such a way as to condition their behaviour to coincide with our beliefs. In some not yet fully charted way, we tend to become what others tell us we are — whether 'academic', 'lazy', 'a right rascal' or a 'real charmer'. Labelling theory incorporates this possibility, but refers to a much broader framework which questions the entire basis on which people put others into categories, particularly moral/legal ones. In contrast to the previous perspectives which have been concerned with the 'causes' of deviant behaviour, it rejects even the assumption that it is clear-cut as to what or who is 'deviant'. Before probing any 'self-fulfilling' effects of labelling another as divergent, we need to identify precisely what rule of 'normality' is being infringed, and who has the power to decide and enforce such distinctions. Definitions of deviance clearly vary between cultures and over time: taking another's life is 'wrong' in our society — except in war-time when it is not only 'right' but courageous, an irony posed by the classic peace poster 'Join The Army and See The World: Meet Interesting Exciting People — And Kill Them'.

The amount and nature of deviance then shifts according to who is making the rules. The only true and clear distinction between a 'normal' and a deviant, between an office stationery 'borrower' and a thief, is that the latter's behaviour has been noticed, defined and condemned. The classic formulation of this is Becker's:

> The central fact of deviance is that it is created by society. I do not mean this in the way it is ordinarily understood, in which causes of deviance are located in the social situation of the

deviant, or the social factors which prompted his action. I mean, rather, that social groups create deviants by making the rules whose infraction constitutes deviance, and by applying those rules to particular people and labelling them as outsiders. From this point of view, deviance is not a quality of the act a person commits, but rather a consequence of the application by others of rules and sanctions to an 'offender'. The deviant is one to whom the label has been successfully applied. Deviant behaviour is behaviour that people so label.   (Becker, 1963)

Increases in the crime rate arise not because we are becoming more evil but because many more acts are now defined as criminal than they were earlier in the century, and also because police activity in apprehending and convicting law-breakers becomes more efficient. Statistics on deviance are themselves to be explained rather than treated as absolutes. On one level any teacher knows that if you tighten up the rules you overnight create a whole new category of deviants to be processed; yet the social construction (and therefore possible deconstruction) of deviance can be ignored, and rules take on a life of their own. A deputy head was quoted in a *Times Educational Supplement* 'No Comment' column as being opposed to abolishing uniform. Uniform, he said, was extremely important: half his time was spent checking up on it.

In order to deal with our social world, we have the urge to slot people and behaviour into manageable categories. This is perhaps summed up best by the bewildered telegram sent to a correspondent by *Time Magazine* in response to a subtle and finely balanced account of happenings in some remote foreign part: 'WHO GOOD GUYS WHO BAD GUYS?' Yet the strength of labelling theory is the insistence that such definitions are *always* subjective and a question of interpretation — that all of us commit deviant acts and, more significantly perhaps, even the most delinquent will conform most of the time. Hence the approach does not seek to find 'causes' of initial deviance, nor 'best' methods of controlling crime, but asks questions such as:

What are the circumstances under which a person gets set apart, henceforth to be considered as a deviant? ... What actions do others take on the basis of this redefinition of the person? ... How does a person judged to be deviant react to this designation? ... How does he adopt the deviant role that may be set aside for him? ... What changes in his group membership result?   (Rubington and Weinberg, 1968)

The concern, then, is the social definition of deviance, and processes of social typing; this is followed by an examination of the implications for the identity of the 'bad guy', and of the likelihood of the self-fulfilling prophecy coming into action because of the problems caused by the label.

> This is one of the major thrusts of the labelling perspective — that forces of social control often produce the unintended consequences of making some persons defined as deviant even more confirmed as deviant because of the stigmatization of labelling. Thus, social reactions to deviance further deviant careers.
> (Rist, 1977)

The movement from one who has broken a rule to one who sees her or himself as a habitual rule-breaker is what has been termed the transition from a 'primary' to a 'secondary' deviant. A secondary deviant is someone who has had to reorganize their whole persona around the deviant role to cope with problems arising from the application of the label. Forced exclusion (as in prison) would be an example of this, as not only does it confront the subject with a collective, legitimized version of themselves as different, but the possibility of alternative, or 'normal' identities is in fact reduced. 'If he suffers the misfortune of being grossly excluded from all occasions promising the temptation of theft, his provisional identity as thief receives considerable affirmation' (Box, 1981). The child sent out of the classroom would be a typical instance of exclusion. Not only is the pupil more likely to violate rules in that more stringent codes of silence and isolation are imposed, and she will have to manage boredom and solitude; but also she has no opportunity to engage in teacher-pleasing behaviour and adopt another identity. She is likely to be 'spotted' by other teachers, and the collective label becomes more probable because of her high visibility. Wilkins' 'deviance amplifying system' uses a cybernetic model to show how social reaction acts as a positive feedback loop. Thus:

less tolerance leads to
more acts being defined as crimes
leads to
more action against criminals
leads to
more alienation of deviants
leads to
more crime by deviant groups
leads to

less tolerance of deviants by conforming groups,
and so on in a circular and expansionary process.

(Wilkins, 1971)

Feedback models can of course be applied to a whole range of phenomena, such as the stock market, but it must be remembered that the vital element of labelling theory is its symbolic component, 'the way in which people are "tagged", pigeon-holed, bottled, stamped, labelled, stigmatized; how they come to bear the mark of Cain' (Pearson, 1975). Our concern here would be the symbolic distinctions within deviance processing whereby boys and girls might come to be differentially labelled. The initial questions to ask, then, are: i) whether different rules apply to females by which their deviance or conformity comes to be defined; and ii) whether there is differential processing of females by official agencies of social control.

In the field of female criminality, these issues have now been relatively well explored. The criminal law is generally held to be equally applicable to both sexes, yet this can be challenged by a glance at the laws on homosexuality, rape, infanticide and prostitution. The second, more widespread question of differential enforcement for men and women has led several criminologists to assert that the administration of the law treats women more favourably than men (see Pollak, 1961; Mannheim, 1965; Walker, 1973). Under labelling theory, this would at least partially contribute to women's smaller prison population and representation in crime statistics. Campbell (1977) found a much more equal sex balance of actual offences than was indicated by the official statistics, and cites various reasons for the 'unrealistically' low crime figures for women. First, certain crimes or individuals are more likely to appear before a court (she instances football violence rather than girls fighting in a playground); secondly, some typically female offences like shoplifting or receiving stolen goods may not get reported to the police; thirdly, there are differential police practices in apprehension (as applies also with regard to social class and race); and finally there is the discretion used by the police in charging: if the motives are circumstantial and unlikely to be repeated, the offender may just be cautioned. Policemen may perceive women as usually more law-abiding, or entertain chivalrous beliefs about the 'gentle sex'.

However, elsewhere it has been argued that there are anomalies and subtle forms of discrimination which have been overlooked up till now:

The existence of 'chivalry' towards women is synonymous with an inequality of power between the sexes in which a woman must depend on a man for her protection. Women must deserve their protection, however, and women and girls of 'bad' moral character who lose their rights in this respect, leave themselves open to the full force of outraged morality.

(Smart, 1977)

The notion of 'outrage' might receive support from a NACRO report (1977) which showed that female first offenders are up to five times more likely to be sent to prison than male first offenders. Reasons for this might well relate to greater suspicion of female character, as noted in the first section of this chapter on 'pathological' theories of women's behaviour. The feminist campaign against bias towards men in rape trials is a long-standing one, notably its attack on questions being raised by the defence about the woman's character and previous sexual relations, with the inference that she either asked for, or deserved what she received. The same 'moral' concerns may condition how female delinquents are processed, for as a writer on the family court points out:

These labels (immoral, incorrigible) allow for the same abuses that characterize the labels of 'sick' or 'insane' — that is, the 'saving' or 'helping' of a girl often justifies more radical or severe 'treatment' than does the punishment of a male law violator. (Chesney-Lind, 1973)

Home Office Statistics on children in approved schools bear this out: Richardson (1969) revealed that 95 per cent of boys compared to 36 per cent of girls were sent for committing offences — in other words, that nearly two-thirds of the girls were there without having committed any criminal offence. Rather, the justification was as a form of protection or as an opportunity for moral guidance; in practice it would seem that juvenile girls are punished severely for behaviour usually overlooked in boys or in adults. Such 'offences' at present include truancy, keeping late hours, resistance to parental authority, and, from a revealing study by Casburn (1979), 'being beyond control' and 'in moral danger'. She found over half the girls were before the court for non-criminal matters initiated by the Education and Social Services Departments. Only one boy, in contrast, appeared on 'care proceedings' — and he was a six month old baby boy on a 'neglect' clause.

Different processing of the female, whether resulting in lighter or harsher treatment, would thus seem to revolve around perceptions of morality and the 'correct' female role. An interesting example was a profile of women appearing before three urban benches, where they were accused mainly of petty thefts and forgeries featuring family allowance books. (One third were single parents, and thus violated the family norm as well.) Yet 27 per cent of the women were remanded for psychiatric reports, in line with Home Office Circular 59, 1971, recommending social enquiry reports should be made on all juveniles and women defendants. The investigator concludes that magistrates courts commonly regard women as 'quasi-juveniles', not fully responsible for their actions (Pearson, 1976). This would coincide with Becker's reflection that rules are generally made for young people by their elders and for women by men. The ethnic dimension to processing points this up too: one study reported by Casburn found the differential court decisions for boys and girls less marked for their black subjects, and speculates that in a white man's society, black women are expected to be strong — they are viewed as less wedded to the designated female role and hence less in need of protection than their white sisters.

Clearly the issue of social reaction to female deviance is more complex than whether or not women are treated more leniently; by looking at females especially, we begin to see the importance of monitoring the entire process of 'becoming deviant'. Fewer girls and women appear before the courts, at least partially because of discriminatory reactions by official agencies (which explains divergences between crime 'statistics' and self-report studies); but once there, they may suffer harsher treatment because of their actual or potential violation of the 'normal' moral/motherly female role. They would then be affected by the resultant labelling and law enforcement procedures. Reiss (1960) suggests for example (apparently within a 'secondary deviance' model) that the labelling of girls as immoral involves them in a vicious circle of status loss, promiscuity, further status loss, aggravated promiscuity, and so on. We shall have to see whether such ideologies and their effects are confined only to court procedures.

School processes

With regard to schools, labelling perspectives seem particularly appropriate because of the long term 'careers' there and the differentials in power between teachers and pupils to define rules. There is also the school's crucial function as a selection agency, together with the strong links between 'behaviour' and 'ability' which are part of institutional control. Yet until comparatively recently, labelling theory was rarely applied to educational processes. Hargreaves was able to claim in 1975:

'To our knowledge there is no major empirical study which applies labelling theory to the study of deviance in school.' He admits there are contributions that are relevant, and quotes Cicourel and Kitsuse (1963), Werthman (1963), Stebbins (1970) and Kounin (1970). But these, together with Hargreaves' own study, refer only to boys, or do not refer to any differentials in labelling for the sexes.

There are admittedly obvious differences between 'routine' deviance in school and the 'criminal' deviance to which labelling theory has so often been addressed. It is usually clear in the latter what rules the delinquent or criminal has broken, for these are codified and stated during arrest and trial. In a classroom the rule being broken may never be made explicit (with a pause and a warning look sufficing to indicate some infringement). It may vary according to teacher, territory, or time of day, and the rule-breaking episode may be processed in two or three seconds. Nonetheless, in investigating differences in pupil deviance, it would seem vital to establish the criteria for definition of it, and the subsequent reaction. Four main questions emerge:

  i)   whether there are different rules for the sexes which define deviance and normality, either at the official or idiosyncratic level;
  ii)   whether there are instances where the rules are the same but differentially applied;
  iii) whether once a deviant act had been labelled, there would be differential treatment;
  iv)   whether the sex of the pupil makes any difference to acceptance of the label and the probability of secondary deviance.

(i) Different rules

We could begin with a simple example, that of uniform. The likelihood of rule violation would hang, at least partly, on the extent to which the rule for each sex's dress deviated from the current dress modes outside. It might be argued that the masculinity of some school uniforms for girls (collars and ties, bans on jewellery and make-up), would engender a greater probability of rule infringement by girls in order to accord to 'feminine' norms within their culture. King (1973) found the prescription of uniform generally more exacting for girls: shoes, for example, were prescribed or proscribed in about half the cases for boys, but nearly three-quarters for girls. Higher standards of dress were expected from girls, although this was balanced by practices like 'turning a blind eye' to discreet make-up. But it is the *meanings* attached to uniform which will prove most significant: the polarization studies mentioned earlier cite uniform, or hair length, taking on a 'symbolic' value for the boys. The meaning for girls would vary according to its symbolism in terms of implied allegiance to the school, the extent to which it reserved their fashionable clothes for the evenings, the amount of consultation about colours and styles. Thus the interpretation of rule-violation, the motives imputed by rule-enforcers to rule-breakers (and *vice versa*) are of equal significance to the original existence of rules. Labelling theory tends to allude to rule-violation rather than rule-bending, and with uniform again as an example, a whole range of responses is possible. The ingenuity which pupils will adopt to make a uniform conform as far as possible to current fashions means a constant negotiation between teachers and taught about skirt lengths, trouser widths, shoe types, even the shape of knots in ties. Each school would have to be examined individually.

What happens is that we have to slot overt instances of rules such as dress into broader 'ideological' school rules about appropriate pupil gender identity. Mostly the school may be concerned to play down sex differences, rather than draw attention to them, or at least to play down sexuality as such. Mixed schools have been observed to contain the most 'impermeable' of staffrooms:

> This may have been due to the teachers' wish to avoid being seen by their pupils as men and women. Many mixed schools have strong taboos on the public demonstration of even the mildest non-professional relationship between teachers of different sexes ... keeping the staffroom door firmly closed to pupils avoids their accidental witnessing of the banter that characterizes the informal relationships between teachers as men and women. (King, 1973)

Nonetheless, the very taboos will show the importance attached to sexual concerns: male student teachers are warned never to be left alone with a girl pupil. The idea that there are specifically 'girls' problems', dealt with by females, leads to a further institutionalization of dual standards. Both the official and the hidden curriculum can be seen to maintain social divisions, including the sexual division of labour. Different curriculum options and careers guidance for the sexes, different sports and games, various forms of physical separation, different duties, all will give messages about appropriate roles for the sexes. The authority structure of the school, where heads of department or house are male, and deputies female, or where female teachers are in charge of pastoral care and males concerned with curriculum, may replicate a view of men and women having dissimilar capabilities, reinforcing acceptance of females in supportive or caring roles, males in instrumental roles.

The problem for labelling theory would be the translation of these hidden 'message systems' into identifiable rules or even expectations which can be adhered to or violated. Vallance (1974), talking of the reproduction of the social relations of capitalism in the past, remarks: 'The hidden curriculum became hidden only when everyone was satisfied it was working.' The same might apply to sex roles. Yet the reason why the term 'hidden curriculum' has become so accepted is that by definition its mechanisms are so difficult to uncover; cause and effect remain largely at the speculative level, and it is a convenient concept to explain the large part of school life rarely open to quantitative research, but full of conjecture. Although teachers will, if asked, produce stereotyped adjectives to describe pupils, one would need detailed linguistic analysis of the spoken exchange between teachers and pupils to be able to guess whether different labels were actually being applied to designate the 'personal front' displayed by boys and girls. Hammersley (1976) does give an example when he draws attention to sex labels in deviance 'imputations': just as teachers will use age-comparisons to communicate expectations (you're behaving like five year olds), they may also juxtapose sex and intelligence. The teacher's rebuke was: 'Now, WILL YOU STOP BEING SO SILLY. The next boy who laughs in that stupid manner like a little girl I shall drop on quickly.' As Hammersley says: 'Silliness, stupidity, childishness and girlishness are all used to characterize the same piece of behaviour. They seem to be used as synonyms, reinforcing the imputed behaviour.' Yet there is still no way of gauging the long-term effects of such aspersions: conveying messages about behaviour is not synonymous with applying personal labels and making them stick.

One possible line of enquiry would be via the question of moral rules. Following the research indicating the 'sexualization' of girls' offences, and the double standards of morality attached to adolescent behaviour, it might be surmised that teachers apply different labels regarding virtue to the sexes. Goffman's concept of 'moral career' is a doubly significant one here; in *Asylums* he describes how an institution offers individuals the framework for the working out of character or reputation, of a particular 'presentation of self'. Most institutions offer an official life trajectory, in terms of which honour can be acquired and reputation gained. The 'career' of the deviant, on the other hand, would be accompanied by a process of 'stigmatization', by which the deviant is discredited, derogated, humiliated, degraded, insulted, mocked, paraded, rejected (Goffman, 1968). The question here is whether such 'spoiled identity' is linked to different moral rules for the sexes. One newspaper report was of girls 'marching' down to the local education office protesting that their headteacher had said their clothes made them look like tarts (*The Guardian*, 5 February, 1976). The fusion of school rule-breaking with sexual rule-breaking may be peculiar to females. Shacklady-Smith (1978) quotes a girl:

> Sometimes at school, like you get mad and go and smash something up. Like this one day, I grabbed hold of this thing and smashed it through the toilet window. Well, I did do wrong, but you should have heard our headmistress. She said I was a common looking slut, and the most vulgar and common girl she had known.

However, this study indicated that the continual reference to the girls as sluts and common prostitutes did not have the cumulative labelling effect that Reiss surmised; most of the girls tended to react with, if anything, aggressive rather than promiscuous behaviour:

> There seemed to be a particular resistance on the part of the girls to seeing themselves as promiscuous, a form of behaviour strongly condemned by most of the girls in the study. What they did develop were self-conceptions as tough, dominant and boyish.   (Shacklady-Smith, 1978)

Matza (1964) has suggested that the attribution of delinquent defini-tions to males leads to exaggerated patterns of masculine behaviour; in the case of girls, it may lead to reactive unfeminine conduct, it seems. The context within which the labelling occurs would be crucial here, in that the actual sexual status of girls is much more a product of out-of-school life (if boyfriends come from outside), and is clearly bound up with the relevant transactions. It is not in fact likely, or even possible, that in the school context sexual labelling will create 'prob-lems' for the girls, to be solved by the response of more sexual 'deviance'. They are more likely to reciprocate the perceived insult in a school-based way, confirming the inappropriateness of the label. But it is interesting that in the quotation given, the sexual imputation seemed to the girl to be far worse than any more suitable accusation could have been. The label causes problems, not so much in any exclusion, or confirmation of behaviour, but as a 'threat' to identity, or to the 'construct system', in Kelly's terms. At the top of many girls' construct systems would presumably be some notion of decent/slut or moral/immoral, a more salient construct than violent/non-violent or responsible/irresponsible. Hence the 'exaggerated' reaction when this construct is threatened in school: the very act of 'taking offence' demonstrates the existence of one's own highly moral code.

Another linked area would be 'rules' about relationships in school, whether with teachers or fellow pupils. There is little empirical work on this with regard to gender, although Wolpe noted how different relationships were permitted and fostered for girls in a mixed school, with female pupils being 'coquettish' towards young male teachers, and encouraged in this behaviour: 'Mr B selected one of the prettiest girls in the class (and also one of the cleverest) for this chore and advised her to go to Mr A, charm him, use a lovely voice, say "thank you Sir" and smile at him when you ask for the books' (Wolpe, 1977). Wolpe calls this 'coaching' the girls, assuring them that these ploys are essential to achieving ends. Similar differences might be expected in teacher rules about interactions between pupils — fighting, bullying, insulting or teasing, whether inter- or intra-sex. Although finding no such explicit models, King (1973) did note control of pupil sexual liaison to be an issue here. Holding hands was approved only between girls. Apart from the possibility of sexual misbehaviour, the fear also seemed to be that such affectively based relationships might distract the partners from the educational process, and if they occupied different age or ability statuses the whole basis of the distribution of honorific status was seen as threatened. In particular, King alleged, the effectiveness of the prefectorial system was thought to be jeopardised by a friendship between a boy prefect and a younger girl.

The complicated issue in schools, then, is not so much the existence of overtly different rules for the sexes leading to marked differences in likelihoods of breaking them, but that the hidden curriculum of school or even of individual classroom may convey messages about appropriate pupil identity by which deviance and normality may be occasionally defined. Yet a note of caution must be expressed about the impact of the hidden curriculum. There have been, for example, some attacks on the Rosenthal and Jacobsen (1968) 'Pygmalion' thesis, and many parallel studies which failed to find a teacher expectancy effect (reported in Rist, 1977). Other studies gave some clues that learners could resist expectation effects or be stimulated into 'confounding' behaviour to prove the teacher wrong (Nash, 1976).

One must be careful not to confuse 'rules' by which deviance is defined and 'expectations' which may or may not be self-fulfilling, or affect the situation at all. As Rist points out:

> What the labelling perspective can provide to the study of educational outcomes as a result of the operationalization of teacher expectations is a model of the study of the *processes* by which the outcomes are produced. The detailing over time of the interactional patterns which lead to changes in self-definition and behaviour within classrooms is sadly lacking in almost all of the expectation research to date. A most glaring example of this omission is the study of Rosenthal and Jacobsen themselves.

For the Pygmalion people indeed have to admit: 'We do not know how a teacher's expectation for a pupil's intellectual growth is communicated to the pupil' (Rosenthal and Jacobsen, 1968). In fact we are now beginning to identify the cues by which pupils can interpret teachers' values and orientations, for example by differences in giving tasks and turns, or by non-verbal communication; but there is still a long way to go in equating, say, different achievement expectations for the sexes with actual discrepancies. We must also take care not to insist on 'sexist practices' as having particular effects: it is the *interpretation* put on these which is paramount. Girls may have to line up separately from boys, but we must establish the attributed meaning, if any, of this before saying with any confidence that processes of 'sex-typing' are occurring.

Above all one would have to query the significance placed on rule-breaking by the teacher. This might vary with the age of the pupil so that 'tomboyish' or 'cissy' behaviour would be tolerated with younger children, but less so with approaching adulthood. Meanings would also vary with individual teachers: in his study of pupil and staff perceptions of school work, Woods (1978) quotes a teacher:

> They're good lads, you know, they're earthy, they're not villains. They're not angels either, you know, they'll break the rules, but they're OK. The girls on the other hand are a bit wishy washy. There's not one character amongst them. Basically they're idle. They'll probably end up with jobs in Woolworths.

The girls had complained how this teacher favoured the boys, and did not care about them. Thus, though the boys may in fact receive more interaction and even more deviance imputations, the girls will have to develop strategies to cope with being ignored, or with infringing the teacher's implicit rule about being a 'character'. Their deviance may take the form of being 'idle', a very different kind of rule-breaking. King was commenting on the lower standard of expectation for behaviour from boys, particularly when young, not so able, or working class, and the parallel or perhaps different standard of behaviour expected for girls, and made the interesting observation:

> The judgments of good behaviour seem to be based less on the breaking of rules and more on the girls' demeanour even when actually observing them. Thus the only girls' school to cane its pupils did so only for cases of deliberate disobedience or repeated rudeness or insolence. Our observations suggest that the look on a girl's face and the way she stands can be interpreted as insolence in some girls' schools.

Here we do have an example of how an expectation can become enshrined in school practice. It is possible that the 'image' of femininity is so undifferentiated in a school's ideology that, as in the courts, infringement of one aspect has implications for the total personality, actual or potential; the girl who breaks school rules will, especially if she is 'attractive', be likely to infringe the most sacred of a patriarchal society's prescriptions — appropriate subdued feminine identity.

A final complexity would be the question of who actually 'makes' the rules. Given the major concerns both of the teacher's 'coping strategies' and of the school's achievement goals, we would expect to find a bank of rules common to any institution. To explain boys' greater violation of these, one might ask the conflict theorist's question — in whose interest do such rules operate? Anatole France drily observed that the law in all its majesty equally forbade the rich as well as the poor to beg in the streets, to sleep under bridges, to steal bread. It is possible that 'neutral' school rules of obedience, passivity or deference suit girls far better on the whole (although they might be more deviant on an Outward Bound course). Thus the girls themselves would be responsible for the 'secondary' rule that females are expected to behave better. This leads to another explanation for 'extremes' of conduct. The higher expectation would normally condition girls to adhere to the rules, but the girl who did not would have doubly offended. She would have broken the common pupil conduct rule, but in addition the girls-are-better presupposition. In short, 'double standards' may well apply in school, but they are not the sole creation of the teacher.

(ii)   Differences in rule application

This second question, of whether similar rules might be differentially applied, has already been hinted at above. Here the relevant issue would be the greater number of sanctions loaded onto boys (as outlined in chapter 6). According to labelling theory, this would imply a greater likelihood of a deviant label being successfully applied:

> Even if high criticism rates for these boys were due entirely to a higher rate of misbehaviour on their part, teachers were using ineffective control strategies to deal with them. Instead of working to eliminate misbehaviour through rewarding appropriate behaviour, and other more effective behaviour-modification techniques, teachers had apparently drifted into a pattern of criticizing but tolerating misbehaviour from the boys. This very problem reinforces negative expectations and increases alienation, while at the same time leaving the rate of misbehaviour unchanged.   (Brophy and Good, 1974)

There is apparently a strong correlation between children's perceptions of themselves and their perceptions of teachers' view of them. As girls in primary schools perceived teachers' feelings towards them to be more favourable than did boys, so their behaviour ratings were more favourable. They lived in a 'climate of approval' for far longer (Davidson and Lang, 1960). Most observers of the acceptance of feminine characteristics in early classrooms are concerned about the effects on later achievement. Thus Bruner writes:

> Observant anthropologists have suggested that the basic values of the early grades are a socialized version of the feminine sex role in society, cautious rather than daring, governed by a lady-like politeness ... girls in the early grades who learn to control their fidgeting earlier are rewarded for excelling in their feminine values. The rewards can be almost too successful in that in later years it is difficult to move girls beyond the orderly values they learned in their first school encounters. The boys, more fidgety in the first grades, get no such reward, and as a consequence may be freer in their approach to learning in the later grades.   (Bruner, 1966)

Silbermann, similarly, sees the young girls 'programmed' into a dependency on rewards and more likely to avoid the possibility of failure and loss of teacher approval. This will mean potential avoidance of academic growth and stimulation: 'The naive young bargainer of 7/8 has made an exchange which will cost her dearly' (Silbermann, 1971).

The notion of a Faustian contract is an interesting one in terms of pupil achievement; it has even more implications for deviance. The conversion from primary to secondary deviance might well be helped by the teacher's reaction, for the behaviour modification theorists suggest that loud reprimands available to the whole class maintain disruptive behaviour, while soft reprimands directed at the individual offender effectively decrease disruption (O'Leary et al, 1970). The larger proportion of loud critical comments towards boys would tend to maintain their disapproved behaviour; it seems inherently less likely that the greater passivity of girls, getting less of the teacher's attention, would disappear as a result of being ignored or discouraged. 'It is possible that much of the "trouble" teaches at least some of the boys that they can create some interesting effects in the classroom by being independent of the teacher' (Sears and Feldman, 1966). Yet Fuller observed that girls, when seeking the teacher's attention, were more noisy and persistent, while boys were more inclined to make one effort, which if ignored, they did not actively pursue. Typically, girls would call loudly from their seats (not always raising their hand first). If this did not work, it was not uncommon to leave their desk, take their query to the teacher and follow him or her about if necessary:

> From the girls' point of view, it was necessary to actively pursue a teacher for his/her attention, and thus their behaviour can be seen as an attempt to gain a measure of control in one aspect of their classroom lives in which they believed they would otherwise be more poorly treated than the boys.
>
> (Fuller, 1979)

Similarly, a study by Brophy and Good (1974) found boys receiving more attention, but girls exceeding boys in tendencies to seek out teachers and create interactions with them. The authors raise the question of whether teachers are compensating for this in their interactions with boys, or whether girls are feeling neglected. Fuller would imply the latter. So within this aspect of differential application of rules, we have an interesting refinement of labelling theory. For boys the deviance amplification would be a straightforward process; for girls it might be primary *conformity* which creates problems leading on to secondary deviance. Their responses to expectations that girls need less attention would contribute to collective female labels of 'fusspots' or 'whiners', a qualitatively different type of deviance, of the 'emotional' type noted earlier.

(iii)   Differences in processing

What do teachers then *do* with deviants, once defined and drawn attention to? My original study had recorded girls perceiving teachers as being 'stricter' or 'harsher' in their punishments with the boys (although again giving them more attention in general). A key issue in this case would seem to be that of corporal punishment. A more recent pilot study I conducted on 101 sixth formers in a Midlands comprehensive found that although two-thirds thought the sexes caused the same amount of trouble in school, 78 per cent thought that if a boy and a girl committed the same offence, the girl would be let off more lightly. Thus less than a quarter thought they would be treated the same; and no pupil thought the boy would be treated more leniently. Here there were no sex differences in *perceptions* of treatment, although a Scottish survey of 1000 pupils had the puzzling finding that only 15 per cent of boys compared with 45 per cent of girls thought the sexes were treated alike for punishment. Did the boys have an unjustified chip on their shoulders about being picked on? Or were the girls, *because* they were less subject to punishment, also less aware of its finer discriminatory practices? Overall, in fact, the prevalent impression was that girls *were* treated more leniently, and either not strapped or strapped less severely. Forty-three per cent of the girls compared with a mere 16 per cent of the boys said they had not been strapped at primary school (Educational Institute of Scotland, 1977). King had found only one boys' school that did not cane, and only one girls' school that did so (although with some authorities abandoning institutionalized violence, and with the advances of the STOPP campaign, this picture is subject to change).

While not commenting on differences in official corporal punishment, Rutter (1979) reports that rates of unofficial physical punishment were low 'especially in girls' and mixed schools', and 'it is clear that in schools where they are at all frequent, pupil behaviour was correspondingly worse'. Reynolds (1976) also demonstrated that high rates of corporal punishment were associated with worse pupil behaviour and wider delinquency for the boys — and he kept other variables constant, so the high rates could not be excused because the pupils were originally 'worse'. Such over-reaction may partially explain why school is associated with delinquency for boys but not for girls. 'Where the initiation of the child into the accepted ways of the adult community is perverse', says Reynolds, 'then so too will be the child's response.' Girls would be less subject to 'perverse' treatment or brutality, less prone to any weakening of the 'moral bind' tying the child to conventional adult life and institutions. Once more we see the linkages between labelling and control theory, and also with wider ideologies about sex roles.

(iv) Differences in label acceptance

It remains to look at the fourth question, of the sex of the pupil influencing the internalization of a deviant identity. Hargreaves (1976) identifies four factors conditioning a pupil's acceptance of a label and the likelihood of a deviant career: the frequency of the labelling; the extent to which the pupil sees the teacher as a significant other whose opinion counts; the extent to which others support the label; and the public nature of the labelling. What happens if we look at each of these in terms of sex difference? With regard to frequency, the studies showing more negative exchanges with boys have already been ear-marked. The relationship with the teacher would be an issue relating to the second factor: if the girls *are* more accepting of authority, as the socialization literature suggests, then they would be more likely to see teachers as significant others, and make a positive reaction of some sort to imputations of deviance. This would either entail avoidance of further imputations and thus of labels, or more strenuous attempts at neutralization and, according to the theory, *further* acts of deviance:

> To stop engaging in a delinquent behaviour constitutes his agreement that he has indeed behaved badly, and by implica-tion, that he is bad; he withholds his agreement and rejects this judgement by offending again.   (Gold, 1970)

There is some evidence that girls do have a greater tendency towards internalization. A study of pupils' satisfaction with their school experi-ence showed dissatisfied boys more frequently than dissatisfied girls used 'extrapunitive' adjectives — words that placed the blame for their condition on others (for example 'misunderstood', 'rejected'). The girls, in contrast, employed more 'intropunitive' adjectives, blaming themselves ('inadequate', 'ignorant') (Jackson and Getzels, 1959). Six to nine-year old girls in one investigation showed little self-confidence and expected to fail in situations where boys expected to succeed. They also took the blame for failures while boys tended to project blame onto something else (Crandall et al, 1962). With an interest in responses to stress, Miller (1966) asked adolescents to complete the sentence 'When I'm in trouble. . . .' He found girls were less likely to seek help from family or other adults (or God), and more likely to take individual responsibility. So this possibility of greater internalization of blame may be yet another clue to the 'extremes' in girls' behaviour. The socialized 'normal' reaction to definitions of deviance would be an avoidance response, a return to conformity; but if the label is viewed as a double rejection of the behaviour and of the girl's personal front, then problems are caused in terms of a consistent self-image, problems solved only by actions confirming the judgment of the significant other.

The support for the label by others, thirdly, would invite connections with the question of morality.

> Where criminal labels are applied to females they are so pervasive that they are more or less bound to force girls into more extreme forms of delinquency. For though a more protective attitude appears to be taken by probation officers, social workers and others, the paradox of their protection is that it leads to more severe labelling of their behaviour as being 'common' or 'sluttish'. Thus, long before they had reached the courts, all the girls interviewed had experienced a continual defining process which classified them as unfeminine.
>
> (Shacklady-Smith, 1978)

Twin issues are conspicuous in this account. One is whether peers as well as teachers support a deviant label, whether (because of the moral implications) there might be ostracism, the rejection by other girls fearful of their own reputation by association, even in school. The other is the nature of the processing of deviance by the school, whether the girl is referred through some pastoral care system (rather than being caned) which makes her subject to a 'continual defining process'. The sex balance of the school could be decisive: if male and female teachers have different interpretations of deviant acts, or pupils exhibit different conduct according to whether teachers are male or female, then this will have implications for the amount of consensus in the staffroom about which pupils are 'trouble-makers'. Here it is individual schools which would create different possibilities for labelling.

Finally, the public nature of the treatment accorded to deviants may vary between the sexes. The louder reprimands directed at boys would obviously make their deviance more public; 'degradation ceremonies' may also be more common for boys, or in boys' schools, given the greater acceptance of corporal punishment for boys. But this is a tentative suggestion, to be tested empirically. One might want to explore Erikson's argument that a society will strive to maintain a certain level of deviance within itself, as deviance is functional to clarifying group boundaries, providing scapegoats, creating out-groups who can be the source of furthering in-group solidarity. Each school might have a different penchant for scapegoats, *'pour encourager les autres'*, and the likelihood that in a mixed school these would be males can only be surmised.

Discussion

After such a wealth of conjecture, the possibilities raised by the labelling perspective should be summarized. We have seen that where different types or levels of rules apply for the sexes (that is, double standards), then clearly different definitions of rule-breaking and therefore who-are-the-deviants will ensue. Pupils with different gender socialization may, however, contribute to expectations and even 'rules' about behaviour. Different punishments for the *same* behaviour will affect pupil attitudes in terms both of the immediate applicability and threat to the person, and of a general comparison with the opposite sex's likely treatment. The probability of acceptance of a deviant label or identity is then related to previous sex role learning, neutralization techniques, avoidance strategies, negotiative or bargaining power, or, returning to sub-cultures, the desire actively to seek out a deviant label as a status symbol. Girls' greater conformity would in this way be simply explained by less frequent deviant labelling, and/or (unlike juvenile courts) more lenient treatment once labelled. The 'careers' of girls who appear to live up to deviant labels, or have internalized them, would have to be examined in terms of the type of label applied and the problems caused by it, especially with regard to the 'moral career' of the deviant girl. 'Extremes' of behaviour would result from this stronger reaction to a deviant label; or from teachers being reluctant to apply deviant labels until serious rule infringements had been noted because of their normative expectations for female behaviour (only the really bad troublemakers being processed anyway); or from percep-tions of the 'normal' female making girls' deviance *seem* more extreme, linked to the double violation of good pupil rules and sex role rules.

A final critical view of the approach is to be expected. There have been many critiques of the labelling perspective (it is not strictly a theory), starting with the 'vacuous tautology' (Plummer, 1979) of the definition 'deviance is behaviour that people so label'. It has sustained attacks on the grounds of relativism, bias towards the underdog, on its smuggling in taken-for-granted categories of deviance by the very subjects chosen for investigation. A major 'gap' could be that it ignores the sources of deviant action; but the criticism is unfair insofar as the perspective does not set out to probe causes, and no labelling theorist would hold that deviance is created by social reaction alone. But theirs is the emphasis that people do not become deviant overnight, and the concentration is on the series of 'shiftings' and 'negotiations' by which people gradually build up a deviant identity. Labelling's main credibility problems would seem to lie in its 'hard' or misinterpreted version — that deviant labels are applied independently of personality or behaviour, and invariably have negative consequences. Instead one can acknowledge the usefulness of the concentration on deviance processing rather than end-product, while recognizing that both boys and girls may contribute to their own labelling; that labelling, especially for girls, may have deterrent or 'positive' consequences; and that 'destigmatization' is possible, particularly in school, where 'settling down' or 'maturity' are recognized happenings.

Interactionist and labelling perspectives imply particular methodologies and tend to be linked with micro level research. Hence the accusation that they ignore structural limits of inequality in the power to apply labels, to negotiate identities, to win character contests. The sociology of 'nuts, sluts and perverts' has been at the expense of looking at covert 'violence' from society and institutions. The interactionist will of course acknowledge that action does take place in a wider social order, referred to by such notions as 'constraints' or even 'sex role ideologies'. Nonetheless the interactionist studies of labelling in schools (for example, Cicourel and Kitsuse, Hargreaves) have yet to develop a deeper analysis of the institutional obligations on teachers which pressure them into applying labels, and of the broad social goals and structures which underpin their classroom typifications. While admittedly the labelling theorist's task is not to uncover such relationships, the problem of over-optimism remains — the implication that more sympathetic, aware, deviance-insulative teachers are the best remedy for pupil deviancy. But can teachers *avoid* labelling pupils, and labelling them in particularized ways? The last section must turn to the structural base both to deviance and to teachers' labelling of it.

The Bad State of Society: Structural Analyses

'I think there's been all this blah about equality and so on, and I think perhaps they've aped what they've seen on TV, Charlie's Angels and all that; I think it's just the influence of the world around them', said one (male) teacher in attempting to explain increases in girls' deviance. Social change, new permissiveness and all-pervasive television are perennials in finding scapegoats for apparent outbreaks of non-conformity; the problem for the sociologist is accounting for social change and deciding in whose interests, or to whose detriment such change operates. We need to trace the previous approaches yet one stage further back to pinpoint *why* socialization cycles perpetuate, *how* inequality leading to 'strain' is permitted to continue, and *what* social function gender ideologies and labels have. We need in effect to locate the structural reasons for our definitions of normality before we can surmise how and why deviation occurs. Two accounts can profitably be contrasted here: the functionalist and the Marxist. (I have the temerity to deal with these most complex analyses very simply and briefly, but fuller accounts can be found in any sociology textbook.)

Basically the functionalist sees 'society' as comparable to a biological organism, with a series of interlocking and interdependent parts which 'contribute' to the whole. A division of labour and of roles helps an advanced society to run more efficiently; inequality between people and groups is not only inevitable but 'functional', as greater contributions to society need to be rewarded more highly in order to maintain the motivation and incentives which keep the system operating. Deviance under this model has been variously analyzed: on the one hand, deviants are seen as sand in an otherwise smoothly running machine, their incidence a phenomenon arising from faulty socialization or from the structured inequalities becoming at certain stages too polarized and intolerable, and hence *dys*functional; on the other hand there is the notion, already cited in the section on labelling, that a certain level of deviance is in fact necessary for a harmonious society in order to clarify, reiterate and remind the majority of what is 'good' and 'normal'. Punishments and definitions of 'crime' are there not only to avenge and protect, but to act as a moral example.

A Marxist analysis would dispute the argument that 'society' is organized and structured for the benefit of the majority, and argue that it operates primarily in the interests of a ruling class. In the struggle for scarce resources, certain groups manage to appropriate not only a greater proportion of *material* wealth, but also come to hold *ideological* supremacy over the rest of society. Their unequal and privileged position is maintained not necessarily by physical force (although this can happen temporarily) and not even only by economic power, but by being able to command the transmission of knowledge, ideas and justifications for the nature of 'society'. Groups suffer from the 'false consciousness' of not being aware of the true reason for their subordinate position and of the potential for changing that position. Deviance again has been seen to have a variety of 'causes' under this model: it is an inevitable, albeit blind reaction to the inequities of the social order; or it is a breakthrough in false consciousness, and hence a form of political resistance. Its distribution stems from the fact that the so-called 'neutral' laws and definitions of 'crime' operate primarily in the interests of the property-owning classes, who make, for example, any attempt to redistribute that property 'illegal' and hence punishable.

But our task is to explain sex differences in deviance, not just economic and social class disparities. For this we must look specifically at the above perspectives' contrasting analyses of the functions of the family. Both would look to historical and industrial developments, in particular to the implications for the family of the separation of work and home, in unravelling our current traditions; but they would diverge in their claims over whose interests were served by a sharper differentiation in roles. For the functionalists (as represented by writers such as Talcott Parsons) a stable family was beneficial to all; it was manifestly impossible for women to be involved equally in the occupational system unless other arrangements were made for taking care of children and managing households. Parsons suggested that the tendency towards differentiated sex roles helped to forestall a possible source of competition and conflict within the family; that middle-class women who worked tended to have jobs with less prestige than their husbands and were hence not competing; the greater instability of lower class marriages (as indicated by a higher divorce rate) might be due in part to the fact that, when lower class women work, their jobs are more nearly equal in prestige to their husbands. He would thus see a particular (and asymmetrical) type of differentiation as directly functional to the smooth running of the family and to social integration. The key concepts are always 'instrumentality' and 'expressiveness': instrumentality encompasses task-orientation, a pragmatic concern with the outside world, and a responsibility for, or vested interest in change and improvement. Expressiveness on the other hand is the concern with the internal affairs of the group, and the responsibility for maintaining equilibrium in within-group interaction (Parsons and Bales, 1955). The father's role is seen as being high on instrumentality and low on expressiveness, the mother's the reverse. The father looks outward to the world of work, the mother inward to relationships and stability within the family. Through socialization, individuals will 'internalize' such a central value system, which becomes a component of personality. Deviance would arise from 'inefficient' socialization or internalization, or would be a dysfunctional consequence of particular role-learning, as for example male aggression resulting from instrumentality. Women's greater conformity would be linked to her essentially conservative 'equilibrating' function in the family.

The Marxists, in particular the feminist-Marxists, would see such internalization of roles as acting not in the interests of social integration but in the interests of the capitalist class. Their analysis would stress the crucial economic and ideological functions of the family for capitalism, in which the woman is the prime mover.

> The family must raise children who have internalized hierarchical social relations, who will discipline themselves and work efficiently without constant supervision ... women are responsible for implementing most of this socialization.
>
> (Morton, 1971)

Not only is the economic job of the family the provision of a certain type of non-questioning but productive labour force, but also it is to act as a consumption unit. The home is the place to enjoy individual private property; the workers will labour socially in the production of the private property of a few capitalists in the hope of individual private property for themselves and their families; and the demand for private goods (nowadays freezers and videos) for each nuclear unit, rather than for shared resources, will further support the expansionary capitalist enterprise. Thus Engels traced the origin of the oppression of women to the demands for individual property: women had to be 'owned' and faithful to marriage to produce an heir for this private property. The feminist analysis takes this further, by pointing to the contradictions inherent in capitalism since industrialization, where the work-place is physically separate from the home, where the man is not working directly *for* his family, where there is an ideology of individualism. 'The woman's task is to hold on to the unity of the family while its separate atoms explode in different directions', claims Mitchell (1971). The family acts as a place of retreat, of sexuality, a haven where the woman must provide free services. Women are socialized to perform 'love labour', to work not for monetary reward, but for love for and duty to others. The 'expressiveness' of the functionalists has in fact an *economic* base: children, too, are 'property', 'love' is blackmail, 'care becomes an investment' (Rowbotham, 1973). Thus the family is of vital importance to capitalism; the woman is of vital importance to the maintenance of the family; and a Marxist analysis would also stress the salience of the conservative mother-daughter-mother cycle, and the conformist and reactionary values that are transmitted.

Is a deviant girl, then, one who has deliberately resisted this 'false consciousness'? Or one for whom the breakdown in mother-daughter bonding has prevented the reproduction of commitments to the ideology and institutions of capitalism? Further complications are the contradictions inherent in contemporary capitalism, and the functions of the school in socializing for both home and work. We noted earlier how the school acts to reproduce the sexual division of labour through both the official curriculum and through the ideologies, practices and expectations of the hidden curriculum. Although pupils pass through different types of schooling and different classroom and teaching experiences, Marxist analysis insists that the reproduction of class and gender distinctions is a fundamental and continuous process. The pupils will learn not only different male and female roles, but ideologies of the family and domesticity essential to patriarchal capitalism. Women also constitute an essential sector of the (albeit at present declining) labour market, and schools must provide socializing experiences for that too, often within a meritocratic ideology. The most useful formulation of this complicated process is one which takes not a totally deterministic view, but argues that while schools and education can be seen as part of the reproductive process, they do not in any way perform a simple function for capital. Thus Meyenn and Miller state their position:

> Historically, the separation of home from work is a creation of capitalist economic and social organization.... It has been women's unpaid labour at home that has secured the reproduction of labour power, while men's and some women's underpaid labour has been the source of capital accumulation and family income. Schools can be seen at least in part as designed to modify the culture of the home to meet the requirements of capital.

They argue that school has two faces, looking to the institutions of family and work. It encompasses the authority of the family, acting '*in loco parentis*', taking over the familial duties of care, nurture, development; but it also looks towards the world of work, the relations within the workplace and between the various hierachies of workers. So:

> There may be a space where the child between family and work, with her peers has a limited amount of room to negotiate

her image of herself, her peers and even parents, and to develop specific orientations to work and family.

(Meyenn and Miller, 1979)

And it is this 'space' which we shall need to examine in considering resistant pupils.

A further contradiction in a capitalist 'democracy' is maintaining competitive market incentives side by side with a welfare ideology which should in no way discriminate. This, for Bricker (1979) is reflected in the education profession's competing principles of meritocracy and egalitarianism, and it is this which forms the structural dilemma underlying teachers' need to label and make imputations of deviance. Teachers must balance ideologies of impartiality, of equal distribution of time and attention with the need to provoke individual achievement (a need which involves comparison and the motivating of children in divergent ways). So they have to tackle the question of how long they are obliged to evoke conformity in a pupil no matter how varied and persistent his deviance has been. If we translate such a problem into the gender dimension, the dilemma for teachers in mixed schools might be the ideology of equal education for boys and girls in the face of overt discrimination in jobs and higher education for which schooling is supposedly a preparation. Boys may receive more negative sanctions in the classroom because teachers feel a longer or stronger obligation to promote conformity because of future careers. What appears as unfair discrimination towards boys in terms of more deviance imputations is in fact a reflection of the differential responsibility felt by teachers with regard to pupil achievement. As I had hypothesized earlier, it is not that girls' deviance is less; it is that it is ignored.

Marxist analyses seem to imply that reproductive processes are unique to capitalism, but the universal, if culturally related nature of social control is demonstrated in Bronfenbrenner's engaging comparative study *Two Worlds of Childhood* (1973). He found Soviet children much less willing to take part in antisocial behaviour than children in three western countries (America, Britain and West Germany). They also believed children should first take personal initiative in correcting the behaviour of their friends and classmates, then invoke the help of other children, then tell an adult. West European children would tell adults, then look the other way, then invoke help. Soviet youngsters placed stronger emphasis than other groups on overt propriety, such as being clean, orderly and well-mannered, but gave less weight than others to telling the truth and seeking intellectual understanding: 'From a cross-cultural perspective, Soviet children, in the process of growing up, are confronted with fewer divergent views both within and outside the family, conform more completely to a more homogenous set of standards.' Yet even though Soviet children in general supported behaviour consistent with adult behaviour, and took personal initiative, it was the girls who showed both the highest level of commitment to adult standards, and least individual variation within the classroom. 'It is Soviet girls in particular who support the society's values and — both as individuals and in the collectives — exert pressures on other to conform to good behaviour' (Bronfenbrenner, 1973).

It would seem that even within 'socialist' societies, females are vanguards of conformity, even though the lack of the contradictions posed by the individualism of private enterprise capitalism means the possibility of all children conforming more to a 'homogenous set of standards'. I would want to examine the particular function of the female in the reproduction and maintenance of socialist societies, and ask whether her greater conformity was merely 'culture lag', a throwback to bourgeois imperialism, or whether she had a particular ideological role in socialist families as well. What might be more crucial to sex role socialization would not be so much whether the economic system was private capitalism, state capitalism or socialism, but the degree to which it was patriarchal. The extent of relegation of women to the domestic or private sphere may influence not only definitions and processing of deviance, but personal acceptance of these. In the private sector (characterized by low public visibility and low mobility), norms, conflict and control are personalized. An argument from feminist criminologists is thus: 'Judicial ideology mystifies women's social reality and thereby reinforces and legitimizes the hidden oppressive character of their lives. The legal rule of the protection of private life is a prime example of such an instrument.' The lack of support for battered wives is cited as a case in point:

> The indifference of the legal system to women's need for protection is partly a result of scepticism regarding the 'worthiness' of the victim. However, women themselves will also often prefer not to press charges against their husbands and bring 'internal' conflicts to court. This attitude should be viewed as a reflection of both the victim's bondage to the

economic basis of her life-support and of the social indoctrina-
tion which transforms the beatings into a personal failure.

(Dahl and Snare, 1978)

And here we return to the questions of 'internalization of blame' and
power to define the law that were raised in the discussion of labelling
theory.

But for whatever purpose, functionalists and Marxists would agree
on the importance of socialization and social control for preserving the
system, a system which would necessitate quite sharply differing sex
roles and ways of seeing self and the world. The two key questions that
have emerged (which, phrased baldly, sound like a magazine competition) are first whether the 'system' serves primarily: everyone; the
ruling class; or men, and secondly whether those young people who do
deviate from school and family norms are: threatening social integration and complementary family roles; actively and rightly challenging
the economic and legal order; or merely confirming in the end their
own subordinate position through failure to 'achieve'.

Answers on a postcard will unfortunately receive no definitive
accolade, as inevitably no approach is without its problems. Within a
theory of complementary roles, functionalists have the difficulty of
handling conflict, except in terms of individual or social pathology, or
in terms of dysfunctions at one level of the system being functional at
another (we need three million unemployed ...). Given the assumption of a high level of moral consensus, or a common value system,
there is the elevation of the 'function' of individuals or groups to the
rank of a moral imperative. Women not fulfilling their maternal or
expressive role (working mothers for example) may cause 'maternal
deprivation' (à la Bowlby) and can be blamed for any subsequent
problems with their offspring. Women are therefore encouraged to stay
at home to consolidate the attachments; socialization theories can
themselves intervene and be a causal factor in the very cycles they are
trying to explain. Deviance has to be seen as individual or family
breakdown rather than structurally produced conflict; thus the 're-
medies' are justified in terms of 'the needs of society' or 'the needs of
the individual', under the assumption that these are synonymous. Just
as 'compensatory education' sought to balance out 'deficits' in home
background and social environment, so the 'treatment' of delinquents
will involve institutionalization, the removal of a child from 'adverse'
home influences; or it will engage in the more subtle, but sometimes
more pernicious methods of therapy and behaviour modification.

While such personalized treatments can be remarkably 'successful', they do nothing to question the system which generated the 'deviation', and indeed, their very success only serves to bolster the idea that breakdowns in social order are individualized and remediable. It is the same dilemma that faces more 'radical' social workers who are aware that their intervention and localized problem-solving will in the end merely prop up a shaky and unjust system.

For Marxists, of course, socialization into acceptance of the (capitalist) social order is not a goal functional for the majority, but is seen as itself a process of distortion and alienation. In the course of producing personalities required for capitalist production and consumption, human potential is underdeveloped; and even deviance from the social mores of consumer capitalism is not necessarily a true realization of oppression, but rather an affirmation of the goals — merely using different means to them (as in burglary or tax evasion). Willis claims that his lads' culture did exhibit 'partial penetrations' of the economic system — that is, they had some idea of why they were to constitute a subordinate class. But in Marxist terminology the use of the terms 'consciousness' and 'unconsciousness' allows the contradictions of capitalism to be seen as 'logged into the very structure of the personality' (Gomm, 1978), and suggests that revolution or change will depend on the practice known as 'consciousness raising'.

Dealing with deviance within a Marxist framework has itself led to conflict. Marx and Engels are noted for their disdain of the *lumpenproletariat*, its promotion of class interests, its openness to bribes. Criminal careers, although the products of capitalism, were not seen as political rebellion, but reaction and accommodation to the political order. Newer Marxist criminological approaches have had both to wrestle with a macro-sociological analysis that can uncover the structural links between the law, its creation and application, the state and the material base of society; and also to come to terms with the interpretive avenue which wants to 'appreciate' the meanings by which people organize their experience. A Marxist analysis of female deviance has also to include women's consciousness within the model. Thus:

> This proposed shift from an etiological concern with female offenders to a model analyzing the relationship between women's current socio-legal status and the repressive state apparatus needs a continuing appraisal and requires the integration of a feminist paradigm with a class analysis.
>
> (Dahl and Snare, 1978)

The book of readings by Smart and Smart (1978) examines aspects of female deviance within a social control model, with social control including the whole range of primary and secondary socialization and the more formal processes of institutional intervention through state legislation, the implementation of the law, the penal system and the criminal process. The terminology throughout the book of coercion, oppression and exploitation tends to reinforce the image of women as acted upon, rather than acting, although of course it may be that the historical dominance of male over female means that social control perspectives are peculiarly appropriate. However, especially in the field of individual and group deviance in those of a relatively young age, it seems important not to replace environmental determinism (it's all in the home background) with a political determinism (it's all in the power structure); for the notion that anything short of a total revolution might be a sop to the system gives little hope to those of us who prefer what the feminists call 'white-anting' — a sort of chipping away at the edges.

Summary

In looking at structural explanations for conformity and deviance, we have replaced 'socialization' by 'reproduction' — which may pose dilemmas for teachers. One is that the possible over-optimism of the previous approaches (the assumption that removal from a bad home, from an influential peer group, from a stigmatizing authority, could 'correct' the deviance) may be replaced by a deep pessimism which believes that both deviance, and sex differences therein, are heavily and historically rooted in the total organization of our capitalist/patriarchal economy, and hence minimally open to change. With current unemployment levels making the school's supposed task of preparation for the world of 'work' increasingly a charade, so pupil deviance (whether resulting from conscious appraisal of, or gut reaction to such contradications) will be a growing possibility. Teachers themselves may feel little power in the face of such anomalies. The options open to them so far seem to be:

    i)   a stand for the 'old' values — achievement for its own sake, acceptance of authority, adherence to the domestication of women;

    ii)   new definitions of conformity, which include the embracing of 'education' for leisure and cooperative rather than competitive classrooms;

iii) the active use of pupil deviance to engender 'consciousness-raising', and a channelling into political appraisal and activity.

In my study I tried to clarify two grey areas before commenting on teacher policy. One was whether pupil deviance could be seen as personalized biography or alternatively whether it stemmed from some sort of immediate and critical assessment of the school's task. The second was how far a school did in fact 'reproduce' class and sex divisions (through its definitions of conformity and deviance), and what the respective contributions of teacher and pupil to such reproduction would be. The relevance of theory and research is that any teacher wanting to be deviant themselves — to resist maintaining social inequalities — would be more effective if informed by a practical analysis of the particular place of their school within the social framework.

8   The Methodology of Researching Gender and School Deviance

Clearly, any chosen methodology of research is the result of two sometimes conflicting factors: what one wants to find out and the means at one's disposal to do it. While a national survey involving teams of researchers and large injections of funds might seem desirable, the small scale case-study is often the most practicable and accessible way into an investigation. It can also yield no less information — and this is especially true in the field of pupil deviance. This chapter will briefly examine possibilities in designs of research, and then give detail on the choices made for this particular study.

Surveys

Social science can be said baldly to concern itself with two major questions: what is there, and why is it there? With regard to the first, there have been various attempts to log the extent and type of pupil disruption through large-scale surveys of schools (see chapter 6 for detail). Heads and teachers can be asked to comment on pupil behaviour in their experience, and to consider, for various categories of conduct, variables — such as age, stream or gender — which serve to indicate how much 'trouble' there is in a school, who causes it, and whether it remains static or not. These reports can then be combined to give an overall picture of pupil reactions to 'schooling' in general, or, conversely, to point up the variation between schools in the extent of perceived misconduct. Broad issues of sampling, of the reliability and validity of surveys, can be found in any methodology text; here we need to be reminded of the self-evident question-marks with regard to surveying school deviance.

First there is the question of definition. What is 'disruptive' behaviour to one head may be simply 'high spirits' to another. Unlike measuring maths achievement, there can be no national criteria laid down for 'standards' of conduct whereby pupils can be charted along a single dimension. Just as the official and unofficial rules for 'normal' conduct vary between schools, teachers and even individual class-rooms, so too must definitions of rule-infringement. Logging 'defiance' or 'not wearing uniform' is not the same as noting reading age or social class background (and even these latter can be accused of some degree of subjectivity).

Secondly, as with criminality, there is little way of knowing what proportion the acknowledged troublemakers represent of the 'deviant' pupil population as a whole. A low incidence of pupil misconduct reported in one school may simply represent inefficient apprehension techniques, or the much maligned 'laissez-faire' attitudes. A higher rate of smoking in school A may merely indicate its greater concern and policing of such an activity.

Similar subjectivity arises, thirdly, with the question of admission. A school or a teacher may not want to 'confess' to high levels of disruption, as it might be seen to reflect badly on them, or to paint a misleading picture of the relationships they do have with pupils. The question of truancy may be viewed as an exception to this, as it infringes a codified and national law regarding school attendance; however, as noted in chapter 6, the official figures on truancy are not so reliable, given the difficulty of ascertaining whether the pupil 'genuinely' has a reason for not attending school, or knowing whether he or she is slipping away after 'getting their mark'.

Offiicial delinquency rates for school pupils do provide useful information, as the comparative yardsticks of 'appearing before a court under the age of 16', or 'cautioned by the police' do have a factual base. Even these are of course influenced by social area and by the extent of police activity; interestingly, a more systematic and organized criminal area may discourage delinquency among its younger apprentices, as it attracts too many police into the area.

Gender differences which may emerge from such surveys of schools must also be treated with caution, for reasons which refer us back to the labelling section of the previous chapter. Deviance, disruption, insolence, violence and even truancy may be defined and interpreted differently when it comes from boys than from girls; and delinquency rates are conditional on police practices and expectations about gender (p. 183), as they are (notoriously) with regard to race. However, at least for survey purposes, the factual distinction between a boy and a girl is uncontroversial, even if that between deviance and normality is not; and the sample surveys can give us a broad picture of what is there, especially if taken in conjunction with pupil admissions.

Self-report Questionnaires and Schedules

Here pupils are asked, anonymously, to log their own behaviour against a list of conduct rules or conduct infractions. Instead of their behaviour being filtered through the perceptions and practices of teachers, the pupils assess directly their responses to schooling. Again, evident problems occur about 'truth' — whether pupils, even anonymously, are reluctant to confess to deviance for a variety of reasons, or conversely will exaggerate their misbehaviour either in line with the norms of the peer group, or to confound the researcher. Clearly, even intentionally 'honest' admissions rely on memory and the way one writes one's own biography; and there is also always the subjectivity of the frequency system — whether 'often' of 'occasionally' mean the same thing to different people. Thus the validity of self-report studies has been widely discussed; in general, however, there is support for the view that respondents are honest (Box, 1971). School children are deemed particularly good subjects as they are less inhibited (Mawby, 1977).

The interesting divergences between official statistics and self-report admissions seem to support the 'iceberg' theories of deviance — that much is necessarily concealed — and also the idea of differential official treatment for the sexes, given that the sex ratios are much closer in admissions than they are in records (p. 135).

Self-report schedules are then an essential balance to teacher perceptions. Possible disadvantages with regard to school deviance and gender must nevertheless be mentioned. First, truants are by definition not represented, and thus the sample could be biased towards those most likely to be at school, or in class — that is, those most 'conformist'. Secondly, although confidentiality is stressed, the adult administrator of the questionnaire may be seen as an authority figure, and some may underestimate or deny their deviancy as a precaution. If surmises about girls' greater 'shame' are correct (p. 155), then this latter case would apply especially to girl pupils. It would depend of course very much on what they were being asked to admit: on my own self-report schedule (p. 234), some of the items like 'chatting in class' were so much part of 'normal' school life that it could be surmised that pupils would not even see them as deviant, still less feel 'shame'. Given that pupils are being given 'permission' to admit behaviour, my own view is that such possible sex differences in response to schedules are in fact minimal.

Comparative Studies

The 'why' question regarding pupil behaviour clearly presents more problems. Given, for example, the 'fact' of different amounts of deviance from different schools, how do we start to attribute cause and effect? This is where variables must be isolated, where enormous care must be taken to ensure that like is really being compared with like. Both Reynolds (1976) and Phillipson (1971) found different delinquency rates, school attendance rates and examination success between schools of apparently very similar catchment areas; their research, often unpopular with local authorities, had to make sure that such divergences were not still due to different social class composition, different ability intakes, different ethnic balance, differing police practices or indeed any combination of these. What they had to focus on in the end were features of the schools themselves in terms of control and discipline factors, and of relationships with children. Rutter (1979) similarly arrived at the individual school 'ethos' as a major contributory factor in children's orientation towards education. Whether this school 'ethos' affects all pupils similarly, or whether it has a further differential effect on boys and girls is a question that still needs much comparative research.

The Case-Study Method

An old war film about submarines shown on television recently, entitled 'Run Silent, Run Deep', forced one bored and deafened reviewer to conclude that it should really have been called 'Run Noisy, Run Shallow'. The larger-scale surveys may attract more noise and publicity, but they can remain at the level of surface generalities; depth can often only be achieved by immersion in a small-scale context. The merits and demerits of the case-study method will at this point be discussed using my own research design as the example (or cockshy).

To engage in a qualitative study of one school had two major justifications in terms of the research questions comparing sex differences in deviance. The first was concern for context and doubts about contextual comparability. The effects of a setting on behaviour are well summarized by Weisstein:

> If subjects under quite innocuous and non-coercive social conditions can be made to kill other subjects and under other types of social conditions will positively refuse to do so; if subjects can react to a state of physiological fear by becoming euphoric because there is somebody else around who is euphoric, or angry because there is someone else angry; if students become intelligent because teachers expect them to be intelligent, and rats run mazes better because experimenters are told that the rats are bright, then it is obvious that a study of human behaviour requires first and foremost a study of the social contexts within which people move, the expectations as to how they will behave and the authority which tells them who they are and what they are supposed to do. (Weisstein, 1970)

What is more, the behaviour itself influences the context: social interaction is not just an arena in which determining factors like class or gender work themselves out into human action, but a formative process in its own right (and one which would have been created anew while I was there, and partially because of my presence). People in interaction are not just giving expression to 'background' factors in forming their respective lines of action, but are directing, checking, bending and transforming their scripts in the light of what they encounter in the actions of others. The networks that comprise an 'institution' are not static 'fields' of interaction, but constantly shifting eddies. Thus, although a study of two schools, or the attempt at a 'survey' method, would have allowed the possibility of comparison, the difficulty is in assuming that one is comparing like with like, that observed differences in phenomena can be 'attributed' to observed differences in school-based factors. With the complexity outlined earlier of interacting facets in girls' behaviour, attempting to hold all the variables constant in order to probe the impact of one (in the tradition of positivist sociology) would not seem fruitful or even possible. Harré and Secord (1972) argue that in fact parameters cannot be held constant in exploring human behaviour:

> Most probably, the attributes of people are not logically independent, but are interactive, and the most important ones of all may not even exist in isolation. Yet the idea of ex-

perimental design relating independent variables to dependent ones requires the assumption of logically independent attributes.

In school terms, the context in which behaviour occurs is not just a background, but a crucial *dependent* variable, itself contingent upon the day-to-day behaviour of the actors. The newer traditions of ethnography, of anthropological immersion in a culture, have led to the realization that negotiation between participants will often be unique to a particular organization, or locality, where particular cultural styles are created and interpreted at least partially in response to that situational setting. Sufficient 'comparison' would be built in by the immersion in a mixed school — that is, by the sex variable.

The second rationale is a linked one: that of the need for depth. One of the reasons ethnographers generally spend a long period of time in a single setting is to try to minimize the chances of misunderstanding others' actions, of misinterpreting cultural styles, and also to minimize any deception involved — the extent to which others are motivated to put on 'fronts' and indeed even to lie directly about beliefs and actions. Participant observation in a single setting is particularly appropriate and popular for deviancy research because of these situationally based and subjective definitions by the individual or group concerning behaviour, because of the specific 'opportunity structures' of the setting, and because of the unique way in which acts of deviance are 'created' in terms of the interaction between the definers and the defined.

Hargreaves (1978) usefully lists the complex strengths and capacities of the symbolic interactionist approach to research, which can be elaborated in terms of my own study. There is first the 'appreciative' capacity: to be able to expose social action from the viewpoint of the actor, with 'empathetic fidelity'. Once can also in a well-known setting display the nature, the meaning and the inherent rationality of pupil conduct to teachers and to others. Although I had originally entered the school claiming no wish to 'interfere' or to make prescriptions, I found in fact that I was *asked* at certain intervals to reveal my findings, explain pupil behaviour, to make recommendations. Secondly there is the 'designatory' capacity, the naming of features normally taken for granted. In this case it was the tacit knowledge of the teachers which was being explored, and staff were interested in each other's reactions to my questions, without being able to predict or generalize what these might be. The 'reflective' capacity, thirdly, refers to the approach acting as a mirror, although this occurs only if reactions to the researcher and the research are followed up. The interactionist would be the last to be surprised to find staff choosing whether to look in the mirror. The fourth capacity is the 'immunological' one, the ability to understand why changes that 'graft' new ideas onto schools without knowledge of the everyday world of teachers and taught merely arouse antibodies. Finally there is the 'corrective' capacity. As Hargreaves puts it: 'Good quality ethnography is always a potential source of correction to macro theories, which frequently oversimplify, underestimate or ignore the complexity of the detailed operation of relevant factors in actual social settings.' The complexity referred to here was initially seen as a problem in the first analysis of my findings. Later the lack of 'patterns' was to become a source of fascination, and indicated the need for a more delicate approach than the over-used notions of 'sub-cultures' or 'the norms of the peer group'. Four of these capacities — appreciation, designation, reflection and immunity — have clear implications for individual school policy; while appreciation, immunity and correction together offer important points of articulation with macro level work. Study at the 'micro' level is not in contrast to, or as substitution for macro theorizing, but acts to inform and refine those generalized models.

An additional vindication of the qualitative mode is that intensive design, although located in one setting, does not preclude a multi-variant research approach. The methodology here had to include the members' subjective experience of the world, but also situational constraints on action: it had to probe the derivation of 'recipe know-ledge' as well as the immediate creative construction of events. The investigation had to include examination of official school 'statistics', traditions, practices; it had to attempt by questionnaires and interviews to explore subjective possibilities which may not have been reflected in particular observed situations or members' accounts of the past. One has to be careful not to 'romanticize' the voice of respondents; a false unity can develop in 'trying to make sense of it', for as Willis admits, the ethnographic account is a 'supremely *ex post facto* account of everyday life'. Thus some attempt to escape the framework imposed by 'pure' ethnography was made by tackling head on some of the hypothesized structural features which might have their effect in different attitudes, self-concepts and so on, and by examining the social constraints on the school itself. A scatter approach was therefore preferred, using on occasion pre-existing constructs and theories — for example 'rules', 'social reaction', 'sex-typing'. It was hoped thereby to engender a critical appreciation of these concepts and their usefulness.

The Research Programme

Research was conducted primarily over a period of two years, 1977/8 and 1978/9, with follow up visits during 1979/80. Because of the split-site nature of the school, and the evidence that deviance increases as pupils become older, most of the investigation was concentrated on the upper school — that is the fourth and fifth year, and the staff who taught them. However, an early phase of the research included a week following the new intake of 11 year olds into lower school. The various avenues of investigation as outlined below do not coincide with any 'phases' of the research, as many of them overlapped.

The framework of the school

Interviews and conversations with administrators, together with examination of the school handbooks for staff and pupils provided relatively clear guidelines as to the official goals, rules and ethos of the school, information essential for locating values by which 'normality' and 'deviance' come to be defined. The lower and the upper school each had a handbook for pupils or parents which set out on the one hand the instrumental goals — learning areas, extra-curricular activities, examinations taken, careers opportunities — and on the other hand the facilitating goals — grouping, timetabling, pastoral care, the social order, the 'consensual and differentiating rituals' of behavioural rules and uniform. The thirty-eight page staff handbook gave clear indications, too, as to 'expected' roles and rules for pupils and teachers, information supplemented or orchestrated by written reports of staff meetings and discussion topics, notice boards and assemblies. I also had access to individual pupil records, and to records of punishments such as canings and detention. The education welfare officer was interviewed on the subject of truancy and pupil orientation to school.

If we take Goffman's analytical framework for looking at establishments, we can distinguish four dimensions: the 'technical' — here the official objectives and their achievement; the 'political' — the actions which each participant can demand of others, and sanctions applied, in this case roles and rules of school life, the pastoral care system, the rights and duties of teachers; the 'structural' — here the groupings and divisions of pupils (and teachers) by age, sex and ability; and the 'cultural' — the moral values which influence activity. However, the inseparable nature of these aspects of a framework is notable from seemingly random juxtaposition in the handbooks of items about fire drills, marking registers, classroom discipline, the use of the minibus, careers guidance. Typologies to analyze institutions infer a static system of goals and norms, whereas in fact these will shift in emphasis according to everyday concerns and events, as noted from interview transcripts. Nonetheless, two years observation in the school enabled some sensitivity to distinctions between rules-on-paper and rules-in-practice. Goffman also adds the 'dramaturgical', employed as the end point of analysis, a final way of ordering facts — techniques of impression management, identity and interrelationships of several performance teams operating in the establishment (Goffman, 1959). Such 'dramaturgy' indeed emerged in my eventual choice of a script analysis.

The teacher interview

All teachers who taught upper school pupils were asked if they would be willing during a free period to talk to me 'about their work in school', and 41 out of a possible 50 teachers (24 male and 17 female) came for 35 minutes each. Conversations were tape-recorded, although occasionally I had to reassure teachers that in spite of the support I was receiving from the head in this research, I was not reporting individual teachers' attitudes and comments about the school directly back to him. Other teachers were obviously hoping that I would.

The interview schedule is reproduced in Figure 1. The aims were to probe teachers' perceptions of the nature and extent of girls' deviance as compared with boys', including their definitions of 'troublesome' pupils; and to elicit their ideologies regarding both explanations for disaffected pupils and suitable 'treatments'. Using relatively open questions, it was hoped to allow 'accounts' of their actions and reactions to pupils (and towards other teachers) to emerge, and while an interview framework of necessity tapped the researcher's own 'second order' constructs', it was felt necessary to make some attempt to get at members' 'first order' constructs, their own interpretive work. Any theoretical concepts, or a sociological register, were thus avoided.

The interview was seen as important back-up to observation in the classroom; as Hargreaves rightly warns' 'too frequently the symbolic interactionists saw their task as identifying the actions of members as exemplifications of the concepts of "rule-breaking" or "labelling" without specifying how they knew this' (Hargreaves, 1978). This

Figure 1   Interview schedule: teachers

As you know, I am doing some research on pupils' conformity and deviance in school, and hope you could help by giving me your views. I'll ask you first of all to fill in a questionnaire; then perhaps you could give me your reactions to some more general items. I'll record the interview if you have no objection, but all results will of course be confidential, and the tape erased once a transcript has been made.

1   Could you tell me first of all how long you have been teaching at this school?

2   Would you say that there has been any increase in 'trouble' over that time?

    If No: Decrease?
    If Yes: In what areas?
             Why do you think this is?

3   Would you say that there are any notable differences between boys' and girls' reactions to school? (Is it possible to generalize?).

    If No: 4
    If Yes: In what ways?
             To what elements? (Prompt: rules, uniform, different teachers, different subjects etc.)
             Why should this be so?

4   Would you say that there was any difference in the ways boys and girls formed friendships? (Prompt: preference for pairs/gangs/shifting groups etc.)

5   How much influence would elder brothers or sisters have on a pupil's behaviour?

6   If you had to teach only boys or only girls, which would you choose? Why?

7   Would you say that boys and girls ever receive different punishments by the school, for doing the same thing?

    (a)   Should there be different ways of punishing, or different rules for boys and girls?
    (b)   Why (not)?

8   Would it be possible for you say what some of the main reasons are for girls' disruptive behaviour in particular?

9   In your opinion, is there anything that the school could do to ease the 'problem' of difficult pupils, boys or girls?

---

interview was, then, an attempt to get teachers to articulate their sometimes tacit knowledge on which they based their actions in the classroom; to elicit directly the definitions, typifications and rules by which deviance imputations were made. This formal interview was continuously supplemented by informal conversations with teachers in staffrooms, classrooms before, during and after lessons, and travelling between sites, from which field notes were made from memory later or at the end of the day.

The teacher questionnaire

The written questionnaire was an attempt to explore in a slightly more positivistic sense the issue of differential school and teacher treatment or expectations for the sexes. Levitin and Chananie (1972) had successfully tested predictions about teachers' responses to certain sex/behaviour pairings in pupils by asking the teachers to react to statements about children in classrooms, with half the teachers being assigned statements about a girl, and the other half receiving identical statments but alluding to a boy. Goldberg's (1968) classic study of gender prejudice in judgments of academic writing used a similar technique. In like vein, the first part of this questionnaire (Figure 2) contained two sections of similar format. Part A was designed to elicit teachers' predictions of the reaction of the school in general to certain rule infringements. The behavioural dimensions were chosen to cover a range of rule-breaking responses and were checked with the head as to

---

Figure 2   School treatment questionnaire to teachers

Part A: You are asked to assume that the pupils described below are in their fourth or fifth year at your school. For each one please say what treatment they are likely to receive from the school, if any.

1   Robert (Sharon) is frequently late for school, although he lives only a short walk away.
     What treatment will he (she) receive?

2   Sharon (Robert) often comes to school in a brightly coloured sweater.
     What treatment will she (he) receive?

3   Andrew and David (Lesley and Janet) have been apprehended carving graffiti on walls.
     What treatment will they receive?

4   Stephen (Diane) often bullies pupils younger than himself (herself).
     What treatment will he (she) receive?

5   Diane (Stephen) has been caught smoking in the toilets for the third time.
     What treatment will she (he) receive?

6   Lesley and Janet (Andrew and David) mess about in assembly.
     What treatment will they receive?

Part B: Now you are asked to assume that the pupils described below are in a class that you teach. For each one please say what you would do, if anything.

1   Martin (Angela) is talking and giggling as usual, and the class is distracted.
     What do you say/do?

2   You go over to tell Angela (Martin) off, and as you return to the front, she (he) mimics you under her breath.
     What do you do?

3   David (Julie) tells you to get stuffed.
     What do you do?

4   Margaret (Tony) hits Susan (John) over the head with a ruler, and Susan kicks and punches Margaret in retaliation.
     What do you do?

5   Barry (Linda) insults Linda (Barry) loudly, using a four letter word.
     What do you do?

6   Julie (David) is taking CSE in your subject this year, but frequently doesn't do her (his) homework. She (he) says there's no point.
     What do you do?

---

whether these were pertinent kinds of school offences. Teachers were assigned randomly to two groups, with the sex/behaviour pairings being reversed for the second group. Part B had a similar structure, but asked teachers to outline what they would do personally if certain behaviours were exhibited by pupils in their classes. Again, boys' and girls' names were reversed in half the questionnaires.

While this 'treatment' part of the questionnaire probed responses to deviance — the question of social reaction — the subsequent 'stereotype' questionnaire was designed to explore teacher definitions of the 'good' pupil, and the relationship of this to gender (Figure 3). As explained previously, it was adapted from a questionnaire to clinicians about their patients by Broverman et al (1970). In my case a set of sex role stereotypes for pupils was elicited by asking a different group of 54 teachers to list attributes which distinguished boys' and girls' response to schooling. Those adjectives appearing more than three times were used as stereotypical, together with selected relevant items from the Broverman questionnaire. (A detailed discussion of the development of a stereotype questionnaire can be found in Rosenkrantz et al, 1968). The resultant 44 items were arranged in bi-polar form with the poles separated by 60 points. Teachers were asked to indicate which pole a well-adjusted, reasonably successful pupil would be closer to; for one third of the teachers the word pupil was replaced by boy, for the remaining third, girl. The wording of the statement was chosen to imply the teacher's perception of the good pupil, and piloted on a group of 29 practising teachers. While 'the pupil you would like to have in your class' was also a possibility, the concern was not so much to tap teachers' prescriptions about model types, but to assess their ideas of reality. As noted in chapter 6 the notion of 'teacher expectations' is sometimes an unclear or confusing one: does it refer to judgments on the pupils' approximations to 'ideal types', or simply forecasts about behaviour? That is to say, are expectations prescriptions or probabilities? Given that no pupil or class would ever act 'ideally', it seemed more profitable to define teacher 'expectations' of the sexes as 'perceived likelihoods'. Even if there emerged no significant differences between expectations for boys and girls, the use of the questionnaire would enable two dimensions of the good pupil to be plotted, and hence the criteria by which deviation is defined. A further consideration was whether the joint responses would verge more towards the masculine pole for each item or the feminine, and thus what the implications were for boys' orientations as well as girls'.

The stereotype questionnaire was also given to a control group of

Figure 3 *Stereotype questionnaire to teachers: schedule and results*

You are asked to think of fourth or fifth year boys/pupils/girls in your school, and then indicate on each item the pole to which a well-adjusted, reasonably successful boy/pupil/girl would be closer.

Item	'boys', 'pupils', 'girls' Means	Between 'pupils', 'girls' — F Probability*	Between 'pupils', 'girls' — Significance	Between sex of teacher		Between Gladstone and other teachers		
1 Not at all aggressive 1...2...3...4...5...6...7 Very aggressive	28.9	0.24						
2 Very talkative 1...2...3...4...5...6...7 Not at all talkative	36.3	0.66						
3 Very hardworking 1...2...3...4...5...6...7 Not at all hardworking	29.5	0.57						
4 Not at all independent 1...2...3...4...5...6...7 Very independent	46.2	0.06						
5 Very responsible 1...2...3...4...5...6...7 Very irresponsible	28.8	0.65						
6 Not at all emotional 1...2...3...4...5...6...7 Very emotional	B33.2 P38.5 G40.1	0.04	5%			G35.37 O40.74	0.025	5%
7 Not at all conformist 1...2...3...4...5...6...7 Very conformist	45.7	0.66				G47.72 O42.14	0.024	5%

*Of significant difference between all three groups

223

	Means	F Probability	Significance
8 Very tactful 1....2....3....4....5....6....7 Very blunt	40.7	0.57	
9 Very subjective 1....2....3....4....5....6....7 Very objective	41.2	0.39	
10 Not at all helpful 1....2....3....4....5....6....7 Very helpful	51.7	0.45	
11 Very gentle 1....2....3....4....5....6....7 Very rough	B40.0 P40.5 B34.8	0.02 / T=0.006*	5% / 1%
12 Not at all easily influenced 1....2....3....4....5....6....7 Very easily influenced	36.1	0.64	
13 Very motivated 1....2....3....4....5....6....7 Not at all motivated	28.6	0.23	
14 Very aware of feelings of others 1....2....3....4....5....6....7 Not at all aware of feelings of others	31.7	0.64	
15 Very submissive 1....2....3....4....5....6....7 Very dominant	42.7	0.43	
16 Very immature 1....2....3....4....5....6....7 Very mature	47.3	0.25	
17 Likes maths and Science very much 1....2....3....4....5....6....7 Dislikes maths and science very much	B35.1 P34.6 G41.1	0.05	5%

*T probability of significant difference between two groups: boys + pupils, and girls

Item	Means	F Proba-bility	Signi-ficance	Means	F Proba-bility	Signi-ficance
18 Not at all conscientious 1.....2.....3.....4.....5.....6.....7 Very conscientious	50.2	0.28				
19 Very interested in own appearance 1.....2.....3.....4.....5.....6.....7 Not at all interested in own appearance	B38.5 P29.0 G25.8	0.001	1%	M34.4 F26.3	0.006	1%
20 Very active 1.....2.....3.....4.....5.....6.....7 Very passive	B33.2 P33.6 G28.4	0.09 T=0.02	5%			
21 Very neat in habits 1.....2.....3.....4.....5.....6.....7 Very sloppy in habits	30.8	0.36				
22 Very oriented towards the peer group 1.....2.....3.....4.....5.....6.....7 Very individualistic	38.9	0.34				
23 Not at all competitive 1.....2.....3.....4.....5.....6.....7 Very competitive	B45.5 P43.0 G49.4	0.11 T=0.03	5%			
24 Very loud 1.....2.....3.....4.....5.....6.....7 Very quiet	B37.4 P39.2 G42.4	0.12 T=0.02	5%			
25 Very illogical 1.....2.....3.....4.....5.....6.....7 Very logical	48.8	0.65		M51.14 F45.48	0.022	5%
26 Enjoys art and literature very much 1.....2.....3.....4.....5.....6.....7 Does not enjoy art and literature at all	B40.9 P35.1 G36.3	0.117 T=0.05	5%			

	Means	F Proba-bility	Signi-ficance
27 Very boisterous 1....2.....3.......4........5........6........7 Very placid	39.2	0.42	
28 Very home oriented 1....2.....3.......4........5........6........7 Very worldly	39.2	0.12	
29 Easily expresses tender feelings 1....2.....3.......4........5........6........7 Does not express tender feelings at all	41.6	0.43	
30 Very disruptive 1....2.....3.......4........5........6........7 Not at all disruptive	51.3	0.39	
31 Feelings easily hurt 1....2.....3.......4........5........6........7 Feelings not easily hurt	40.9	0.36	
32 Very adventurous 1....2.....3.......4........5........6........7 Not at all adventurous	35.3	0.60	
33 Cries very easily 1....2.....3.......4........5........6........7 Never cries	B54.3 P50.1 G44.9	0.003 T=0.005	5% 1%
34 Very keen on sport 1....2.....3.......4........5........6........7 Not at all keen on sport	36.9	0.41	
35 Almost never acts as a leader 1....2.....3.......4........5........6........7 Almost always acts as a leader	43.8	0.60	
36 Very career-oriented 1....2.....3.......4........5........6........7 Not at all career-oriented	35.2	0.36	

Item	Means	F Probability	Significance	Means	F Probability	Significance	Means	F Probability	Significance
37 Not at all self-confident 1......2......3......4......5......6......7 Very self-confident	48.8	0.53					G47.04 O51.96	0.019	5%
38 Does the minimum work 1......2......3......4......5......6......7 Does the maximum work	49.6	0.42							
39 Very ambitious 1......2......3......4......5......6......7 Not at all ambitious	B28.37 P35.84 G30.50	0.57 T=0.013	5%						
40 Very interested in the opposite sex 1......2......3......4......5......6......7 Not at all interested in the opposite sex	31.4	0.42					G33.32 O28.07	0.02	5%
41 Unable to separate feelings from ideas 1......2......3......4......5......6......7 Easily able to separate feelings from ideas	41.9	0.69							
42 Uses harsh language 1......2......3......4......5......6......7 Never uses harsh language	43.7	0.29					G46.23 O39.18	0.013	5%
43 Thinks boys are superior to girls 1......2......3......4......5......6......7 Does not think boys are superior to girls	B35.56 P39.83 G49.50	0.001	1%						
44 Very conceited about appearance 1......2......3......4......5......6......7 Never conceited about appearance	43.7	0.69		M46.32 F39.86	0.016	5%			

227

31 teachers from a range of other schools. All results were subject to a one-way analysis of variance, a contrast coefficient matrix and a Scheffe multiple range test, in order to identify any significant differences (a) between the teachers given 'boy', 'girl' or 'pupil'; (b) between male and female teachers; and (c) between Gladstone teachers and others.

The pupil interview

An early phase of the research involved the structured interviewing of 112 fourth year pupils (66 boys, 56 girls) across the whole ability range. This constituted a 40 per cent sample of the fourth year. An interview schedule and example of opening remarks and assurances is reproduced in Figure 4. Like the teacher questionnaire, questions were framed in as open a way as possible, and expanded only if necessary. For example, the question 'What do you do if a lesson is boring?' sometimes prompted the reply 'maths' or 'history', where the pupil was obviously interpreting the structure of the question differently from that in-

Figure 4   *Interview schedule: pupils*

Introduction

Many people are asking teachers and experts what they think about education; I think it's important to find out what pupils think about school, and I'd be very grateful if I could have your views on life in school. I'll tape this conversation if you don't mind, to save me scribbling notes, but the tape will be erased afterwards, and nobody else will hear it.

1   Could you tell me when you want to leave school?
2   Do you know what you want to do when you leave?
3   What do you like about school?
4   What do you dislike about school?
5   What do you think about school rules?
6   What sort of teachers do you like?
7   What sort of teachers do you dislike?
8   Do you ever feel a teacher has a down on you?
9   What do you do if a lesson is boring?
10   Does anything make you mad in school?
11   Do you think boys and girls cause the same amount of trouble in school?
12   Do you think boys and girls are treated differently?
13   Do you think boys and girls should be caned if they cause trouble?
14   What do you think of the sorts of punishments there are in the school?
15   Are you happy with the subjects and options you are doing this year?
16   If you could change anything in the school, what would you change?

tended. The interviews took place in a small office and were tape-recorded. The pupils were assured of confidentiality, and there was no possibility of being overhead. There seemed no objection to the tape, and it added 'seriousness' to the setting.

The pupils were interviewed in pairs. Although this does introduce the possibility of bias, it also served as a validity check, as they would correct each other. In addition, the group setting stimulated additional recall, and highlighted any disagreements; it was appropriate in that I was seeking publicly shared perspectives in order to identify and explain pupil cultures. While individual members' subjective experiences of the world were also important, I was obviously looking to compare boys and girls, and seeing pupils as representative of a gender; except on one occasion, the pupils arrived in same sex pairs.

The pupil interview was done at an early stage so that I would be relatively unknown to them, and therefore not necessarily associated with the teaching staff. When I prefaced my questions with the request to explore *their* views of school (as opposed to educationalists'), many pupils wanted to know what I wanted this information *for*; the explanation already given to some by the deputy head, that I was writing a book, seemed a suitable one to concur with, and this was the rationale I was to use to pupils throughout the research period. Adult fears about anonymity were not apparent in the pupils; many of them wanted assurances that their names *would* be in the book, and were disappointed if I indicated that names would have to be changed in any published material.

The pupil questionnaire

This was completed shortly after the interviews by 219 of the fourth year pupils (114 girls and 105 boys), representing a 78 per cent sample of the whole fourth year. The reasons for tapping into fourth year perceptions for both interview and questionnaire was to enable comparison and some extended familiarity with these pupils over the two year period; and also because the feeling was from the 'hierarchy' that the problems lay there, rather than in the fifth year where the pupils were looking forward to the world of work and were 'settling down' (either that, or they had stopped coming).

The first three sections (see Figure 5) contained questions reproduced from the Schools Council Enquiry *Young School Leavers* (1968). The reasons for using this material were twofold: first, it had already

Figure 5   Pupil perceptions of school — sex difference: schedule and results[1]

	School should:	Direction of difference	Values of x^2	d.f.	Significance level
1	Help you to become independent		1.10	2	
2	Help you to do well in examinations		2.19	2	
3	Help you to develop personality	G — more important	9.52	2	1%
4	Teach things of use in job		0.49	2	
5	Help you to know about the world		3.43	2	
6	Teach you plenty of subjects		1.65	2	
7	Teach you things to get a job		3.71	2	
8	Teach about right and wrong		5.89	2	
9	Teach things useful in the home	G — more important	7.97	2	5%
10	Teach how to manage money	G — more important	6.16	1	5%
11	Give you sex education		0.03	2	
12	Teach you behaviour for confidence		5.08	2	
13	Help you with appearance	G — more important	8.50	2	5%
14	Help you to get on with people	G — more important	6.94	2	5%
15	Give you interests and hobbies		3.60	2	
16	Teach about different jobs		3.03	2	
17	Teach about what work is like		4.55	2	
18	Run clubs after school	G — less agreed	10.64	2	5%
19	Take you on cultural outings		0.43	2	
20	Take you to places of work		1.18	2	
	I feel that:				
1	Mostly look forward to going to school	G — more 'yes'	6.33	2	5%
2	Get fed up with teachers' orders		0.53	2	
3	School is always the same		0.22	2	
4	Teachers take much interest		0.41	2	
5	Delighted when can stay away		0.66	2	
6	Lots of interesting things going on	G — more 'no'	10.50	2	1%
7	Teachers forget growing up		1.54	2	
8	Most of friends come from near home		5.96	2	
9	Most of what taught very useful		0.50	2	
10	Would like to stay later each day		1.89	2	
11	Will like being at work better		0.96	3	

[1] For full wording of the questionnaires used, see Schools Council (1966)

been piloted and validated; and secondly it enabled comparison both with pupil responses in 1966 and with responses elicited in two other schools in my previous research in 1973. The age group was approximately the same, in that the Schools Council survey was conducted when the leaving age was 15.

Figure 5b   Personal concerns to the pupil — sex difference: schedule and results

		x^2	d.f.	Significance level
1	Getting a job which you like	3.40	1	
2	To be earning money	0.46	—	
3	Clothes, hairstyles, appearance	26.10	1	1%
4	Being treated as grown up	14.25	1	1%
5	Dancing	33.71	2	1%
6	Pop music	6.15	2	5%
7	Having a boy/girl friend (opposite sex)	0.30	2	
8	Starting work as soon as possible	0.73	2	
9	Having friends to go around with	3.14	2	
10	Sport	67.01	2	1%
11	Your family	8.55	1	1%
12	Getting married	8.80	1	1%
13	Having a good time while you are young	2.51	2	

The next section (Figure 6) was a self-concept questionnaire, where pupils were asked to respond to 20 statements as being 'like me' or 'unlike me'. The form was an adaptation of Coopersmith's 'self-esteem inventory' (SEI) (1967), but incorporated eleven items from Waetjen's 'self-concept as a learner scale' (SCAL) (1963). The eight items from SEI (for example, 'I often feel upset in school') were selected as being particularly likely to evoke either sex differences or to be associated with deviant responses; the eleven items from SCAL comprised three items regarding motivation, four regarding task orientation and two concerned with class membership. A final item was incorporated on perception of liking by the teacher, in order to parallel the investigation into teacher preference for boys or girls. The aim of this section was to probe differences in self-concept between the sexes (or between streams), and through items such as 'I never ask teachers to explain something again', to test hypotheses about girls' passivity, quietness, lesser assertiveness and so on, which had been indicated in the socialization literature.

Figure 6 Pupil self-concept — sex and stream difference: schedule and results

		Sex difference (% scores)				Values of x^2 (raw scores)	Significance level	Stream difference	Values of x^2	Significance level
		Like me		Unlike me						
		G	B	G	B					
1	I find it very hard to talk it front of the class	75	77	25	23	0.07			26.23	1%
2	Things are all mixed up in my life	28	27	72	73	0.01				
3	Kids usually follow my ideas	19	33	81	67	5.73	5%	Low stream girls more 'like me'		
4	I often feel upset in school	34	24	66	76	0.28				
5	I'm not as nice looking as most people	56	33	44	67	9.42	1%	Top stream girls more 'like me'	11.95	1%
6	If I have something to say I usually say it	65	66	35	34	0.07				
7	I often get discouraged in school	50	47	50	53	0.24				
8	I usually feel as if my parents are pushing me	29	37	71	63	4.92	5%			
9	I never ask teachers to explain something again	52	44	48	56	2.37				
10	I do things without being told several times	65	61	35	39	0.56				
11	I like school jobs which give me responsibility	62	56	38	54	0.61				
12	I sometimes use unfair means to do my school work	54	58	46	42	0.39				
13	I try to be careful about my work	73	64	27	36	1.67				
14	I get tense when I'm called on in class	73	58	27	42	4.96	5%	Low stream girls more 'like me'	5.79	5%
15	I make mistakes because I don't listen	45	43	55	57	0.17				
16	I change my mind a lot	73	59	27	41	4.75	5%			
17	I know the answer before the rest of the class	16	26	84	74	2.94				
18	I find it easy to get along with people in the class	83	82	17	18	0.02				
19	I take an active part in group projects and activities	30	60	70	40	15.23	1%			
20	I usually feel that the teachers like me	31	41	69	59	2.29				

The final part of the questionnaire (Figure 7) was a self-report schedule asking pupils to indicate the frequency with which they had committed various rule-violations. The validity of such schedules was discussed earlier. For administration of the questionnaire, I was able to take various classes for a whole period. When this was too long, pupils wrote additional comments pertaining to 'My Ideal School', 'My Ideal Teacher' and 'The Ideal Pupil'; or we chatted informally. There was no resistance from pupils to completing the questionnaire; on the contrary, they enjoyed being asked their views, and many asked if I 'had any more' to fill in when they had completed it. All results were subjected to a chi-square statistical analysis to test for any significant differences between boys and girls.

Classroom observation

Observations in classrooms were carried out over the whole two year period, with approximately 400 hours spent in mainly fourth and fifth year classes. Notes were taken during the lessons, and supplemented from memory afterwards. No tape recorder was used, in order to maximize the 'naturalness' of the setting. The pupils were, however, often interested in what I was writing, and would instruct me to note certain events and things said. No attempt was made at any structured interaction analysis, as the various critiques of the limitations of such data seem irrefutable (see Robinson, 1974) — especially when one is concerned with the unique contexts which provide motivations for, and interpretations of, deviance. Thus an ethnographic approach was preferred, where the aim was to discover the 'interpretive procedures' in classrooms by which participants were able to understand one another and coordinate their actions. The strategy is to retain an anthropological strangeness in order to learn the vocabulary, the dictionary of action. Hammersley (1977) cites the methodological themes at the heart of the 'preferred methods' of ethnography as discovery, understanding, naturalism and deception. Related to my classroom observations, this meant discovery of the surface rules and meanings of 'deviance' and 'conformity' displayed by boys and girls in specific teaching and learning settings, and discovery too of how pupil identities may be formed and reformed. It necessitated understanding of the shared language and styles through which the culture of the classroom was identified and recreated for each lesson. It meant that the naturalism of classroom settings was a useful and essential balance to the artificiality of other aspects of the research such as interviews; and it

Figure 7   Self-report schedule for fourth year pupils: example and results

Class . . . .   (PLEASE DO NOT WRITE YOUR NAME)
Could you please tick if you have ever done any of these things. Please be as honest as you can;
it does not matter whether anyone ever knew about it or not.

a) *Example*

	Never	Once or twice	Several times	Quite often
1 Being late for school				

b) *Results: Differences by sex*

	Values of x^2	d.f.	Significance level	Sex admitting more offences
1 Being late for school	4.24	3		
2 Fighting	29.69	2	1%	B
3 Not wearing proper uniform	4.26	3	—	
4 Skipping school without an excuse	7.85	2	5%	B
5 Telling teachers what you think of them	4.30	2	—	
6 Taking something that didn't belong to you	22.08	2	1%	B
7 Chatting in class	2.27	2	—	
8 Staying out all night without your parents' permission	15.64	2	1%	B
9 Hurting someone who hadn't done anything to you	5.99	2	5%	B
10 Throwing things in class	3.93	3	—	
11 Smoking in school	4.42	2	—	
12 Disobeying your parents	1.60	3	—	
13 Coming home late	5.80	3	1%	
14 Drinking alcohol in school	1.56	1	—	
15 Making jokes in class	3.72	3	—	
16 Setting fire to something	7.04	2	5%	B
17 Taken part in a gang fight	13.60	2	1%	B
18 Run away from home	0.58	1	—	
19 Damaging or breaking something in school deliberately	10.36	2	1%	B
20 Chewing in class	4.51	2	—	
21 Not paying attention in class	2.77	3	—	
22 Damaging or breaking something out of school deliberately	14.85	2	1%	B
23 Fooling about in class	0.31	3	—	
24 Writing on the desks	17.81	3	1%	G
25 Skipping lessons	0.12	3	—	
26 Writing on the walls at school	7.05	2	5%	G

was a check on the deceptive 'fronts' teachers and pupils might put on in face to face interaction with a researcher asking specific questions. 'Participant' observation may thus refer to the observer as far as possible 'experiencing' the field as does the 'native'.

There are also various methodological difficulties about participant observation to which attention must be paid here. One is the 'Hawthorne effect' — the possibility of the observer's presence distorting the situation. Another is the selection of events for recording, and the retaining of some objectivity. I was obviously on the look-out for differences in teacher treatment, in pupil response; with pupils I knew well I would be watching out for predictable (or unpredictable) actions. I found myself concentrating on watching the girls, which may have communicated itself. Linked to this is the immediate interpretation of events in the process of recording or coding of them. Gill (1978) points out the tendency of the researcher to think that all conversations he/she has and all interactions witnessed will support the theme of deviant behaviour, but the vast majority of events, of things said, are 'conventional'. Having been both a pupil and a teacher, I would share many of the taken-for-granted typifications of what was going on, and fail to note important interpretative work because it seemed 'usual'. The difficulty for the observer is to decide when a rule or a meaning is new or old, spontaneous, changeable or fixed. Yet another issue is the subsequent interpretation of data, once recorded. How are the researcher's accounts superior to the actors'? Ideally some 'triangulation' method is preferable, where the three versions of events from pupils, teacher and researcher can be contrasted as soon as possible after the lesson. With the structure of school timetabling, this is rarely possible. The final point is the generalizability of such material. Ethnography is admittedly poor with regard to 'representativeness' — the very essence of studying natural settings with minimal intervention and manipulation means that one cannot 'control' as in experimental designs. But as Delamont (1976a) argues, while concepts or hypotheses are generated in a restricted range of contexts, they are then developed, modified, rejected through comparison with further social settings. At least some proliferation of ethnography is to be encouraged to develop a cumulative base of comparative sources.

The Sub-cultural study

Much of the second year was spent with the group of fifth year girls identified by the school as 'difficult'. While classroom observation helps in locating patterns of action between participants, one aim of small group study is the anthropological quest — not just to observe action, but to investigate 'meaningful action', the meaning-loaded exchange between actors. How does their world work? What are the 'generative mechanisms' which give rise to their behaviour as observed in school settings? To probe this entails obtaining 'accounts': the actors' own statements about why acts were performed and what social meanings were given to their own and others' behaviour. This involves the retrospective monitoring of performance, and as such may incur the need to show oneself in a favourable light — to find a *post hoc* motive, to neutralize antisocial behaviour. There may thus be no consistent set of rules discernible; but the tradition of ethogenics (obtaining accounts) insists that the commentaries are authentic, if revisable, reports of phenomena. The claim is that the same social knowledge and skill is involved in the genesis both of behaviour and of the accounts of that behaviour.

> Ethogenics is not introspection under another name. Rather we suppose that in both accounts and in actions, the same know-ledge of what is socially potent and proper is revealed ... [the actors'] meanings and their rules have priority in the scientific analysis of the phenomena.　　(Marsh, Rosser and Harré, 1978)

The girls would thus be the best authorities on what the action 'actually' was. People's capacity to monitor their own self-monitoring is a distinctly human feature; and in ethogenics one attempts to restore 'humanity' to the subjects under discussion. Even then it may be difficult to avoid patronage or 'refinement' in the final writing up.

Although the accounts are direct, there are obvious representation-al problems. One is that we have entered the world of the taken-for-granted, no longer available for conscious inspection; much will remain unaccounted for. In addition, drawing inferences from conversations presents the same problems of interpretation as does participant observation. We cannot ever directly 'know' or empirically present the world of somebody else. Yet however imperfect the presentations of accounts are, no theory of behaviour is complete without them:

> In particular the ethogenic account, without always knowing how, can allow a degree of the activity, creativity and human agency within the object of study to come through into the analysis and the reader's experience. This is vital when we view the cultural not as a set of transferred internal structures (c.f.

socialization), nor as a passive result of action of the dominant ideology downwards (c.f. kinds of Marxism) but at least in part as collective human praxis.   (Willis, 1977)

It was just this 'praxis' of girls which had so rarely been given life in sex role research.

The generation of theory

In their advocacy of grounded theory, Glaser and Strauss (1968) reject the narrowness of positivist research, with its highly refined methods; they claim that the problem is chosen to suit the method, not *vice versa*, with the result that the problem is often trivial from the theoretical and practical point of view. They advocate the comparative analysis of data — that is, simply the observation of the phenomena under question in more than one setting — as the appropriate methodology for 'generation' of theory.

My problem (differences in pupil deviance) was certainly not narrow, and one would hope not trivial. My comparative data was not different schools, but teachers and pupils, boys and girls. Questions of who decides what counts as data have already been noted; the major concern is the relationship between theory, method and data, and the level at which data can be used not only to test or illustrate theories, but generate and inform theory. I attempted in this methodology to accommodate this two-way process — to illustrate theories about labelling, about sub-cultures, but also to generate some sort of theoretical model which would link micro and macro features - which in my case became script analysis.

There are dangers in remaining at the micro level, as Karabel and Halsey warn:

> Stress on the fact that relations in educational institutions are humanly constructed is a welcome antidote to the determinism and reifying tendencies of some of the 'old' sociology of education. But emphasis on 'man the creator' often fails to take account of the social constraints on human actors in everyday life.   (Karabel and Halsey, 1977)

I have argued that emphasis on 'woman the creator' might in fact be a better entry to those social constraints. Yet making the synthesis is no easy task. The two sociological perspectives and appropriate methodologies are seen as stemming from perceptions of the 'ultimate determiner':

> It can be argued that 'in the end' the interactionist sees the individual and his ability to negotiate as the ultimate level while the structuralist sees the social structural forces as the ultimate determiner. This does *not* mean that interactionists are not concerned with power or institutional and structural constraints (although it is conceded that some may well not be.
>
> (Meyenn and Miller, 1979)

Even with interactionist or qualitative methodologies it seems essential to include power considerations of whose definitions of the situation will prevail; to recognize how interaction may occur in repetitive and seemingly immutable patterns.

Hence there is the need to look at social control, not just social interaction. Social groups do not simply interact, they interact to some end. And one of the most salient ends is the exercise of control by one group over another, and thereby the maintenance of social or school order. The ethnographic work in this study had to be informed by an examination of one specific type of social construction — the power to define situations for others and to label others. The question is whether one can shift from ethnographies of school deviance or school control to the level of the social formation as a whole without a break with the fundamental tenets of symbolic interactionism. Banks gives a sharp warning here, when discussing bridge building: 'What I think we must at all costs guard against is the adoption of any viewpoint which takes the micro level as simply the reflection of macro level forces' (Banks, 1978). It would certainly go against the tenets of grounded theory to enter research seeking refinements of the 'correspondence principle' (in this case, that the structures and relationships of schools 'correspond' to the structures and relationships of the capitalist economy). We do have to uncover sexual and domestic ideologies, to look at when the school appears to select or legitimate gender and class structures, but we also have to discover when it appears to do so least (that is, to appear autonomous). One must then find a way graphically to describe the relationship between constraint and independence, between social structure and localized choice. My own version was a script analysis; but ideally each piece of research should generate its own synthesis.

Bibliography

ADLER, F. (1975) *Sisters in Crime*, New York, McGraw Hill.

ANYON, J. (1983) 'Intersections of gender and class: accommodation and resistance by working-class and affluent females to contradictory sex-role ideologies', in WALKER, S. and BARTON, L. *Gender, Class and Education* Lewes, Falmer Press.

BALL, S. (1981) *Beachside Comprehensive: a case study of secondary schooling*, Cambridge, Cambridge University Press.

BANDURA, A., ROSS, D. and ROSS, S. (1961) 'Transmission of aggression through imitation of aggressive models', *Journal of Abnormal and Social Psychology*, 63, pp. 575–82.

BANDURA, A. (1965) 'Influence of model's reinforcement contingencies on the acquisition of imitative responses', *Journal of Personality and Social Psychology*, 1, pp. 589–5.

BANKS, O. (1978) 'School and society', in BARTON, L. and MEIGHAN, R. (Eds.) *Sociological Interpretations of Schooling and Classrooms*, Driffield, Nafferton.

BANNISTER, D. and MAIR, J. (1968) *The Evaluation of Personal Constructs*, London, Academic Press.

BANNISTER, D. (1977) 'The child's construing of self', reported in F. FRANSELLA and K. FROST (1977) *On Being a Woman*, London, Tavistock.

BECKER, H.S. (1963) *Outsiders: Studies in the Sociology of Deviance*, New York, Free Press.

BELLABY, P. (1974) 'The distribution of deviance among 13–14 year old students', in EGGLESTON, J. (Ed.), *Contemporary Research in the Sociology of Education*, London, Methuen.

BERKSHIRE ASSOCIATION OF SECONDARY HEADTEACHERS (1975) 'Disruptive pupils', *Education*, 145, pp. 320–321.

BERNE, E. (1976) *Beyond Games and Scripts: selections from his major writings*, C. STEINER and C. KERR, (Eds.) New York, Grove Press.

BLAND, L., BRUNSDON, C., HOBSON, D. and WINSHIP, J. (1978) 'Women "inside and outside" the relations of production', in Women's Studies Group, University of Birmingham CCCS (Eds.) *Women Take Issue: Aspects of Women's Subordination*, London, Hutchinson.

BLYTH, W.A.L. (1960) 'The sociometric study of children's groups in English schools', *British Journal of Education Studies*, 8, 2, May, pp. 127–147.

BOWLBY, J. (1947) *Child Care and the Growth of Love*, Harmondsworth, Penguin.

BOX, S. (1981) *Deviance, Reality and Society*, New York, Holt, Rinehart and Winston.

BRAKE, M. (1980) *The Sociology of Youth Culture and Youth Sub-cultures*, London, Routledge and Kegan Paul.

BRANDIS, W. and BERNSTEIN, B. (1974) *Selection and Control: Teachers' Ratings of Children in Infant School*, London, Routledge and Kegan Paul.

BRICKER, D.C. (1979) 'Social dilemmas involved in a teacher's deviance imputations', in BARTON, L. and MEIGHAN, R. (Eds.) *Schools, Pupils and Deviance*, Driffield, Nafferton.

BRONFENBRENNER, U. (1973) *Two Worlds of Childhood: United States and USSR*, New York, Pocket Books.

BROPHY, J. and GOOD, T. (1974) *Teacher — Student Relationships: Causes and Consequences*, New York, Holt, Rinehart and Winston.

BROVERMAN, I.K., BROVERMAN, D. and CLARKSON, F. (1970) 'Sex-role stereotypes and clinical judgements of mental health', *Journal of Consultative and Clinical Psychology*, 34, pp. 1–7.

BROWN, V. (1972) 'Social Relations in a Girls' Secondary School', unpublished BEd dissertation, University of Birmingham, reported in SHAW, J. (1972).

BRUNER, J. (1966) *Toward a Theory of Instruction*, Cambridge, Mass, Harvard University Press.

BUSWELL, C. (1981) 'Sexism in school routines and classroom practices', *Durham and Newcastle Research Review*, IX, 46, pp. 195–200, Spring.

CAMPBELL, A. (1977) 'What makes a girl turn to crime', *New Society*, 27 January, pp. 172–173.

CASBURN, M. (1979) *Girls will be Girls: Sexism and Juvenile Justice in a London Borough*, Explorations in Feminism no. 6, London: Women's Research and Resources Centre.

CHESLER, P. (1972) *Women and Madness*, New York, Doubleday.

CHESNEY-LIND, M. (1973) 'Judicial enforcement of the female sex-role: the family court and the female delinquent', *Issues in Criminology*, 8, 2.

CHETWYND, S.J. (1976) 'Sex differences in stereotyping the roles of wife and mother', in SLATER, P. (Ed.) *Explorations of Personal Space*, London, John Wiley and Sons.

CICOUREL, A.V. and KITSUSE, J.I. (1963) *The Educational Decision Makers*, Indianapolis, Bobbs-Merrill.

CLOWARD, R.A. and OHLIN, L.E. (1961) *Delinquency and Opportunity: A Theory of Delinquent Gangs*, London, Routledge and Kegan Paul.

COHEN, A. (1955) *Delinquent Boys: The Culture of the Gang*, New York, The Free Press.

COHEN, P. (1972) 'Subcultural Conflict and Working-class Community', *Working Papers in Cultural Studies*, no. 2, University of Birmingham, CCCS.

COHEN, S. and TAYLOR, L. (1976) *Escape Attempts: The Theory and Practice of Resistance to Everyday Life*, Harmondsworth, Penguin.

COLEMAN, J. (1961) *The Adolescent Society*, New York, The Free Press.

COLLINS, R. 'A conflict theory of sexual stratification', *Social Problems* (1971), 19, pp. 3–21, Summer.

COOPERSMITH, S. (1967) *The Antecedents of Self-Esteem*, San Francisco, Freeman.

CORRIGAN, P. (1979) *Schooling the Smash Street Kids*, London, Macmillan.

COWIE, J., COWIE, V. and SLATER, E. (1968) *Delinquency in Girls*, London, Heinemann.

CRANDALL, V., KATKOVSKY, W. and PRESTON, A. (1962) 'Motivational and ability determinants of young children's intellectual achievement behaviours', *Child Development*, 33.

DAHL, T.S. and SNARE, A. (1978) 'The coercion of privacy: a feminist perspective', in: SMART, C. and SMART, B. (Eds.) *Women, Sexuality and Social Control*, London, Routledge and Kegan Paul.

DAVIDSON, H. and LANG, G. (1960) 'Children's perceptions of their teachers' feelings towards them, related to self-perception, school achievement and behaviour', *Journal of Experimental Education*, 29, pp. 107–8.

DAVIE, R., BUTLER, N. and GOLDSTEIN, H. (1972) *From Birth to Seven*, London, Longman.

DAVIES, L. (1973) 'The Contribution of the Secondary School to the Sex-typing of Girls', unpublished MEd dissertation, University of Birmingham.

DAVIES, L. and MEIGHAN, R. (1975) 'A Review of Schooling and Sex Roles', *Educational Review*, 27, 3, June.

DAVIES, L. (1980) 'Deviance and Sex Roles in School', unpublished PhD thesis, University of Birmingham.

DEEM, R. (Ed.) (1980) *Schooling for Women's Work*, London, Routledge and Kegan Paul.

DELAMONT, S. (1976a) *Interaction in the Classroom*, London, Methuen.

DELAMONT, S. (1976b) 'Beyond Flanders' fields: the relationships of subject matter and individuality to classroom style', in STUBBS, M. and DELAMONT, S. (Eds.) *Explorations in Classroom Observation* Chichester, Wiley 1976b.

DITKOFF, G.S. (1979) 'Stereotypes of adolescents towards the working woman' *Adolescence*, 14, 54, Summer.

DOUGLAS, J., ROSS, J. and SIMPSON, J. (1968) *All Our Future*, London, Davies.

DOWNES, D. (1966) *The Delinquent Solution*, London, Routledge and Kegan Paul.

DRIVER, G. (1980) 'How West Indians do better at school (especially the girls)', *New Society*, 17 January, pp. 111–14.

EDUCATIONAL INSTITUTE OF SCOTLAND (1977) Report of Scottish Council for Research in Education, quoted in 'Two out of three Scots pupils favour the strap' *The Times Educational Supplement*, 22 April.

EGGLESTON, J. (1977) *The Ecology of the School*, London, Methuen.

ENGELS, F. (1962 edition) *The Origin of the Family, Private Property and the State*, in MARX-ENGELS, Selected Works II, Moscow, Progress Publishers

EPPEL, E. and EPPEL, M. (1966) *Adolescents and Morality*, London, Routledge and Kegan Paul.

ERIKSON, K. (1966) *Wayward Puritans*, New York, Wiley.

Essex County Teachers Association (1975) *Education*, 145, 350.

Eysenck, H. (1965) *Fact and Fiction in Psychology*, Harmondsworth, Penguin.

Fransella, F. and Frost, K. (1977) *On Being a Woman*. London, Tavistock.

Frye, N. (1971) 'The definition of a university' in Rusk, B. (Ed.) *Alternatives in Education*, London, University of London Press.

Fuller, M. (1979) 'Dimensions of Gender in a School', unpublished PhD thesis, University of Bristol.

Fuller, M. (1980) 'Black Girls in a London comprehensive school' in Deem, R. *Schooling for Women's Work*, London, Routledge and Kegan Paul.

Furlong, V. (1976) 'Interaction sets in the classroom: toward a study of pupil knowledge', in Hammersley, M. and Woods, P. *The Process of Schooling*, London, Routledge and Kegan Paul.

Gagnon, J. and Simon, W. (1974) *Sexual Conduct: The Social Sources of Human Sexuality*, London; Hutchinson.

Galloway, D. (1982) 'A study of pupils suspended from school' British *Journal of Educational Psychology*, 52, 2, pp. 205–2.

Gannaway, H. (1976) 'Making sense of school', in Stubbs, M. and Delamont, S. *Explorations in Classroom Observation*, London, John Wiley and Son.

Garfinkel, H. (1956) 'Conditions of successful degradation ceremonies', *American Journal of Sociology*, 61, pp. 420–4.

Gill, O. (1978) *Luke Street: Housing Policy, Conflict and the Creation of the Delinquent Area*, London. Macmillan.

Glaser, B. and Strauss, A.L. (1968) *The Discovery of Grounded Theory*, London, Weidenfeld and Nicolson.

Goffman, E. (1959) *The Presentation of Self in Everyday Life*, Harmondsworth, Penguin.

Goffman, E. (1967) *Interaction Ritual*, Harmondsworth, Penguin.

Goffman, E. (1968) *Asylums*, Doubleday, Penguin.

Gold, M. (1970) *Delinquency in an American City*, Berkeley University of California Press.

Goldberg, S. (1968) 'Are women prejudiced against women?' *Transaction*, 5, p. 28.

Gomm, R. (1978) 'Perspectives on Socialization', *The Social Science Teacher*, 8, 2, p. 51, December.

Good, T.L. and Brophy, J.E. (1972) 'Behavioural expression of teacher attitudes', *Journal of Educational Psychology*, 63, pp. 617–24.

Good, T.L., Sikes, J.N. and Brophy, J.E. (1973) 'Effects of teacher sex and student sex on classroom interaction', *Journal of Educational Psychology*, 65, 1, pp. 74–87.

Hacker, H. (1969) 'Women as a Minority Group', in Roszak, B. and Roszak, T. *Masculine/Feminine*, New York, Harper and Row.

Hadfield J.A. (1962) *Childhood and Adolescence* Harmondsworth, Penguin.

Hagan, J., Simpson, J.H. and Gillis, A.R. (1979) 'The sexual stratification of social control: a gender-based perspective on crime and delinquency', *British Journal of Sociology*, 30, 1, pp. 25–38, March.

Halsey, A., Heath, A. and Ridge, J. (1980) *Origins and Destinations*, Oxford, Clarendon.

HAMMERSLEY, M. (1976) 'The mobilization of pupil attention', in HAMMERS-LEY, M. and WOODS, P. (Eds.) *The Process of Schooling*, London, Routledge and and Kegan Paul.

HAMMERSLEY, M. (1977) *Ethnography*, 1, Milton Keynes, Open University Occasional Publications, September.

HAMPSON, J. and HAMPSON, J. (1965) 'Determinants of 'psychosexual orientation', in F. BEACH (Ed.), *Sex and Behaviour*, New York, John Wiley.

HANSARD PARLIAMENTARY DEBATES (1973) London HMSO 863, p. 105.

HARGREAVES, A. (1978) 'Towards a theory of classroom coping strategies' in BARTON, L. and MEIGHAN, R. *Sociological Interpretations of Schooling and Classrooms*, Driffield, Nafferton.

HARGREAVES, D. (1967) *Social Relations in a Secondary School*, London, Routledge and Kegan Paul.

HARGREAVES, D., HESTOR, S. and MELLOR, F. (1975) *Deviance in Classroom*, London, Routledge and Kegan Paul.

HARGREAVES, D. (1976) 'Reactions to labelling', in HAMMERSLEY, M. and WOODS, P. (Eds.) *The Process of Schooling*, London, Routledge and Kegan Paul.

HARGREAVES, D. (1976a) 'What are little boys and girls made of?', *New Society*, 9 September.

HARGREAVES, D. (1978) 'Whatever happened to symbolic interactionism?', in BARTON, L. and MEIGHAN, R. (Eds.), *Sociological Interpretations of Schooling and Classrooms*, Driffield, Nafferton.

HARGREAVES, D. (1979) 'Durkheim, deviance and education', in BARTON, L. and MEIGHAN, R. (Eds.) *Schools, Pupils and Deviance*, Driffield Nafferton.

HARRÉ, R. and SECORD, P.F. (1972) *The Explanation of Human Behaviour*, Oxford, Blackwell.

HARRIS, A. (1977) 'Sex and theories of deviance: towards a functional theory of deviant typescripts', *American Sociological Review*, 42, 1, February.

HARTLEY, D. (1978), 'Teachers' definitions of boys and girls: some comparisons', *Research in Education*, 20, November.

HEAL, K.H. (1978) 'Misbehaviour among school children: the role of the school in strategies for prevention', *Policy and Politics*, 6, pp. 321–32.

HENNIG, M. and JARDIM, A. (1978) *The Managerial Woman*, London; M. Boyars,

HIRSCHI, T. (1969) *The Causes of Delinquency*, Berkeley, University of California Press.

HOCHSCHILD, A.R. (1973) 'A review of sex role research'; *American Journal of Sociology*, 78, 4, pp. 1011–29.

HOFFMAN-BUSTAMANTE, D., (1973) 'The nature of female criminality'; *Issues in Criminology*, 8, 2.

HOGHUGHI, M. (1978) *Troubled and Troublesome*, London, Burnett Books.

HUTT, C. (1979) 'Why do girls underachieve?', *Trends in Education*, 4, Winter.

INGLEBY, J.D. and COOPER, E. (1974) 'How teachers perceive first year school children: sex and ethnic differences', *Sociology*, 8, pp. 463–72.

JACKSON, P. and GETZELS, J. (1959) 'Psychological health and classroom functioning: a study of dissatisfaction with school among adolescents', *Journal of Educational Psychology*, 50, pp. 295–300, December.

JACKSON, P. (1968) *Life in Classrooms*, New York, Holt, Rinehart and Winston.

JACKSON, P. and LAHADERNE, A. (1977) 'Inequalities of teacher–pupil contacts', in SILBERMAN, M. (Ed.) *The Experience of Schooling*, New York, Holt, Rinehart and Winston.

JEPHCOTT, P. (1962) *Married Women Working*, London, George Allen and Unwin.

JONES, V. (1971) 'The Influence of Teacher-student Intraversion, Achievement, and Similarity on Teacher-student Dyadic Classroom Interactions', unpublished doctoral dissertation, University of Texas at Austin.

KAGAN, J. and MOSS H. (1962) *Birth to Maturity: A Study in Psychological Development*, New York, Wiley.

KARABEL, J. and HALSEY, A.H. (1977) *Power and Ideology in Education*, New York, Oxford University Press.

KEDDIE, N. (1971) 'Classroom knowledge', in YOUNG, M. (Ed.) *Knowledge and Control*, London, Collier-Macmillan.

KELLMER-PRINGLE, M.L., BUTLER, N.R. and DAVIE, R.V. (1966) *11,000 Seven Year Olds*, Essex. Longman.

KELLY, G.A. (1970) 'Behaviour is an experiment', in BANNISTER, D. (Ed.) *Perspectives in Personal Construct Theory*, London, Academic Press.

KEMER, B.J. (1973) 'A Study of the Relationship between the Sex of the Student and the Assignment of Marks by Secondary School Teachers', PhD dissertation, Michigan State University, 1965, quoted in N. FRAZIER and M. SADKER, *Sexism in School and Society*, New York, Harper and Row.

KING, E. (1978) 'The social construction of ethnic identity — everyone has scripts', *The Social Science Teacher*, 7, 4, pp. 21–5.

KING, J.S. (1974) 'Women and Work: Sex Differences and Society', Department of Education and Science, *Manpower* no. 10, London HMSO.

KING, R. (1973) *School Organization and Pupil Involvement*, London, Routledge and Kegan Paul.

KOHLBERG, L. (1967) 'A cognitive-developmental analysis of children's sex role concepts and attitudes', in MACCOBY, E. (Ed.) *The Development of Sex Differences*, London, Tavistock.

KONOPKA, G. (1966) *The Adolescent Girl in Conflict*, New Jersey, Prentice Hall.

KOUNIN, J.S. (1970) *Discipline and Group Management in Classrooms*, New York, Holt, Rinehart and Winston.

KREUZ, L., ROSE, R. and JENNINGS, J.R. (1972) 'Psychological stress results in suppression of androgen activity', *Archives of Generad Psychiatry*, 26, pp. 479–82.

LACEY, C. (1970) *Hightown Grammar*, Manchester University Press.

LAHADERNE, H. and JACKSON, P. (1970) 'Withdrawal in the classroom: a note on some educational correlates of social desirability among school children', *Journal of Educational Psychology*, 61, 2, pp. 97–101.

LAMBART, A.M. (1976) 'The Sisterhood', in HAMMERSLEY M. and WOODS, P. *The Process of Schooling*, London, Routledge and Kegan Paul.

LENSKI, G. (1966) *Power and Privilege: A Theory of Social Stratification*, New York, McGraw Hill.

LEVENTHAL, D.B., SHEINBERG, K.M. and VAN SCHOELANDT, S.K. (1968)

'Effects of sex-role adjustment upon the expression of aggression', *Journal of Personality and Social Psychol*, 8, pp. 393–7.

LEVITIN, T.E. and CHANANIE, J.D. (1972) 'Responses of female primary school teachers to sex-typed behaviours in male and female children', *Child Development*, 43, pp. 1309–16.

LLEWELLYN, M. (1976) 'Girls at school,' paper read to BSA Sexual Divisions Study Group, Lanchester Polytechnic, reported in R. DEEM, (1980). *Schooling for Women's Work*, London, Routledge and Kegan Paul.

LLEWELLYN, M. (1980) 'Studying girls at school: the implications of confusion' in DEEM, R. (Ed.) *Schooling for Women's Work*, London, Routledge and Kegan Paul.

LOBBAN, G. (1978) 'The influence of the school on sex-role stereotyping', in CHETWYND, J. and HARTNETT, O. *The Sex Role System: Psychological and Sociological Perspectives*, London, Routledge and Kegan Paul.

LOMBROSO, C. and FERRERO, W. (1895) *The Female Offender*, London, Fisher Unwin.

LOWENSTEIN, L.F. (1975) *Violent and Disruptive Behaviour in Schools*, National Association of Schoolmasters.

MACCOBY, E.E. and JACKLIN, C.N. (1974) *The Psychology of Sex Differences*, California, Stanford University Press.

MANNHEIM, H. (1965) *Comparative Criminology*, London, Routledge and Kegan Paul.

MARSH, P., ROSSER, E. and HARRÉ, R. (1978) *The Rules of Disorder*, London, Routledge and Kegan Paul.

MARTIN, R. (1972) 'Student sex and behaviour as determinants of the type and frequency of teacher-student contacts', *Journal of Social Psychology*, 10, pp. 339–47.

MATZA, D. (1964) *Delinquency and Drift*, London, Wiley.

MAWBY, R.I. (1977) 'Truancy: data from a self-report survey', *Durham and Newcastle Research Review*, 8, 39, pp. 21–34.

McGUIRE, W.J. (1968) 'Personality and susceptibility to social influence', in BORGATTA, E. and LAMBERT, W. (Eds) *Handbook of Personality Theory and Research*, Chicago, Rand McNally.

McROBBIE, A. and GARBER, J. (1975) 'Girls and sub-cultures', in S. HALL and T. JEFFERSON (Eds) *Resistance Through Rituals*, London, Hutchinson.

McROBBIE, A. (1978) 'Working-class girls and the culture of femininity', in Women's Studies Group, CCCS University of Birmingham, *Women Take Issue: Aspects of Women's Subordination*, London, Hutchinson.

MEAD, M. (1935) *Sex and Temperament in Three Primitive Societies*, New York, William Morrow.

MEAD, M. (1966) 'Sex and temperament', in SCHUR, E.M. (Ed.) *The Family and the Sexual Revolution*, London, Allen and Unwin.

MEEKER, B.D. and WEITZEL-O'NEILL, P.A. (1977) 'Sex roles and interpersonal behaviour in task-oriented groups', American Sociological Review, 42, pp. 91–105, February.

MEYENN, R.J. (1979) 'School girls' peer groups', in WOODS, P. (Ed.) *Pupil Strategies*, London, Croom Helm.

MEYENN, R. and MILLER, H. (1979) *The relationship between theory, method and data in a piece of school research*, conference paper, Pupils In and Out of School Conference, Hertford College, Oxford.

MEYER, W. and THOMPSON, G. (1963) 'Teacher interactions with boys as contrasted with girls', in KUHLENS, K. and THOMPSON, G. (Eds) *Psychological Studies of Human Development*, New York, Appleton Century Crofts.

MILLER, D. (1966) 'Personality', in RAISON, T. (Ed.) *Youth in New Society*, London, Rupert Hart Davis.

MILLER, W.B. (1958) 'Lower class culture as a generating milieu of gang delinquency', *Journal of Social Issues*, 14, 3, pp. 5–19.

MITCHELL, J. (1971) *Woman's Estate*, Harmondsworth, Penguin.

MITCHELL, J. (1975) *Psychoanalysis and Feminism*, Harmondsworth, Penguin.

MITCHELL, S. and SHEPHERD, M. (1967) 'The child who dislikes going to school', *British Journal of Educational Psychology*, 37.

MORRIS, R. (1965) 'Attitudes towards delinquency by delinquents, non-delinquents and their friends', *British Journal of Criminology*, 5.

MORTON, P. (1971) *A woman's work is never done*, Leviathan, II, 1, quoted in J. MITCHELL, (op. cit.).

MURDOCK, G. and PHELPS, G. (1973) *Mass Media and the Secondary School*, Schools Council Publications, Macmillan.

MUSGROVE, F. (1971) *Patterns of Power and Authority in English Education*. London, Methuen.

MYRDAL, G. (1969) 'Women, servants, mules and other property', in B. ROSZAK and T. ROSZAK, *Masculine/Feminine*, New York, Harper and Row.

NACRO (1977) *Children and Young Persons in Custody: Report of a Working Party*, National Association for the Care and Resettlement of Offenders, Chichester, Rose.

NAS/UWT, (1979) *Action on Indiscipline: A Practical Guide for Teachers*, National Association of Schoolmasters.

NASH, R. (1976) *Teacher Expectations and Pupil Learning*, London, Routledge and Kegan Paul.

NEWSON, J. and NEWSON, E. *Seven Years Old in the Home Environment*. London: Allen and Unwin, 1976.

NEWSON, J., NEWSON, E., RICHARDSON, D. and SCAIFE, J. (1978) 'Perspectives in sex role stereotyping', in CHETWYND, J. and HARTNETT, O. *The Sex Role System: Psychological and Sociological Perspectives*, London, Routledge and Kegan Paul.

O'LEARY, K.D., KAUFMAN, K., KASS, R. and DRABMAN, R. (1970) 'The effects of loud and soft reprimands on the behaviour of disruptive students', *Exceptional Children*, 37, pp. 145–55.

PACK REPORT, THE, (1977) *Truancy and Indiscipline in Schools in Scotland*, Scottish Education Department, HMSO.

PAHL, R.E. (1978) 'Living without a job: how school leavers see the future', *New Society*, 2 November.

PAIGE, K. (1969) 'The Effects of Oral Contraceptives on Affective Fluctuations Associated with the Menstrual Cycle', unpublished PhD dissertation, University of Michigan.

PARRY, K. (1976) 'Disruptive children in school', in DAVIES, J. (Ed.) *The*

Disruptive Pupil in the Secondary School, London, Ward Lock.

PARSONS, T. (1942) 'Age and sex in the social structure of the United States', *American Sociological Review*, 7.

PARSONS, T. and BALES, R.F. (1955) *Family, Socialization and Interaction Process*, Glencoe, Free Press.

PEARSON, G. (1975) *The Deviant Imagination*, London, Macmillan.

PEARSON, R. (1976) 'Women defendants in magistrates courts', *British Journal of Law and Society*, Winter.

PHILLIPSON, (1971) 'Juvenile delinquency and the school', in CARSON, W. and WILES, P. (Eds) *Crime and Delinquency in Britain*, London, Martin Robertson.

PLUMMER, K. (1979) 'Misunderstanding labelling perspectives', in DOWNES, D. and ROCK, P. (Eds) *Deviant Interpretations*, London, Martin Robertson.

POLLAK, O. (1961) *The Criminality of Women*, New York, A.S. Barnes.

POWELL, R. and CLARKE, J. (1975) 'A note on marginality', in HALL, S. and JEFFERSON, T. (Eds) *Resistance Through Rituals*, London, Hutchinson.

REISS, A. (1960) 'The marginal status of adolescents', in 'Report from the Select Committee on Violence in Marriage', *Law and Contemporary Problems*, 1, session 1974–5, London, HMSO.

REYNOLDS, D. (1976) 'The delinquent school', in HAMMERSLEY, M. and WOODS, P., *The Process of Schooling*, London, Routledge and Kegan Paul.

RICHARSON, H. (1969) *Adolescent Girls in Approved Schools*, London, Routledge and Kegan Paul.

RICKS, F.A. and PYKE, S. (1973) 'Teacher perceptions and attitudes that foster or maintain sex role differences', *Interchange*, 4, 1.

RIST, R.C. (1977) 'On understanding the processes of schooling: the contributions of labeling theory', in KARABEL, J. and HALSEY, A.H. (Eds), *Power and Ideology in Education*, New York, Oxford University Press.

ROBINS, D. and COHEN, P. (1978) *Knuckle Sandwich: Growing Up in the Working-class City*, Harmondsworth; Penguin.

ROBINSON, P.E.D. (1974) 'An ethnography of classrooms', in EGGLESTON, J. (Ed.) *Contemporary Research in the Sociology of Education*, London, Methuen.

ROSENKRANTZ, P., VOGEL, S. BEE, H. BROVERMAN, I. and BROVERMAN, D. (1968) 'Sex role stereotypes and self-concepts in college students', *Journal of Consultative and Clinical Psychology*, 32, 3, pp. 287–95.

ROSENTHAL, R. and JACOBSEN, L.C. (1968) *Pygmalion in the Classroom*, New York, Holt, Rinehart and Winston.

ROWBOTHAM, S. (1973) *Woman's Consciousness, Man's World*, Harmondsworth, Penguin.

RUBINGTON, E. and WEINBERG, M.S. (1968) *Deviance: The Interactionist Perspective*, New York, Macmillan.

RUTTER, M., MAUGHAN, B., MORTIMORE, D. and OUSTON, J. (1979) *15,000 Hours: Secondary Schools and their Effects on Children*, London, Open Books.

SAMPSON, R. (1966) *The Psychology of Power*, New York, Pantheon.

SAMPSON, S. (1979) 'Sex stereotypes: some evidence from Australian schools', *Australian Journal of Education*, 2, June.

SCHOOLS COUNCIL (1968) *Enquiry One: Young School Leavers*, London, HMSO.

SCHOOLS COUNCIL (1970) 'Teaching English to West Indian Children', *Working Paper* 29, London, Evans and Methuen.

SEARS, P. and FELDMAN, D. (1966) 'Teacher interactions with boys and girls', *Nat. Elementary Principal*, 46, 2, pp. 30–35.

SERBIN, L.A., O'LEARY, K.D., KENT, R.N. and TONICK, I.J. (1973) 'A comparison of teacher response to the pre-academic and problem behaviour of boys and girls', *Child Development*, 44, pp. 796–804.

SHACKLADY-SMITH, L. (1978) 'Sexist assumptions and female delinquency', in SMART, C. and SMART, B., *Women, Sexuality and Social Control*, London, Routledge and Kegan Paul.

SHARPE, S. (1976) *Just Like a Girl*, Harmondsworth, Penguin.

SHAW, J. (1976) 'Finishing school', in BARKER, D. and ALLEN, S., *Sexual Divisions and Society: Process and Change*, London, Tavistock.

SILBERMAN, M. (1971) 'Classroom rewards and intellectual courage', in SILBERMAN, M. (Ed.) *The Experience of Schooling*, New York, Holt, Rinehart and Winston.

SMART, C. (1976) *Women, Crime and Criminology: A Feminist Critique*, London, Routledge and Kegan Paul.

SMART, C. (1977) 'Criminological theory: its ideology and implications concerning women', *British Journal of Sociology*, 28, 1, March.

SMART, C. and SMART, B. (Eds) (1978) *Women, Sexuality and Social Control*, London, Routledge and Kegan Paul.

SPAULDING, R. (1963) 'Achievement, creativity, and self-concept correlates of teacher-pupil transactions in elementary schools', *Co-operative Research Project* no. 1352, US Department of Health, Education and Welfare Office, Washington DC.

STAFFORDSHIRE EDUCATION COMMITTEE (1977) *Disruptive Pupils in Schools*, Report of Working Party, February.

STEBBINS, R.A. (1970) 'The meaning of disorderly behaviour: teacher definitions of a classroom situation', *Sociology of Education*, 44, pp. 217–36, Spring.

SUGARMAN, B. (1967) 'Involvement in youth culture, academic achievement and conformity in school', *British Journal of Sociology*, 18, 2, June.

TATTUM, D. (1982) *Disruptive Pupils in Schools and Units*, Chichester, John Wiley.

TEDESCHI, J., SCHLENKER, B. and BONOMA, V. (1973) *Conflict, Power and Games: The Experimental Study of Interpersonal Relations*, Chicago, Aldine Publishing Co.

THOMAS, H. and ALBRECHT-HEIDE, A. (1977) *Schools and Professional Inequality of Women in the European Community*, ECID, contract no. 233–75, 12, Berlin.

THOMAS, W.I. (1907) *Sex and Society*, Boston, Little Brown.

TURNER, R.H. (1962) 'Role-taking: process and conformity', in ROSE, A. (Ed.) *Human Behaviour and Social Processes*, London, Routledge and Kegan Paul.

TYERMAN, M.J. (1968) *Truancy*, London, University of London Press.

VALLANCE, E. (1974) 'Hiding the hidden curriculum', *Curriculum Theory Network*, 4, 1, pp. 5–22.

WAETJEN, W. (1972) *The Self-Concept as a Learner Scale (SCAL)*, Bureau of Educational Research and Field Services, University of Maryland, 1963, and *O.U. E281*, Unit 10 (1972), Milton Keynes, Open University.

WALKER, N. (1973) *Crime and Punishment in Britain*, University of Edinburgh Press.

WALKER, R. and ADELMAN, C. (1976) 'Strawberries', in STUBBS, M. and DELAMONT, S. (Eds) *Explorations in Classroom Observation*, Chichester, Wiley.

WALL, W.D. (1973) 'The problem child in school', *London Education Review*, 2, 2, pp. 3–21, Summer.

WARD, J. (1976) *Social Reality for the Adolescent Girl*, Faculty of Education, University of Swansea.

WARNER, R.S., WELLMAN, D.T. and WEITZMAN, L.J. (1973) 'The hero, the Sambo and the operator: three characterizations of the oppressed', *Urban Life and Culture*, 2, pp. 53–84.

WEISSTEIN, N. (1970) 'Kinder, küche and kirche as scientific law: psychology constructs the female', in MORGAN, K. (Ed.) *Sisterhood is Powerful*, New York, Random House.

WERTHMAN, C. (1963) 'Delinquents in school: a test for the legitimacy of authority', *Berkeley Journal of Sociology*, 8, pp. 39–60.

WEST, G.W. (1979) 'Adolescent autonomy, education and pupil deviance', in BARTON, L. and MEIGHAN, R. (Eds) *Schools, Pupils and Deviance*, Driffield, Nafferton.

WILKINS, L.T. (1971) 'The deviance — amplifying system', in CARSON, W.G. and WILES, P. *Crime and Delinquency in Britain*, London, Martin Robertson.

WILLIS, P. (1977) *Learning To Labour*, Farnborough, Saxon House.

WISE, N.B. (1967) 'Juvenile delinquency among middle-class girls', in VAZ, W. (Ed.) *Middle-Class Juvenile Delinquency*, New York, Harper and Row.

WOLPE, A.M. (1977) 'Some Processes in Sexist Education', *Explorations in Feminism*, no. 1, Women's Research and Resources Centre Publications.

WOODS, P. (1976) 'Having a laugh: an antidote to schooling', in HAMMERSLEY, M. and WOODS, P. *The Process of Schooling*, London, Routledge and Kegan Paul.

WOODS, P. (1978) 'Relating to schoolwork: some pupil perceptions', *Education Review*, 30, 2, pp. 167–75, June.

WOODS, P. (1983) *Sociology and the School*, London, Routledge and Kegan Paul.

WRONG, D. (1961) 'The oversocialized conception of man in modern sociology', *American Sociological Review*, 26, pp. 183–93.

ZINNECKER, J. et al (1972) *Emanzipation der Frau und Schulausbildung* Weinheim.

Author Index

Subject Index

acculturation, 164
  see also cultural factors;
    sub-cultures
aggression
  and sex role socialization, 154–6,
    162–3
anthropology, 149–50, 179, 233, 236
Association of Education
  Committees, 134
authority, 14
  and teachers, 2, 34

banding, 4
Beachside Comprehensive school,
  174
biology
  and deviance, 14, 120, 145–53, 163
boys
  and aggression, 154–5
  attitudes of, 17–26
  as 'good' pupils, 59–75, 86, 92,
    124, 138–9
  and institutional attachments,
    17–21
  and role traits, 21–6
  and rules, 186–94
  socialization of, 17–26
  teacher appreciation of, 6, 73,
    142–3
  and type-scripts, 108–14, 123–9
Britain, *passim*

Canada, 159

caning
  see corporal punishment
careers
  and schooling, 19–20, 35–6, 50–1,
    53–4, 179, 203–4, 208–9
case-study method, 1–129, 211,
  214–18, 218–38
  see also methodology
clinical psychology, 149–51
comparative studies, 214
  see also methodology
comprehensive schools, 1–129, 174
conformity, 14, 17–26, 41, 52–3, 54,
  71–2, 93, 95, 105, 106, 124, 136,
  143, 145, 146–9, 154–5, 156–60,
  194, 198, 204, 205, 208–9, 213,
  233
control, 1, 2, 14, 17–21, 32–4,
  38–40, 46–8, 52–4, 79–86,
  153–64, 167, 196, 238
  see also power; status
corporal punishment, 7, 75–9, 80,
  81–2, 195
criminality, 118, 145–9, 181, 183–5,
  207
cultural capital, 126
  see also cultural factors
cultural factors, 28, 120, 124–6, 142,
  151–3, 164, 176–8
  see also culture contact; sub-cultures
culture contact, 17–26
  see also cultural factors;
    sub-cultures